Apocalyp
and/or
Metamorphosis

Apocalypse and/or Metamorphosis

Norman O. Brown

University of California Press

Berkeley · Los Angeles · Oxford

University of California Press
Berkeley and Los Angeles, California

University of California Press, Ltd.
Oxford, England

© 1991 by
The Regents of the University of California

Library of Congress Cataloging-in-Publication Data

Brown, Norman Oliver, 1913–
    Apocalypse and/or metamorphosis / Norman O. Brown.
        p.   cm.
    Contents: Apocalypse—Daphne, or Metamorphosis—My georgics—
Metamorphoses II—The prophetic tradition—The apocalypse of
Islam—Philosophy and prophecy—The turn to Spinoza—
Metamorphoses III—Revisioning historical identities—Dionysus
in 1990.
    ISBN 0-520-07298-7 (alk. paper)
    ISBN 0-520-07828-4 (ppb.)
    1. Civilization—Philosophy.   2. Civilization—Psychological
aspects.   3. Intellect.   I. Title.
CB19.B685 1991
901—dc20   90-47940
                                                           CIP

Printed in the United States of America

9 8 7 6 5 4 3 2 1

καὶ μὴ συσχηματίζεσθε τῷ αἰῶνι τούτῳ, ἀλλὰ μεταμορφ-
οῦσθε τῇ ἀνακαινώσει τοῦ νοὸς ὑμῦν.

And be not conformed to this world [*be nonconformists*]; but be
ye transformed [*metamorphose yourselves*] by the renewing of
your mind.

Romans 12:2

Contents

Preface

These essays, from the work of thirty years (1960–1990), were selected as bearing on the story begun in *Life Against Death* (1959) and continued in *Love's Body* (1966). They are efforts to live with the consequences of the post-Marxist revisioning that began with the defeat of the Henry Wallace campaign for the Presidency in 1948 and the beginning of the Cold War. The first ("Apocalypse," 1960) registers the surprising turn taken between *Life Against Death* and *Love's Body*. The last two ("Revisioning Historical Identities," 1989, and "Dionysus in 1990") are partly retrospective, at the end of an era.

Apocalypse
The Place of Mystery in the Life
of the Mind

Columbia University
May 31, 1960

I didn't know whether I should appear before you—there is a
time to show and a time to hide; there is a time to speak and also
a time to be silent. What time is it? It is fifteen years since H. G.
Wells said Mind was at the End of its Tether—with a frightful
queerness come into life: there is no way out or around or
through, he said; it is the end. It is because I think mind is at the
end of its tether that I would be silent. It is because I think there
is a way out—a way down and out—the title of Mr. John Se-
nior's new book on the occult tradition in literature—that I will
speak.

Mind at the end of its tether: I can guess what some of you are
thinking—*his* mind is at the end of its tether—and this could be;
it scares me but it deters me not. The alternative to mind is
certainly madness. Our greatest blessings, says Socrates in the
Phaedrus, come to us by way of madness—provided, he adds,

Phi Beta Kappa Speech, Columbia University, May 1960. *Harpers Magazine*
(May 1961), 46–49. Anthologized in C. Muscatine and M. Griffith, *Borzoi College Reader* (New York, 1966, 1971), 54–59; L. Baritz (ed.), *Sources of the
American Mind* (New York, 1966), vol. 2, 380–385; H. Jaffe and J. Tytell, *The
American Experience: A Radical Reader* (New York, 1970), 207–211; L. Ha-
malian and F. R. Karl, eds., *The Radical Vision* (New York, 1970), 104–111.
Also in R. Kostelanetz (ed.), *Esthetics Contemporary* (revised New York, 1989),
114–118. German translation, "Dionysos in Amerika," *Neue Deutsche Hefte*, no.
89 (September–October 1962). Reprinted by permission of *Harper's Magazine*,
copyright 1961.

that the madness comes from the god. Our real choice is between holy and unholy madness: open your eyes and look around you—madness is in the saddle anyhow. Freud is the measure of our unholy madness, as Nietzsche is the prophet of the holy madness, of Dionysus, the mad truth. Dionysus has returned to his native Thebes; mind—at the end of its tether—is another Pentheus, up a tree. Resisting madness can be the maddest way of being mad.

And there is a way out—the blessed madness of the maenad and the bacchant: "Blessed is he who has the good fortune to know the mysteries of the gods, who sanctifies his life and initiates his soul, a bacchant on the mountains, in holy purifications." It is possible to be mad and to be unblest; but it is not possible to get the blessing without the madness; it is not possible to get the illuminations without the derangement. Derangement is disorder: the Dionysian faith is that order as we have known it is crippling, and for cripples; that what is past is prologue; that we can throw away our crutches and discover the supernatural power of walking; that human history goes from man to superman.

No superman I; I come to you not as one who has supernatural powers, but as one who seeks for them, and who has some notions which way to go to find them.

Sometimes—most times—I think that the way down and out leads out of the university, out of the academy. But perhaps it is rather that we should recover the academy of earlier days—the Academy of Plato in Athens, the Academy of Ficino in Florence, Ficino who says, "The spirit of the god Dionysus was believed by the ancient theologians and Platonists to be the ecstasy and abandon of disencumbered minds, when partly by innate love, partly at the instigation of the god, they transgress the natural limits of intelligence and are miraculously transformed into the beloved god himself: where, inebriated by a certain new draft of nectar and by an immeasurable joy, they rage, as it were, in a bacchic frenzy. In the drunkenness of this Dionysian wine, our Dionysius (the Areopagite) expresses his exultation. He pours forth enigmas, he sings in dithyrambs. To penetrate the profundity of his meanings, to imitate his quasi-Orphic manner of speech, we too require the divine fury."

At any rate the point is first of all to find again the mysteries. By which I do not mean simply the sense of wonder—that sense of wonder which is indeed the source of all true philosophy—by mystery I mean secret and occult; therefore unpublishable; therefore outside the university as we know it; but not outside Plato's Academy or Ficino's.

Why are mysteries unpublishable? First, because they cannot be put into words, at least not the kind of words which earned you your Phi Beta Kappa keys. Mysteries display themselves in words only if they can remain concealed; this is poetry, isn't it? We must return to the old doctrine of the Platonists and Neo-Platonists that poetry is veiled truth; as Dionysus is the god who is both manifest and hidden; and as John Donne declared, with the Pillar of Fire goes the Pillar of Cloud. This is also the new doctrine of Ezra Pound, who says: "Prose is not education but the outer courts of the same. Beyond its doors are the mysteries. Eleusis. Things not to be spoken of save in secret. The mysteries self-defended, the mysteries that cannot be revealed. Fools can only profane them. The dull can neither penetrate the secretum nor divulge it to others." The mystic academies, whether Plato's or Ficino's, knew the limitations of words and drove us on beyond them, to go over, to go under, to the learned ignorance, in which God is better honored and loved by silence than by words, and better seen by closing the eyes to images than by opening them.

And second, mysteries are unpublishable because only some can see them, not all. Mysteries are intrinsically esoteric, and as such are an offense to democracy: is not publicity a democratic principle? Publication makes it republican—a thing of the people. The pristine academies were esoteric and aristocratic, self-consciously separate from the profanely vulgar. Democratic resentment denies that there can be anything that can't be seen by everybody; in the democratic academy truth is subject to public verification; truth is what any fool can see. This is what is meant by the so-called scientific method: so-called science is the attempt to democratize knowledge—the attempt to substitute method for insight, mediocrity for genius, by getting a standard operating procedure. The great equalizers dispensed by the scientific method are the tools, those analytical tools. The miracle of genius is replaced by the standardized mechanism. But fools with tools are still fools, and don't let your Phi Beta Kappa key fool you. Tibetan prayer wheels are another way of arriving at the same result: the degeneration of mysticism into mechanism—so that any fool can do it. Perhaps the advantage is with Tibet: for there the mechanism is external while the mind is left vacant; and vacancy is not the worst condition of the mind. And the resultant prayers make no futile claim to originality or immortality; being nonexistent, they do not have to be catalogued or stored.

The sociologist Simmel sees showing and hiding, secrecy and publicity, as two poles, like yin and yang, between which societies oscillate in their historical development. I sometimes think I see that civilizations originate in the disclosure of some mystery, some secret; and expand with the progressive publication of their secret; and end in exhaustion when there is no longer any secret, when the mystery has been divulged, that is to say, profaned. The whole story is illustrated in the difference between ideogram and alphabet. The alphabet is indeed a democratic triumph; and the enigmatic ideogram, as Ezra Pound has taught us, is a piece of mystery, a piece of poetry, not yet profaned. And so there comes a time—I believe we are in such a time—when civilization has to be renewed by the discovery of new mysteries, by the undemocratic but sovereign power of the imagination, by the undemocratic power which makes poets the unacknowledged legislators of mankind, the power which makes all things new.

The power which makes all things new is magic. What our time needs is mystery: what our time needs is magic. Who would not say that only a miracle can save us? In Tibet the degree-granting institution is, or used to be, the College of Magic Ritual. It offers courses in such fields as clairvoyance and telepathy; also (attention physics majors) internal heat: internal heat is a yoga bestowing supernatural control over body temperature. Let me succumb for a moment to the fascination of the mysterious East and tell you of the examination procedure for the course in internal heat. Candidates assemble naked, in midwinter, at night, on a frozen Himalayan lake. Beside each one is placed a pile of wet frozen undershirts: the assignment is to wear, until they are dry, as many as possible of these undershirts before dawn. Where the power is real, the test is real, and the grading system dumfoundingly objective. I say no more. I say no more: Eastern yoga does indeed demonstrate the existence of supernatural powers, but it does not have the particular power our Western society needs; or rather I think that each society has access only to its own proper powers; or rather each society will get only the kind of power it knows how to ask for.

The Western consciousness has always asked for freedom: the human mind was born free, or at any rate born to be free, but everywhere it is in chains, and now at the end of its tether. It will take a miracle to free the human mind: because the chains are magical in the first place. We are in bondage to authority outside ourselves: most obviously—here in a great university it must be said—in bondage to the authority of books. There is a Transcendentalist anticipation of what I want to say in Emerson's Phi Beta Kappa address on the American Scholar:

"The books of an older period will not fit this. Yet hence arises a grave mischief. The sacredness which attaches to the act of creation, the act of thought, is transferred to the record. Instantly the book becomes noxious: the guide is a tyrant. The sluggish and perverted mind of the multitude having once received this book, stands upon it, and makes an outcry if it is destroyed. Colleges are built on it. Meek young men grow up in libraries. Hence, instead of Man Thinking, we have the bookworm. I had better never see a book than to be warped by its attraction clean out of my own orbit, and make a satellite instead of a system. The one thing in the world, of value, is the active soul."

How far this university is from that ideal is the measure of the defeat of our American dream.

This bondage to books compels us not to see with our own eyes; compels us to see with the eyes of the dead, with dead eyes. Whitman, likewise in a Transcendentalist sermon, says, "You shall no longer take things at second or third hand, nor look through the eyes of the dead, nor feed on the specters in books." There is a hex on us, the specters in books, the authority of the past; and to exorcise these ghosts is the great work of magical self-liberation. Then the eyes of the spirit would become one with the eyes of the body, and god would be in us, not outside. God in us: *entheos*: enthusiasm; this is the essence of the holy madness. In the fire of the holy madness even books lose their gravity, and let themselves go up into the flame: "Properly," says Ezra Pound, "we should read for power. Man reading should be man intensely alive. The book should be a ball of light in one's hand."

I began with the name of Dionysus; let me be permitted to end with the name of Christ: for the power I seek is also Christian. Nietzsche indeed said the whole question was Dionysus versus Christ; but only the fool will take these as mutually exclusive opposites. There is a Dionysian Christianity, an apocalyptic Christianity, a Christianity of miracles and revelations. And there have always been some Christians for whom the age of miracle and revelation is not over; Christians who claim the spirit; enthusiasts. The power I look for is the power of enthusiasm: as condemned by John Locke; as possessed by George Fox, the Quaker; through whom the houses were shaken; who saw the channel of blood running down the streets of the city of Litchfield; to whom, as a matter of fact, was even given the magic internal heat—"The fire of the Lord was so in my feet, and all around me, that I did not matter to put on my shoes any more."

Read again the controversies of the seventeenth century and discover our choice: we are either in an age of miracles, says Hobbes, miracles which authenticate fresh revelations; or else we are in an age of reasoning from already received scripture. Either miracle or scripture. George Fox, who came up in spirit through the flaming sword into the paradise of God, so that all things were new, he being renewed to the state of Adam which he was in before he fell, sees that none can read Moses aright without

Moses' spirit; none can read John's words aright, and with a true understanding of them, but in and with the same divine spirit by which John spake them, and by his burning shining light which is sent from God. Thus the authority of the past is swallowed up in new creation; the word is made flesh. We see with our own eyes, and to see with our own eyes is second sight. To see with our own eyes is second sight.

> Twofold Always. May God us keep
> From single vision and Newton's sleep.

2

Daphne, or Metamorphosis

Metamorphosis, or Mutabilitie. *Omnia mutantur*. Mutation everywhere. *The Book of Changes*.

ॐ

Metamorphosis, or transubstantiation: we already and from the first discern him making this thing other. His groping syntax, if we attend, already shapes:

Fac nobis hanc oblationem ascriptam, ratam, rationabilem, acceptabilem, quod figura est corporis et sanguinis Christi. Make for us this offering consecrated, approved, reasonable, and acceptable, which is a figure of the body of Christ. *Mutando perde figuram.* Transubstantiate my form, says Daphne.

D. Jones, *Anathemata*, 49.
Auerbach, "Figura," *Scenes from the Drama of European Literature*, 60, 235.
Ovid, *Metamorphoses*, I, l. 547.

ॐ

Metamorphosis, or symbol-formation; the origin of human culture. A laurel branch in the hand, a laurel wreath on the house, a laurel crown on the head; to purify and celebrate. Apollo after slaying the old dragon, or Roman legions entering the city in triumph. As in the Feast of Tabernacles; or Palm

Paper read at meeting of American Philological Association, 1966. Printed in J. Campbell, ed., *Myth, Dreams, and Religion* (New York, 1970), 62–94. Anthologized in R. Gross and G. Quasha, *Open Poetry* (New York, 1973), 28–39. Spanish translation, *Plural* (Mexico D.F.), no. 8 (May 1972).

Sunday. The decoration, the mere display is poetry: making this thing other. A double nature.

Leviticus 23:40.
Mannhardt, *Antike Wald und Feldkulte*, 1:296–298.

෬

Daphnephoria, carrying Daphne. A ceremony of Apollo carrying Daphne, with a choir of maidens. They decorate a piece of olive wood with laurel branches and all kinds of flowers; at the top is tied a bronze ball with smaller balls hanging from it; at the middle they tie another ball not so big as the one on top, with purple ribbons attached; the lower part of the wood they cover with saffron-colored cloth. The ball at the top signifies the sun; the lower one, the moon; the lesser balls, the stars; and the ribbons, the cycle of the year. The Daphne-bearer is made like unto Apollo himself, with hair flowing, and wearing a golden crown, and clothed in a shining robe that reaches down to his feet.

Nilsson, *Griechische Feste*, 164–165.

෬

One branch is the spring. *Pars pro toto*: the tree is a symbol.

෬

The metamorphosis is a trope, or turning: a turn of phrase or figure of speech. *Corpus illud suum fecit "hoc est corpus meum" dicendo, "id est, figura corporis mei."* He made it his own body by saying, "This is my body, that is, the figure of my body." Every sentence is bilingual, or allegorical: saying one thing and meaning another. *Semper in figura loquens.* Every sentence a translation. Of bread and wine, this is my body. Or, of my body, this is a house and this is a steeple.

Tertullian in Auerbach, "Figura," 31.
Salutati, *Epistolario* 4:235: poetry is a *facultas bilinguis, unum exterius exhibens, aliud intrinseca ratione significans, semper in figura loquens.* Cf. Dante, letter to the Can Grande.

෬

Saying makes it so. Poetry, the archetypal fiat; or creative act.

ஜ

Poetry, the creative act, the act of life, the archetypal sexual act. Sexuality is poetry. The lady is our creation, or Pygmalion's statue. The lady is the poem; Laura is, really, poetry. Petrarch says that he invented the beautiful name of Laura, but that in reality Laura was nothing but that poetic laurel which he had pursued with incessant labor.

Petrarch letter in Wilkins, "The Coronation of Petrarch," *The Making of the Canzoniere*, 26.

ஜ

To love is to transform; to be a poet. Together with Apollo's help, the aim is to see, amazed, our lady sitting on the grass, making with her arms a thick shade; as in Pollaiulo's painting. She is the gentle tree whose shade made my weak genius flower.

Petrarch, *Rime*, XXXIV, LX.

ஜ

To love is to transform, and be transformed. The lover must be flexible, or fluxible. There are a thousand shapes of girls, their figures, or *figurae*; the lover, like Proteus, will now melt into flowing water, will be now a lion, now a tree, now a bristling boar.

Ovid, *Ars Amatoria*, I, ll. 759–762.

ஜ

To transform and be transformed. Love and the lady transform him, making out of living man a green laurel, which through the frozen season still loses not its leaves.

Petrarch, *Rime*, XXIII, l. 39.

ஜ

> Apollo's laurel-bough
> That sometime grew within this learned man—

The first stage of spiritual deliverance in yoga is to discover in oneself the tree; the upright surge of the spinal column. Wisdom in Ecclesiastes 29:17: like a cedar I am exalted in Lebanon, and like a cypress on Mount Zion. *Sapientia* is a lady; the *anima* in all of us; the *aura* in Laura. The lady and the lover are one tree.

J. Onimus, "La poétique de l'arbre," *Revue des Sciences Humaines* 101 (1961): 107.
Ovid, *Metamorphoses*, VII, l. 813.

The metamorphosis of sexuality: sublimation.

> The gods that mortal beauty chase
> Still in a tree did end their race.

Instead of the girl, the laurel. *Hanc quoque Phoebus amat.* Orpheus sings, and a tree goes up; in pure sublimation. Or are they one and the same, the tree and the girl, Laura—*remanet nitor unus in illa*—or the tree and the girl and the song. The tree is in the ear; or is it a girl that makes herself a bed in my ear.

Rilke, *Die Sonette an Orpheus*, I, nos. i–ii.
Ovid, *Metamorphoses*, I, ll. 552–553.

From the sensual ear to the spirit ditties of no tone. The spiritualization of the senses; a purification. The laurel purifies. Laurel leaves; Laura laves. Daphne is art, or through art, the still unravished bride. In sublimation the sexuality is not consummated—

> Bold Lover, never, never canst thou kiss,
> Though winning near the goal—yet, do not grieve;
> She cannot fade, though thou hast not thy bliss;
> For ever wilt thou love, and she be fair!

M. B. Ogle, "The Laurel in Ancient Religion and Folklore," *American Journal of Philology* 31 (1910): 287–311.

The still unravished bride. The struggle stilled. The mad pursuit is deathly still. The chase arrested. The immobile running girl, with no carnal motion.

Ovide Moralisé, I, l. 3178.

The chase arrested, the chase goes on forever. As in those gothic novels described by Leslie Fiedler: "Through a dream landscape, usually called by the name of some actual Italian place, a girl flees in terror. . . . She escapes and is caught; escapes again and is caught; escapes and is caught. . . . The Maiden in flight representing the uprooted soul of the artist . . . the girl on the run and her pursuer become only alternate versions of the same plight. . . . Each is a projection of his opposite—*anima* and *animus*."

Fiedler, *Love and Death in the American Novel*, 107, 111.

The still unravished bride, the ever-green. A virginal viridity.
Ovide Moralisé, I, l. 3108.

Ever-green is golden: *grün des Lebens goldner Baum*. The *aurum* in Laura; a golden crown. The alchemical gold of sublimation. The green girl is a golden girl.

Goethe, *Faust*, I, l. 2039.

Ever-green is ever-burning. Daphne a fire-brand; the laurel is full of fire. The branches of that tree which antiquity dedicated to the sun in order to crown all the conquerors of the earth, when shaken together give out fire. The laurel is the burning bush, the Virgin Mary; ardent busshe that did not waste. In the office of the Virgin: *rubum quem viderat Moyses incombustum conservatam agnovimus tuam laudabilem virginitatem*. In the bush that Moses saw burning but unconsumed we recognize the conservation of thy glorious virginity.

Eusebius, *Praeparatio Evangelii*, III, § 112: the laurel sacred to Apollo, ὅτι πυρὸς μεστὸν τὸ φυτόν.
Bacon in Bachelard, *The Psychoanalysis of Fire*, 69–70.
Greene, *Early English Carols*, no. 199.
E. Harris, "Mary in the Burning Bush," *Journal of the Warburg Institute* 1 (1937–1938): 281–282 (Froment triptych, 1476).
L. Réau, *Iconographie de l'Art Chrétien*, vol. 2, part 1, p. 187.
Daphne, δαΐς (δαίω). Cf. H. Boas, *Aeneas' Arrival in Latium*, 98.

Vel rubus incombustus humanitas Christi a divinitate non absorpta; vel ecclesia probata vel turbata tribulatione non consumpta. Or the bush is the humanity of Christ not devoured by his divinity; or the church tried or troubled but not consumed by tribulation.

Harris, "Mary in the Burning Bush," 286.

May she become a flourishing hidden tree. *Virgo, virga,* the rod out of the stem of Jesse. The maiden is a may, a May-branch; thy moder is a may.

> He cam also stylle
> There his moder lay
> As dew in Aprille,
> That fallyt on the spray.

Yeats, "A Prayer for My Daughter."
Greene, *Early English Carols,* nos. 172, 182.

The symbolic equation Girl = Tree; the symbolic equation Girl = Phallus. The virginity is virility; the viridity is virility. We harden like trees.

> I loathe the lewd rake, the dress'd fopling despise:
> Before such pursuers the nice virgin flies;
> And as Ovid has sweetly in parables told,
> We harden like trees, and like rivers grow cold.

O. Fenichel, "The Symbolic Equation Girl = Phallus," *Collected Papers.*
Lady Mary Wortley Montague, "The Lover: A Ballad."

Mascula virgo; going against the grain of her sex. Daphne was a huntress, like Diana; and the only boy she ever loved was a boy disguised as a girl.

S. Sontag, *Against Interpretation,* 279.
Parthenius, *Narrationes Amatoriae,* no. 15.

Metamorphosis into a tree. The sublimation is at the same time a fall, into a lower order of creation; an incarnation. The way up is the way down. The sublime Apollo is desublimated, descends; in love with human nature he takes on human, all-too-human form—the hound of heaven, *ut canis in vacuo lep-orem cum Gallicus arvo*—to be united with the Virgin. And what she finally gives him is wood, the maternal material. The Virgin is his mother; Osiris, Adonis, born of a tree. In her womb he puts on wood; in her womb he is surrounded with wood, crowned with the laurel, embraced by the Virgin.

Ovid, *Metamorphoses*, I, l. 533.
Ovide Moralisé, I, ll. 3245–3250.

What she finally gives him is the wood of the cross.

> The gods that mortal beauty chase
> Still in a tree did end their race.

In a tree or on a tree. Sublimation is crucifixion. Even so shall the Son of Man be lifted up. There is a Coptic tapestry fragment from a fifth-century tomb showing the tree-girl, naked and sexed, handing to Apollo a flower which is a cross. Ovid says, *oscula dat ligno*. He kisses the cross.

In the Louvre Museum.
Ovid, *Metamorphoses*, I, l. 556.

She is his mother; the Great Mother; the naked goddess rising between two branches.

E. Neumann, *The Great Mother*, 241–256.

She is his mother; she may have been a whore. Laura, Laurentia; some say she was the nurse of Romulus and Remus; others say she was a whore.

Freud, "A Special Type of Choice of Object Made by Men," *Collected Papers* 4:199.
Varro, *De Lingua Latina*, V, § 152; VI, § 23.

From the vagabond maiden to the family tree: she settled down; in the Laurentian land. Laura becomes Lar. On Augustus' doorstep—

> postibus Augustis eadem fidissima custos
> ante fores stabis.

> like some green laurel
> rooted in one dear perpetual place.

Vico, *New Science*, § 533.
Cato, *Originum*, Frag. no. 10.
Ovid, *Metamorphoses*, I, ll. 562–563.
Vergil, *Aeneid*, VII, ll. 59–62.

≈&

Metamorphosis into a tree. A fall, into the state of nature. The spirit, the human essence, hides, buried in the natural object; "projected." Great Pan is dead. Ovid's *Metamorphoses*, the death of the gods, and the birth of poetry.

Schiller, "Die Götter Griechenlands."

≈&

Dead and buried. The Muses as museum; art as sarcophagus

> with brede
> Of marble men and maidens overwrought.

Like the laurel, promising immortality.

≈&

Promising immortality, or awaiting resurrection. Not dead but sleeping. The maiden is not dead, but sleepeth. The tree is the sleeping beauty. She made herself a bed in my ear and went to sleep. And everything is her sleep.

Matthew 9:24.
Rilke, *Die Sonette an Orpheus*, I, no. ii.

≈&

To waken the spirit from its sleep. Orpheus or Christ, saying to stem and stone,

> trees
> And the mountain-tops that freeze—

Maiden I say unto thee, arise.

> Shakespeare, *Henry VIII*, act 3, scene 1.
> Luke 8:54.

ào

We shall not all sleep, but we shall all be changed. The resurrection is the revelation of the sons of God. In the Apocalypse

> Daphne hath broke her bark, and that swift foot
> Which th' angry Gods had fast'ned with a root
> To the fix'd earth, doth now unfettered run
> To meet th' embraces of the youthful Sun.

Running to meet the son from whom she originally fled. *Nescis, temeraria, nescis quem fugias.*

> Romans 8:19.
> Carew, "The Rapture."
> Ovid, *Metamorphoses*, I, ll. 514–515.

ào

The triumphant laurel. *In hoc signo vinces.* Be thou faithful unto death and I will give thee a crown of life. A crown of glory that fadeth not; a golden crown. The laud in Laura. The laurel on Caesar's brow; the coronation of Petrarch, the poet laureate. The emperor, the poet, and the triumphant lover:

> Ite triumphales circum mea tempora laurus!
> vicimus, in nostra est, ecce, Corinna sinu.

> Revelation 2:10; 1 Peter 5:4.
> Danielou, "The Palm and Crown," *Primitive Christian Symbols.*
> Kantorowicz, "On Transformations of Apolline Ethics," in *Selected Studies,* 399–408.
> Wilkins, "The Coronation of Petrarch," *The Making of the Canzoniere.*
> Isidorus, *Etymologiarum Lib.*, XVII, § vii. *Laurus a verbo laudis dicta.... Apud antiquos autem laudea nominabatur ... ut in auriculis, quae initio audiculae dictae sunt, et medidies quae nunc meridies dicitur.*
> Ovid, *Amores*, II, no. xii, ll. 1–2.

ào

To restore to trees and flowers their original animality; their original spirituality; their original humanity. Erasmus Darwin in the Proem to his *Loves of the Plants:* "Whereas P. Ovidius Naso, a great necromancer in the famous court of Augustus Caesar did by art poetic transmute Men, Women, and even Gods and Goddesses, into Trees and Flowers; I have undertaken by similar art to restore some of them to their original animality, after having remained prisoners so long in their respective vegetable mansions."

E. Sewell, *The Orphic Voice*, 228.

ॐ

The spirit is human; the invisible reality is human. *Ecce homo; ecce Daphne.* Instead of a stone or tree displayed, a statue; a transfiguration of the stone or tree, disclosing the human essence.

ॐ

The final metamorphosis is the humanization of nature. It is a question of love: the transformation of the Bear into a Prince the moment the Bear is loved. The identification is a change of identity; the magic is love.

Novalis, in Hartman, *The Unmediated Vision*, 135.
Ficino, *Commentarium in Convivium Platonis de Amore*, chapter VI, § 10; cf. F. Yates, *Giordano Bruno and the Hermetic Tradition*, 127.

ॐ

Overcoming the distinction between *Naturwissenschaft* and *Geisteswissenschaft:* "I know what it is to look like a tree but I cannot know what it is to be a tree."

I. Berlin, "The Philosophical Ideas of Giambattista Vico," *Art and Ideas in Eighteenth-Century Italy*, 172.

ॐ

The Tree
Ezra Pound

I stood still and was a tree amid the wood,
Knowing the truth of things unseen before;
Of Daphne and the laurel bow
And that god-feasting couple old
That grew elm-oak amid the wold.

ॐ

A Girl
Ezra Pound

The tree has entered my hands,
The sap has ascended my arms,
The tree has grown in my breast—
Downward,
The branches grow out of me, like arms.

Tree you are,
Moss you are,
You are violets with wind above them.
A child—so high—you are,
And all this is folly to the world.

&

A spiritualization of nature; an invisible spirit in the tree—

Casting the body's vest aside
My soul into the boughs does glide.

The transfiguration is a transmigration.

&

As Karl Marx said, the humanization of nature is the naturalization of man.

The gods that mortal beauty chase
Still in a tree did end their race.

The tree is the teleological end, the *eschaton*. We shall all be changed, in the twinkling of an eye. Resurrection is metamorphosis, from the natural to the supernatural or spiritual body. It is raised a spiritual body. Casting the body's vest aside. The harps that we hung on the willow trees, the organs, are our natural bodies, the sexual organizations.

K. Marx. "The Philosophic-Economic Manuscripts."
G. H. Hartman, "Marvell, St. Paul, and the Body of Hope," *English Literary History* 31 (1964): 175–194.
Methodius, in Rahner, *Greek Myths and Christian Mystery*, 317.

&

The supernatural body reunites us with nature; with rocks and stones and trees. It gives us the flower body of Narcissus, or the tree body of Daphne. Love's best retreat. It is the resurrection of nature in us; nature transformed into invisible spirit. As Rilke says, Earth, is that not what you want, to rise again, invisible, in us. *Unsichtbar in uns zu erstehen.*

Rilke, in Heller, *The Disinherited Mind,* 169.

ᔥ

Love's best retreat. The spiritualization of sensuality is love: a great triumph over Christianity, says Nietzsche. Sensuality is not abolished, but fulfilled.

> No white nor red was ever seen
> So amorous as this lovely green.

Kaufmann, *Nietzsche,* 202.

ᔥ

The reconciliation of spirit and nature; the opposition of sexuality and sublimation overcome. When our eyes are opened, we perceive that in sexuality the object is not the literal girl; but the symbolic girl, the tree. It is always something else that we want. The object is always transcendent.

ᔥ

"Up till now—as is right—my tastes, my feelings, my personal experiences have all gone to feed my writings; in my best contrived phrases I still felt the beating of my heart. But henceforth the link is broken between what I think and what I feel. And I wonder whether this impediment which prevents my heart from speaking is not the real cause that is driving my work into abstraction and artificiality. As I was reflecting on this, the meaning of the fable of Apollo and Daphne suddenly flashed upon me: happy, thought I, the man who can clasp in one and the same embrace the laurel and the object of his love."

A. Gide, *The Counterfeiters,* trans. D. Bussy, 83–84.

ᔥ

The humanization of nature—not in some single herb or tree. In all the flowers and trees. Hierophanies everywhere.

> Each herb and each tree,
> Mountain, hill, earth and sea,
> Cloud, Meteor and Star,
> Are Men Seen Afar.

Blake, letter to Butts, October 2, 1800.

₰

In the meantime, the whole creation groaning. In the meantime, vision is to perceive the tree as Parthenon or maiden's chamber; to perceive the Caryatid in the pillar. To hear the silent speech, or under the bark the beating of a heart. To catch the trembling of her head—

> tremere omnia visa repente
> liminaque laurusque dei.

Glimpses that can make us less forlorn.

Vergil, *Aeneid*, III, ll. 90–91.

₰

To make the tree speak. I am leafy speafing. The oracular tree, or tree of dreams. The sylvan historian, telling a leaf-fringed legend. The *silva* or garden of verses. These trees shall be my book. Book is beech in German (*Buch* and *Buche*); a tree on which we carve our mistress's name. The maidens stray impassioned in the lettering leaves. Laura is really poetry.

Joyce, *Finnegans Wake*, 619.
Fulgentius, *Mitologiae*, I, § 14.
Eliade, *Patterns of Comparative Religion*, 284.
Curtius, *European Literature and the Latin Middle Ages*, 337.

₰

Thus, the whole story from Genesis to Apocalypse in any event; in any metamorphosis. Therefore it is important to keep changing the subject. The subject changes before our very eyes. It is important to keep changing our mind—

> The mind, that ocean where each kind
> Does straight its own resemblance find.

The mind, or the imagination, the original shape-shifter: Thrice-Greatest Hermes.

≥∌

Leo Spitzer said that "in Christian art earthly images easily appear to melt away and vanish. There is a parallel in modern 'poetics by alchemy' exemplified by the practice of a Góngora, who may lead us by metaphors from a maid adorning herself for marriage to Egyptian tombstones; or we may think of the famous passage in which Proust, by the use of metaphors, transforms lilac into fountain—or of Valéry's *Cimetière marin*, that sea cemetery which becomes successively a roof covered with white pigeons, a temple of Time, a flock of sheep with a shepherd dog, a multicolored hydra; all this," says Spitzer, "is based on the same Christian poetics of kaleidoscopic transformation of symbols." A Christian transfiguration, or a pagan orgy: a Bacchanalian revel of categories in which not one member is sober; a protean flux of metamorphosis. As in *Finnegans Wake*.

L. Spitzer, "Classical and Christian Ideas of World Harmony," *Traditio II* (1944), 426.

≥∌

Not everyone can play *Finnegans Wake*. But professors can. James Joyce is the apostle unto the professors. And the message is: Let's play. Or, let's practice metamorphosis. Or, let's change the subject.

≥∌

In any case it is necessary to have faith. To believe what the Bible tells us. Only beleaf. The Bible; *Le Livre*; it is all one book. Literature is as collective as the unconscious; private authorship or ownership is not to be respected. It is all one book, which includes the gospel according to Ovid, Saint Ovid the Martyr (*Ovide Moralisé*); and Petrarch, and Marvell, and Keats, and Rilke, and Yeats, and Gide, and Pound. And also the ravings of every poor Crazy Jane. Every poor schizophrenic girl is a Delphic priestess; or a Daphne, saying, "I am that tree." "That's the rain—I could be the rain. That chair—that wall. It's a terrible thing for a girl to be a wall." It's a terrible thing for a girl to be a Delphic priestess. In the cave the priestess raves: she still resists the brutal god, to shake from her hapless breast his breast; all the more his pressure subjugates her wild heart, wears down her rabid mouth, shapes her mouth into his mouthpiece.

R. D. Laing, *The Divided Self*, 217.
Vergil, *Aeneid*, VI, ll. 77–80.
L. K. Born, "Ovid and Allegory," *Speculum* 9 (1934): 362–379.

 ❧

It is all one book; blossoms on one tree,

>   Characters of the great Apocalypse
>   The types and symbols of Eternity.

One tree, in kaleidoscopic metamorphosis.

Wordsworth, *Prelude*, VI, ll. 637–639.

 ❧

[Added, July 1990]

>   we that were wood
>   when that a wide wood was

>   In a physical Universe playing with

>   words

>   Bark be my limbs my hair be leaf

>   Bride be my bow my lyre my quiver

Susan Howe, "Pythagorean Silence," *The European Trusts* (Los Angeles: Sun and Moon, 1990), 17.

3

My Georgics

A Palinode in Praise of Work

Georgics: a didactic poem. For my students. The assignment is to write.

Georgics: celebrating George. Who is George? George is a farmer. *Gê*, earth, as in geology. *Org* or *erg*, as in organ or energy, is work. Hesiod's *Works and Days, Erga kai Hemerai.* Farmer is earth-worker. My *Georgics*, celebrating earth-work, as in the Garden Project.

My *Georgics*, a palinode in praise of work. A *palin-ode*, or second song. *Palin*, again, against; as in palindrome. Stesichorus' palinode, or recantation: the second song that undoes the first. I was blind and now I see again. My best thoughts are second thoughts. I once praised *Homo ludens*, the play-principle in human culture. I was an abolitionist; a bolshevik, aboleshqvik; abolishing work. But, as Hegel said, "The life and knowledge of God may doubtless be described as love playing with itself; but this idea sinks into triviality if the seriousness, the pain, the patience and the labor of Negation are omitted."[1]

Hannah Arendt's three staples in the Human Condition: labor, work, action. Labor in the fields; work of our hands (making artifacts); and political or historical action. Perhaps we can abolish action along with politics and history. And fall again into

Speech delivered in 1970. A homage to the Garden Project at the University of California at Santa Cruz, in which countercultural dropouts learned the meaning of work from the magus of the garden, Alan Chadwick.

that paradise in which humans have no history. That paradise, that garden. But in that garden there is always work to be done; to dress it and keep it.

There is always work to be done; psychic work to be done; dream-work. Psychoanalytic interpretation works through the repressed materials to turn the stream of consciousness back into useful, into irrigation channels, so that none of this power be wasted. To clean the Augean stables, capture the Erymanthian boar, clear the Stymphalian birds from the marshes of the unconscious mind—these things must be done. "Until we have completed our 12 labours, we (mankind) have no right to rest on cloud-cushion phantasies and dreams of an after-life."[2] "It is reclamation work, like the draining of the Zuyder Zee," says Freud.[3]

There is reclamation work to be done: we are not in Hell; we are in Purgatory. Apropos of Dante's sentence, "The proper functioning is not for the sake of the being which functions, but rather the being for the sake of its function," Charles Williams writes, "This is the primal law for all the images, of whatever kind; they were created for their working, and in order to work. Hell is the cessation of work and the leaving of the images to be, without any function, merely themselves."[4] Just to be ourselves is Hell; just doing our own thing. The ideal state, each doing his own work; functioning organically; members of one body.

To find meaning is to find work. "The confusions which occupy us arise when language is like an engine idling, not when it is doing work."[5] In alchemy, the Great Work of Transformation: transform the nature of work. Two ways of never ending: the scientist continues; the alchemist starts all over again. Recycling.

Transform the nature of work. Return it to life, to labor, the labor of childbirth. Making all men into women; I mean in our work. Giving birth in beauty, as Plato said. My great travail, so gladly spent. The pain, too.

> The sky will be much friendlier then than now,
> A part of labor and a part of pain,
> And next in glory to enduring love.[6]

Labor is fertility: Marx and Freud reconciled. Marx's productive process is really a reproductive process. Life goes on: man makes himself; produces, reproduces, giving birth in beauty to himself. Instead of Gross National Product, reproduction; reproduction of the eternal earth. Ecology instead of economy.

Instead of productivity, reproduction. The proletariat, prolific reproducers, reproduces the organic base of civilization, the sober reality. The proletariat is the human condition: earth-born, earthy, giants of the earth. Human, humility: from *humus*, from the earth.

"My great travail, so gladly spent." The lover too. The Lover Beseecheth his Mistress not to Forget his Steadfast Faith and True Intent:

> Forget not yet the tried intent
> Of such a truth as I have meant;
> My great travail so gladly spent,
> Forget not yet!

To learn to love is to learn to love labor; love's labor loved. Sex is labor. John Donne, "To his Mistress going to Bed":

> Come, Madam, come, all rest my powers defy,
> Until I labour, I in labour lie.

"Until I labour, I in labour lie." The bed is child-bed. Couvade; in which he plays the woman's part.

And labor to be an act of love. *Homo laborans*, man in labor, is man *amans amare*, in love with loving, and seeking an object for his love. Freud on the origin of language: "The first sounds uttered were a means of communication and of summoning the sexual partner; in the later development the elements of speech were used as an accompaniment to the different kinds of work carried on by primitive man. This work was performed by associated efforts, to the sound of rhythmically repeated utterances, the effect of which was to transfer a sexual interest to the work. Primitive man thus made his work agreeable, so to speak, by treating it as the equivalent of and substitute for sexual activities."[7] Freud and Marx reconciled. Labor to be an act of love. And singing makes it so.

Return culture to agriculture. Agriculture, the root; commerce, the branch; rediscover our roots, the radicalism. The Great Cultural Revolution, overcoming the antinomy of town and country. "Rustic" is not the opposite of "cultured."

Agri-culture: *ager*, a field. *The Opening of the Field*, by Robert Duncan; unfolding the field, that is a field folded. Bhagavad Gita, chapter 13: Arjuna said, "Prakriti and Purusha, the Field and the Knower of the Field, knowledge and that which is to be known—all this, O Keśava, I desire to learn." And Hamann, the Magus of the North: "Man is therefore not only a living field, but also the son of the field, and not only the field and the seed (as in the system of the materialists and the idealists) but also the king of the field, who plants good seed and hostile tares in his field: for what is a field without seed, and a prince without land and produce? These three in us are therefore one, namely, God's field."[8]

The city is a field. Marriage, as all statesmen agree, is the seed-bed (*seminario*) of the family, as the family is the seed-bed of the commonwealth. Vico's plough: civilization is a plough.[9] *Polis*, city; *poleuo*, to plough, back and forth; civilization reproducing itself. Imperial paradigm was by ploughing. The Emperor's furrow. From ploughing of fields is justice.[10]

The founders of cities traced out the walls with a plough. The first cities were all founded on cultivated fields. The ploughed lands were the first altars of the Gentiles; the first fire lighted on them was that which served to clear the forests of trees and bring them under cultivation. *Ara*, altar; *arare*, to plough, as in arable.[11] Civilization is an altar on which a sacrifice is being made. And the sacrifice is cultivation; cult is cultivation. Immolation: to sprinkle the victim with ground meal.

Cadmus opened up the furrows with his plough, and planted therein the dragon's teeth. Cadmus's seed-bed, or seminary. The birth of a nation. Open the field, and see the soldiers growing in it, springing up from the furrows; first the points of spears appear; then helmets with colored plumes waving; next shoulders, breasts, and arms loaded with armor.[12]

The field becomes a battle-field. A field of Mars; a Campus Martius; a campus, or armed camp. The flower of the nations mowing each other down.

It could be the Elysian fields. Or Saturn's reign. Saturn the sower, of satisfaction. The age of gold, to gold unknown. The first gold, the golden harvests.

The interpretation of culture is the science of heraldry. The first shield in the world was the ground of the field in which the dead were buried.[13] What we have to interpret is a field. What we have to make is a shield, the shield of Achilles, a field sown with signs and images, the likeness of everything that is in heaven above, or that is in the earth beneath, or that is in the water under the earth.

Culture is agriculture. The Garden Project. A Garden of Verses. The poet says, "There is a garden in her face." There is a garden in the mind. Cultivate your own garden. Cultivate your own psyche. Keats' "Ode to Psyche." "Yes, I will be thy priest," he says to Psyche. Yes, psychotherapy is the cult of the psyche.

Yes, I will be thy priest, and build a fane
    In some untrodden region of my mind,
Where branched thoughts, new grown with pleasant pain,
    Instead of pines shall murmur in the wind:
Far, far around shall those dark-cluster'd trees
    Fledge the wild-ridgèd mountains steep by steep;
And there by zephyrs, streams, and birds, and bees,
    The moss-lain Dryads shall be lull'd to sleep;
And in the midst of this wide quietness
A rosy sanctuary will I dress
With the wreath'd trellis of a working brain,
    With buds, and bells, and stars without a name,
With all the gardener Fancy e'er could feign,
    Who, breeding flowers, will never breed the same:
And there shall be for thee all soft delight
    That shadowy thought can win,
A bright torch, and a casement ope at night,
    To let the warm Love in!

The garden of the mind. There is planting and hoeing and tilling to be done. Energy, *energeia*, the work of self-realization. Two kinds of energy: atomic energy, explosion, ecstasy, mushroom-cloud-in-the-head; and agriculture, patient, enduring, day after day. Hesiod's *Georgics*, his *Works and Days*. Works and days. The hours, the seasons. What a wonder is man. Earth, the foundation; unwearied indestructible Earth; he wears her down. The ploughs go back and forth, year after year.[14] Year in, year out; the earth cycle. There is no end to it. No *telos*, no goal; no teleology.

To plough is to write. *Boustrophedon*, ox-strophe-wise, ox-turning-wise; the word for archaic Greek writing, meaning from left to right and right to left on alternate lines, as the ox ploughs. A strophe, or turning, or verse; back and forth, in field-composition. At any rate, not straightforward. That's prose: *prorsus*, straight forward. Prose goes straight forward without verses.

To plough is to write. In a manuscript of the eighth or ninth century, preserved at Verona (a Mozarabic prayer book), the following notation was discovered in 1924: "Se pareva boves alba pratalia araba et albo versorio teneba et negro semen seminaba"; that is, "He urged on the oxen, ploughed white fields, held a white plough, and sowed black seed." An attempt was made to turn this into a rhymed quatrain in early Italian, and it was given out to be a precious relic of popular bucolic poetry. As a matter of fact it is a scribal adage of erudite origin. The white fields are the pages; the white plough, the pen; the black seeds, the ink.[15]

Thinking drives furrows in the ground of being. *De-lirium:* out of the furrow. Only where there is a furrow is there any point in going straight.

Work, then; for the gods keep life hidden from humans. You have to dig in order to dig it. The treasure is buried in a field. Consciousness is an archaeological dig. Consciousness is an agricultural dig. Go down to the underworld: it is no deeper than a ditch.[16]

Write, then. A Book of Hours; of Works and Days; of Seasons. Hours were seasons, before there were clocks; how things have speeded up! A Book of Ours. I need Thee, O I need Thee, I need Thee every hour.

Work is mystical. A Book of Hours is still a book of prayers. *Laborare est orare,* to labor is to pray. The garden and the monastery or university: "idle monks." The Garden Project: overcoming the distinction between the active and the contemplative life. Overcoming the distinction between works and grace. The seasonal cycle of ritual is the seasonal cycle of work.

A Book of Hours. A Garden of Verses. Sow, then; or let yourself be sown; in your own seminar or seminary. How does your garden grow? What "branched thoughts, new grown with pleasant pain"? And let us gather together the harvest. The sheaves. The leaves. A harvest of poetic gold.

NOTES

1. G. W. F. Hegel, *Phenomenology of Spirit*, Preface § 19.

2. H.D., *Tribute to Freud* (New York, 1956), 156–157.

3. S. Freud, *New Introductory Lectures on Psycho-Analysis* (London, 1949), 106.

4. C. Williams, *The Figure of Beatrice* (New York, 1961), 40.

5. L. Wittgenstein, *Philosophical Investigations*, § 132.

6. W. Stevens, "Sunday Morning."

7. S. Freud, *General Introduction to Psycho-Analysis*, chapter 10.

8. R. G. Smith, *J. G. Hamann* (New York, 1960), 99.

9. G. Vico, *The New Science*, trans. T. G. Bergin and M. H. Fisch (Ithaca, 1968) §§ 11, 15–16.

10. E. Pound, *Cantos* (New York, 1970), 95/643, 98/692, 89/601, 100/715.

11. Vico, *New Science*, §§ 549, 775.

12. Vico, *New Science*, § 679; Ovid, *Metamorphoses*, III, ll. 106–110.

13. Vico, *New Science*, § 563.

14. Sophocles, *Antigone*, 338–340; Pound, *Cantos*, 88/584.

15. E. R. Curtius, *European Literature and Latin Middle Ages* (New York, 1963), 314.

16. Hesiod, *Works and Days*, 42; Matthew 13:44; Vico, *New Science*, § 712.

4

Metamorphoses II
Actaeon

Human culture is human sacrifice, together with symbolic substitution: a ram, caught in a thicket by his horns, to take the place of Isaac. Symbolic substitution, or metamorphosis: turning the human victim into an animal totem: man into stag.

B. Brophy, *Black Ship to Hell*, 437.

Actaeon; alien horns added to his forehead; the dogs that sated themselves in the blood of their own master; all for the sin of seeing. *Cur aliquid vidi?* Why did I have to see something?

Ovid, *Metamorphoses*, III, ll. 139–140; *Tristia*, II, l. 103.

Actaeon, the sacred heart, hart. Gargaphie and Golgotha are the same place: the place of skulls, and the mountain stained with the blood of beasts of every kind.

> O world, thou wast the forest to this hart,
> And this indeed, o world, the heart of thee.
> How like a deer, stricken by many princes,
> Dost thou here lie.

Ovid, *Metamorphoses*, III, l. 143.
Shakespeare, *Julius Caesar*, act 3, scene 1, ll. 205–210.

Actaeon, the Holy Son of God, who took upon him the form of a servant, serf, cerf. And his own knew him not: the Jews,

Published in *New American Poetry*, vol. 1, no. 1 (November–December 1972): 38–40.

worse than dogs, did not recognize their master. The ghost of Actaeon appeared in a dream to his father Aristaeus, and begged him not to punish the dogs, saying Father, forgive them; for they knew not what they did.

Ovide Moralisé, III, ll. 624–630.
Philippians 2:7; Acts 13:27.
Nonnus, Dionysiaca, V, ll. 442–445.

જ

The dogs sated themselves in their own master's blood; Christ feeds his own with his own transubstantiated flesh. One version gives Actaeon's dogs the power of human speech; after they eat their master's tongue, the word made flesh.

Des Périers, Cymbalum Mundi, Dialogue IV.

જ

Devoured by his own dogs; host eaten by parasites. *Fortune par les miens me chasse*. Actaeon, *akteanos*, who wasted his own substance; violent against himself. The wood was filled with black bitches, eager and fleet, as greyhounds that have escaped the leash; into him they thrust their teeth and tore him piece by piece. Like King Lear: he wasted his own substance; was torn to pieces by his own bitches; dehumanized, metamorphosed into a bear; and hunted down till they get Cordelia, his hart; his speechless heart, breaks.

M. Scève, Délie, ed. I. D. McFarlane, 211.
S. Reinach, Cultes, Mythes, et Religions 3:52.
Dante, Inferno, XIII, ll. 124–129.

જ

The dogs that know not their own master are mad dogs; the dogs of madness that tore Pentheus to pieces. Agave, his mother, knew not her own son. Lear's daughters knew not their own father. There is a vase-painting of the stag-man, attacked by his own bitches, with Lady Madness driving them on. Sweet heavens, do not make me mad.

Euripides, Bacchae, 977.
Reinach, Cultes 3:24, fig. 5.

જ

The dogs of madness are bitches, *canes satiatae.* Lear's daughters or Agave's maenads. The pack of hounds is Diana's troop of maidens, metamorphosed into maenads; minions of the moon, or lunatics; Hecate's or Hell's angels, a coven of witches or bitches. Or the hounds of spring on winter's traces. Diana, queen and huntress, chaste and fair, is also Lady Madness.

Ovid, *Metamorphoses*, III, l. 140.
E. Rohde, *Psyche*, 298, 324.
H. Rahner, *Greek Myths and Christian Mystery*, 237.
K. Dilthey, "Die Artemis des Apelles und die Wilde Jagd," *Rheinisches Museum* 25 (1870): 321–336.

è**

Actaeon and Diana: he is her lover. Some give as the reason for his misfortune that presuming upon his dedication to Artemis of the first fruits of his hunting, he proposed to consummate marriage with the goddess in her own temple.

Diodorus, book IV, chap. 81, sec. 4.

è**

He is her lover. She is Circe, who transforms men into stags—

> y los hombres avanzan
> como ciervos heridos—

Or La Belle Dame Sans Merci—

> aliis violentior aequo
> visa dea est.
> Vénus toute entière à sa proie attachée.

F. Garcia Lorca, *Yerma*, II, i.
Ovid, *Metamorphoses*, III, l. 253.

è**

The goddess Kali, or Nature: she feeds with fresh blood the innumerable insatiable mouths suckled at her milkless breast. The Mountain Mother—

> mons erat infectus variarum caede ferarum.

Swinburne, in M. Praz, *Romantic Agony*, 223.
Ovid, *Metamorphoses*, III, l. 143.

è**

Merciless Beauty:

> Your eyen two wol sleye me sodenly
> I may the beauté of hem not susteyne.

Ishtar and Tammuz: Ishtar, who for Tammuz, the lover of her youth, has ordained yearly wailing—

> Then thou didst love the keeper of the herd,
> Who ash-cakes ever did heap up for thee,
> Daily slaughtered kids for thee;
> Yet thou smotest him, turning him into a wolf,
> So that his own herd boys drive him off,
> And his own dogs bite his thighs.

E. Pound, *Cantos*, 81/520.
Gilgamesh, VI.

❧

Madness: Actaeon and Pentheus; their fate is dismemberment, *sparagmos*, and raw-eating, *omophagy*. Diana's minion is moonstruck, a lunatic.

❧

Madness, or masochism. Von Sacher-Masoch organized nightly games of hide-and-seek in the park; the young ladies, dressed in fur wraps (*Venus im Pelz*) had to hunt him down, throw themselves upon him, and scratch and bite like animals.

R. Eisler, *Man into Wolf*, 69–70.

❧

Young ladies dressed in fur wraps: expensive bitches. In the *Ovide Moralisé* Actaeon wasted his substance on dogs. Dogs, or bitches; ravenous and riotous sycophants, or witches; what difference does it make? He went to the dogs. *Fortune par les miens me chasse.*

G. Sandys, *Ovid's Metamorphoses*, 100.

❧

Hunted by his own dogs, his companions, ravenous and riotous sycophants; a stag party, a wild hunt. Initiation is hazing: blind-man's buff, with metamorphosis; bear baiting or stag baiting. Lucius turned into an ass, or Bottom in *Midsummer Night's Dream*. Sir John Falstaff in *Merry Wives of Windsor*, disguised as Herne the Hunter, with great ragged horns on his head. Falstaff: "I do perceive that I am made an ass." Falstaff's great ragged horns are his crown of thorns. The first step in the imitation of Christ: to be mocked. God is mocked. The stag is the hairy fool in the leather coat, much marked of the melancholy Jaques.

> To-day my Lord of Amiens and myself
> Did steal behind him as he lay along
> Under an oak, whose antique root peeps out
> Upon the brook that brawls along this wood,
> To the which place a poor sequestered stag,
> That from the hunter's aim had ta'en a hurt,
> Did come to languish; and indeed my lord,
> The wretched animal heaved forth such groans
> That their discharge did stretch his leathern coat
> Almost to bursting, and the big round tears
> Coursed one another down his innocent nose
> In piteous chase; and thus the hairy fool,
> Much marked of the melancholy Jaques,
> Stood on th' extremest verge of the swift brook,
> Augmenting it with tears.

Lacrima Christi: a rich, sweet Neapolitan wine.

Shakespeare, *As You Like It*, act 2, scene 1, ll. 29–43.

ᘒ

The Wild Hunt, ghostly hunters who ride through the sky on stormy evenings, known in nearly all parts of the world.

> Herne the Hunter
> Sometime a keeper here in Windsor Forest
> Doth all the winter-time, at still midnight
> Walk round about an oak with great ragg'd horns.

G. Roheim, *Gates of the Dream*, chapter 10.
Shakespeare, *The Merry Wives of Windsor*, act 4, scene 4, ll. 27–30.

ᘒ

Ghosts at midnight, or highwaymen. Falstaff as Herne the Hunter in *The Merry Wives of Windsor* is the same as Falstaff the highwayman in *Henry IV*: both are Sir Actaeon. "Let not us that are squires of the night's body be called thieves of the day's beauty; let us be 'Diana's foresters,' 'gentlemen of the shade,' 'minions of the moon' . . . our noble and chaste mistress the moon, under whose countenance we steal."

Shakespeare, *Henry IV, Part I*, act 1, scene 2, ll. 23–26, 28–29.

❧

Sir John Falstaff wears the horns, the cuckold's horns. The complacent husband is a secure and willful Actaeon. The plot of *The Merry Wives of Windsor* is to

> leave proof by that which we will do,
> Wives may be merry, and yet honest too.

The cuckoo meets the fate of the cuckold. For his rendezvous with the Merry Wives, Falstaff disguises himself as Herne the Hunter, with great ragged horns, and then is hunted down in Windsor Forest by the Merry Wives turned maenads, with their fairy-hounds, who

> Pinch him for his villainy,
> Pinch him, and burn him, and turn him about
> Till candles, and starlight, and moonshine be out.

Shakespeare, *The Merry Wives of Windsor*, act 4, scene 2, ll. 109–110; act 5, scene 5, ll. 98–100.

❧

The unchaste wife is chaste Diana; who throws water into his face; to make him blind, or to drive him mad; horn-mad. To make a fool of her husband; the hairy fool. The cuckold, one of the masks of God; the humiliated God.

Ovid, *Amores*, III, xi, l. 6.
R. B. Onians, *Origins of European Thought*, 243.

❧

The mystery of the horn. Shakespeare, *As You Like It*, act 4, scene 2:

The Forest

Enter Jaques and Lords dressed as foresters.

Jaques: Which is he that killed the deer?

A lord: Sir, it was I.

Jaques: Let's present him to the Duke like a Roman conqueror, and it would do well to set the deer's horns upon his head for a branch of victory. Have you no song, forester, for this purpose?

Forester: Yes, sir. . . .

Lords (*sing*): What shall he have that killed the deer?
His leather skin and horns to wear.
Then sing him home; the rest shall bear
        This burthen.
Take thou no scorn to wear the horn;
It was a crest ere thou was born,
            Thy father's father wore it,
            And thy father bore it.
The horn, the horn, the lusty horn,
Is not a thing to laugh to scorn.

Shakespeare has everything. Who is it that wears the horns? The victor or the victim? The emperor or the clown? And the scene changes in a moment from under the greenwood tree to a Roman triumph; and then to the parental bedroom, the primal scene.

ह

Or is it the god that wears the horns? Cernunnus, the Celtic god of witches, with his horned head; or the devil: you shall know him by his horns. Dionysus, lunate, horned like the moon, as well as lunatic; or the horned Moses: *cornuta facies ex consortio sermonis Domini.*

Shakespeare, *The Merry Wives of Windsor*, act 5, scene 2, l. 16.
Exodus, 34:29–35.
T. C. Lethbridge, *Witches*, 35, 41.
E. G. Suhr, "The Horned Moses," *Folklore* 74 (1963): 387–395.

ह

The horn of madness: let the proverb go with me, I'll be horn-mad. Actaeon, alien horns added to his head, is out of his mind.

Shakespeare, *The Merry Wives of Windsor*, act 3, scene 5, end.

૨ଈ

The horn of erection,

> The horn, the horn, the lusty horn
> Is not a thing to laugh to scorn.

Horny, of satyrs; or Faunus, the foolish god who spies on Diana bathing in Spenser's *Cantos of Mutabilitie*; the horn of river gods, those ravishers.

૨ଈ

English *horn* is Latin *cornu*, therefore English *corn*. Greek *keras* ("horn") is English *kern* and *kernel*; also *grain* (*granum*), *garner*. *Cornucopia*, horn of plenty.

But also *cornu* ("horn") is *corona* ("crown"); *coronis*, a curved line or flouish at the end of a chapter. And Greek *keras* ("horn") is Greek *kras*, English *cranium*, a head. Greek *kratos*, a head of power, an authority (aristo-cracy, demo-cracy); *krainein*, "authorize."

Herne the horny hunter is German *Hirn* ("brain"). Herne was brainy; like the horned Moses, crescent, cresting. *Cerebral* ("brainy") is from the same root as *Ceres* ("goddess of growth"), *cresco* ("grow"), *creo* ("create"). Soul substance is seminal substance; the genius is the genital in the head. A swollen or horny head; insane. *Cerebrosus* (*cerritus*), which ought to mean "brainy," means "mad." Greek *keras* and *keraunos*, "horn" and "thunder," horn-mad and thunderstruck.

Herne is also a bird, a heron or hern; also crane or crow; Greek *geranos* and *korone*, Latin *cornix* and *corvus*. "Why these birds should derive their names from *horn* I cannot presume to say" (G. M. Hopkins).

And a tree: cornel tree, Latin *cornus*, Greek *kraneia*.

And a rock: the Hernici were rock-men, Rocky; Matterhorn. English *corner* and *cranny*; Greek *kranaos* is rocky.

Actaean Attica: *akte,* "promontory," "horn"; *akte,* "grain," "corn."

G. M. Hopkins, *Diary,* September 24, 1863: "Horn."
Onians, *Origins of European Thought,* 148–150.
N. O. Brown, *Love's Body,* 136.

ॐ

The mystery of the horn; the gates of horn. He hath raised up a horn of salvation for us. My horn shalt thou exalt like the horn of a unicorn.

For I prophecy that we shall have our horns again.

Luke 1:69; Psalms 92:10.
C. Smart, *Jubilate Agno,* XXIV, l. 38.

ॐ

The Guru Nagarjuna told the thief: "Imagine all things you desire as horns growing in your head. If you meditate in this way you will see a light like that of an emerald." Keats' branched thoughts new grown with pleasant pain . . . the wreathed trellis of a working brain. *Cervi,* Latin for stags, also means forked stakes that support the vine.

A. Govinda, *Foundations of Tibetan Mysticism,* 55.

ॐ

Horn of the beast and horn of prophecy. Instead of the swollen head of the nation, poetry pressing forth like Pegasus; horns of sublime sound. Daniel 7:7–8: After this I saw in the night visions, and behold, a fourth beast, dreadful and terrible, and strong exceedingly; and it had great iron teeth: it devoured and brake in pieces, and stamped the residue with the feet of it: and it was diverse from all the beasts that were before it; and it had ten horns. I considered the horns, and, behold, there came up among them another little horn, before whom there were three of the first horns plucked up by the roots: and behold, in this horn were eyes like the eyes of a man, and a mouth speaking great great things.

R. Duncan, "*Passages 30.*"

ॐ

Those are horns that were his eyes. Antlers in the place of eyes: antler, *antollier*, *ante ocularem ramum*. In German *Augensprosse am Hirschgeweih*: antlers as eye-sprout. The branches that he parted to get a better view now grew in the place of eyes. Caught in a thicket by his horns, the cornea of his eyes. Some interpret the gates of horn as the eyes, taking the part for the whole, in that the outermost covering of the eye is horny.

J.-P. Sartre, *Being and Nothingness*, 578.
Eustathius on *Odyssey*, XIX, ll. 560–586.

Caught in a thicket by his horns: an eclipse; Actaeon, *aktis*, sun-beam, eye-beam. As the golden sun-animal, the stag proceeds through the air spreading light which illuminates the mountain gorges.

A. Salmony, *Antler and Tongue*, 20.

The Actaeon complex: he stole a glance—

> So that an yhe is as a thief
> To love, and doth ful gret meschief.

Gower, *Confessio Amantis*, I, ll. 319–320.

Love at first sight; he loses his soul to the woman in the water—

> Alas, the moon should ever beam
> To show what man should never see!
> I saw a maiden on a stream,
> And fair was she!
>
> I staid to watch, a little space,
> Her parted lips if she would sing,
> The waters closed above her face
> With many a ring.
>
> I know my life will fade away,
> I know that I must vainly pine,
> For I am made of mortal clay,
> But she's divine!

Actaeon is also Narcissus. *Tantus tenet error amantem*; it's all a big mistake. La Belle Dame sans Merci is a reflection, a projection, of our own soul.

J. G. Frazer, *Golden Bough* 3:94.
Ovid, *Metamorphoses*, III, l. 447.

٭

Cur aliquid vidi? Why did I have to see something? We are punished for our unconscious errors: Actaeon, and Ovid, unintentionally saw too much. An ensample touchende of mislok (Miss Luck; miss-look).

Fortunae crimen in illo
non scelus invenies.

Ovid, *Tristia*, II, ll. 103–106; *Metamorphoses*, III, ll. 141–142.
Gower, *Confessio Amantis* 1:333.

٭

The naked truth. Woe is me, for I am undone: for mine eyes have seen the Queen. All knowledge is guilty knowledge, and the consequence is flight; a divided self, alien horns or alienation; a double nature, or schizophrenia; the timid heart of a stag.

Isaiah 6:5.
Ovide Moralisé, III, ll. 635–640.
E. Panofsky, *Studies in Iconology*, 152–153.
Callimachus, *Hymns*, V, ll. 101–102.

٭

The wild hunt, an allegory of civilization. The origin of civilization, madness. It is the tale of Actaeon, who, seeing Diana naked (the living spring) and being sprinkled with water by the goddess (to signify that the goddess cast over him the great awe of her divinity), was changed into a stag (the most timid of animals) and torn to pieces by his dogs (the remorse of his own conscience for the violation of religion). Hence *lymphati* (properly, sprinkled with *lympha* or pure water) must have been originally a term applied to the Actaeons who had been maddened by superstitious terror.

G. Vico, *New Science*, §528.
M. Foucault, *Madness and Civilization*.

ॐ

The Coming of War: Actaeon (Ezra Pound).

ॐ

Civilization, a wild hunt; a fugue or flight, on the wings, the pennants of penance. Remorse, the bite of a mad dog. Conscience, the superego, the introjected father or animal; now eating us even as we ate him.

Epistle of Othea to Hector, ed. J. D. Gordon, 105–107.

ॐ

Conscience, or consciousness, a scapegoat, or Actaeon, expelled into the wilderness. Ovid, or Ezra Pound, exiled poets—

> dicas, inter mutata referri
> fortunae vultum corpora posse meae.

You could call the figure of my fate another metamorphosis.

Ovid, *Tristia*, I, i, ll. 119–120; II, ll. 103–106.

ॐ

Ovid, or Ezra Pound, or Peire Vidal:

> Actaeon: Vidal,
> Vidal. It is old Vidal speaking,
>   stumbling along in the wood,
> Not a patch, not a lost shimmer of sunlight,
>   the pale hair of the goddess.
>
> The dogs leap on Actaeon.
> Stumbling, stumbling along in the wood,
> Muttering, muttering Ovid

Poetry is masochism. The poet Peire Vidal (c. 1150–1210), in honor of a lady named La Loba, The She-Wolf, had himself sewn into the skin of a wolf, and then, provoking a shepherd's dogs, ran before them until pulled down, nearly dead—after which the countess and her husband, laughing together, had him doctored until well.

E. Pound, *Cantos*, IV.
J.Campbell, *Creative Mythology*, 175.

❧

Or Shelley. The agony of consciousness; the Romantic agony:

Midst others of less note, came one frail form,
A phantom among men; companionless
As the last cloud of an expiring storm
Whose thunder is its knell; he, as I guess,
Had gazed on Nature's naked loveliness,
Actaeon-like, and now he fled astray
With feeble steps o'er the world's wilderness,
And his own thoughts, along that rugged way,
Pursued, like raging hounds, their father and their prey.

Shelley, *Adonais*, XXXI.

❧

The passion of the poet is his poetry. His own thoughts pursue their father and their prey. Lear's daughters are his own thoughts. *Fortune par les miens me chasse.*

❧

The poet, the lunatic, and the lover—

O when my eyes did see Olivia first
Methought she purged the air of pestilence;
That instant was I turned into a hart,
And my desires, like fell and cruel hounds
E'er since pursue me.

Shakespeare, *Twelfth Night*, act 1, scene 1, ll. 18–22.

❧

To love is to be hunter hunted. *The Heart Is a Lonely Hunter.* The lover pursues the cruel fere, both beauty and the beast; only to become himself estranged and fugitive. Petrarch-Actaeon, the anchorite or eremite of love. One day hunting, as I used to do, I went, and that beast, beautiful and savage, in a fountain naked stood, at the time when the sun was burning strongest. I, since no other sight contents me, stood to gaze at her; at which she felt ashamed, and to punish me or to hide herself, with her hand she threw water in my face. I will tell the truth, perhaps it will seem a lie: I felt myself turned from my proper shape, and I was transformed into a solitary wandering stag, running from wood to wood; and I am still fleeing from the rage of my own hounds.

Petrarch, *Rime*, XXIII.

ðā

Love like a shadow flies when substance love pursues;
Pursuing that that flies, and flying what pursues.

The stricken hart, emblem of love incurable. The god of love, or Dionysus, the great hunter, is Apollo chasing Daphne. To free us from our servitude: it is we who are the stag; the soul haunted by the hound of heaven. In Eden, the two sources of life are war and hunting; in paradise, the park, the deer-park.

ðā

The dogs of madness must be the mad god himself; transform these dogs into gods. In heroic frenzy, the great hunter sees, and he himself becomes the prey. Actaeon, who with these thoughts, his dogs, searched for wisdom, beauty, and the wild beast outside himself, attained them this way: once he was in their presence, ravished outside of himself by so much beauty, he became the prey of his own thoughts and saw himself converted into the thing he was pursuing. Predator of the marvelous, searching for wisdom, beauty, the wild beast. She is the unicorn.

G. Bruno, *Heroic Frenzies*, trans. P. E. Memmo, 125.
F. Yates, *Giordano Bruno*, 278, 282.

ðā

Saint Actaeon, the hermit; initiate wearing the horns of consecration; like the sorcerer in the paleolithic cave at Trois Frères, a man masked in a stag's head. Antlers as tines, or tongues, or branched thoughts, new grown with pleasant pain; a ladder of perfection.

R. Levy, *Gate of Horn*, 17, 22–23.

ê

Very few are the Actaeons to whom destiny gives the power to contemplate Diana naked, and the power to become so enamored of the beautiful harmony of the body of nature that they are transformed into deer, inasmuch as they are no longer the hunters but the hunted. Therefore, from the vulgar, civil, and ordinary man he was, he becomes as free as a deer, and an inhabitant of the wilderness; he lives like a god under the protection of the woods in the unpretentious rooms of cavernous mountains, where he contemplates the source of the great rivers, vigorous as a plant, intact and pure, free of ordinary lusts; and converses most freely with the divinity, to which so many men have aspired, who in their desire to taste the celestial life on earth have cried with one voice, *Ecce elongavi fugiens, et mansi in solitudine.* Psalms 55:7: "Lo, then would I wander far off, and remain in the wilderness. *Selah.*"

Bruno, *Heroic Frenzies*, 225.

5

The Prophetic Tradition

for David Erdman

We will not get "Blake and Tradition" right until we see the tradition as the Prophetic Tradition, including Judaism, Christianity and Islam; and heresies in Judaism, Christianity and Islam. To bring Islam into the picture is a Copernican revolution; our Copernicus (University of Chicago!), still not sufficiently recognized, is Marshall Hodgson, *The Venture of Islam.*[1] It is a Copernican revolution in our notion of world history; not merely an (ecumenical) acquisition of tolerance or charity toward separated brethren in the Abrahamic (monotheistic) tradition; it is to recover the prophetic sense of the unity of world history, discredited by its association with Westernizing triumphalism, the idea of progress, and Hegelian teleology. It is to recover in the twentieth century, spite of despondence, as Blake did in also dark days, the original prophetic realism and radicalism.

Prophecy is a critical response to the "urban revolution," that irreversible commitment of the human race to the city and civilization which spread outward from the "Nile to Oxus" heartland beginning around 3000 B.C. Prophecy is the perception of

Published in *Studies on Romanticism*, no. 21 (1982), 367–386. Reprinted by permission of the Trustees of Boston University.

This is a risky attempt to anticipate, for this occasion in honor of David Erdman, the results of a much larger undertaking. I undertook in 1980 at the University of California at Santa Cruz, and in 1981 at Tufts University, a lecture series on "The Prophetic Tradition: The Challenge of Islam." The individual lecture titles were: (1) Universal History with Cosmopolitan Intent; (2) Islam and Judaism; (3) Islam and Christianity; (4) The Book; (5) The Succession (Sunni and Shiite); (6) Revolutionary Islam; and (7) Mystic Islam. To condense this train of thought and focus it on the reinterpretation of Blake's theology naturally raises more questions than it answers.

the potentialities, both for "good" and for "evil," inherent in the new social structure. The urban complex makes a process of world unification in one sense—commercial, technological—inevitable, and makes world unification in another sense—the peaceable Kingdom—ever more problematical. The whole prophetic tradition is an attempt to give direction to the social structure precipitated by the urban revolution; to resolve its inherent contradictions; to put an end to the injustice, inequality, anomie, the state of war (within the city, between cities, between city and uncivilized) that has been its history from start to finish.[2]

Ecumenical prophetic history made "scientific" in the work of Marshall Hodgson—he is both a Quaker and, in some sense, a Marxist—differs *toto caelo* from Hegelian triumphalism. World history is as much a story of failure as of success; including, especially including, the failures of the prophetic tradition. And human failure is not compensated by providential interference or the Cunning of Reason. There is no providentially preordained pattern, no teleological structure, to the world-historical process; *Weltgeschichte* is not *Weltgericht*. And modernization, the triumph of modern technology and capitalism, "the Great Western Transformation," represents no solution but rather, as a result of the destruction of traditional institutions, Islamic and Christian, an apocalyptic crisis.

In effect, with Marshall Hodgson we are moving out from under the schema of Christocentric world history, stamped on the minds of orthodox Westerners including Hegel, into ampler, and more Islamic, air. The inscrutable will of Allah determines all outcomes: it does not alter the human obligation to strive, to seek, to find, and not to yield. But there is no particular divine interference in the course of world history, establishing a pattern of B.C. as distinct from A.D., and giving assurance of salvation or any providentially determined outcome. There is no world-historical drama of original sin and subsequent redemption. The human race needs Divine instruction and admonition; the human race like sheep is prone to stray and is brought back to the right path by another manifestation of the one true voice of prophecy. There is no progress in prophetic revelation, no New Testament

to take the place of (or "fulfill") the Old. "The Islamic conception of history is one of a series of cycles of prophecy, each cycle
followed by a gradual decay leading to a new cycle or phase."[3]

It is no accident that Hegel's meditations on world-spirit,
world-history, and world-religion, yield only a caricature of
Islam.[4] In the prophetic tradition, properly understood, Islam
must be perceived as a legitimate dialectical response to the failure of orthodox Christianity. Protestants should be able to see
that the need for a Protestant Reformation was there already in
the seventh century C.E., to be perceived by prophetic eyes.
Blakeans should be able to see that there is no way to accept
"Again He speaks" in Blake unless we accept that again He
speaks in the Koran. It is time to discard the time-honored prejudice that treats Koranic theology as a confused echo of half-
understood Jewish or Christian traditions, selected and polemi-
cally distorted to concoct a new-fangled monotheism to supply
"backward" Arabs with a "cultural identity."[5] New light is coming from two directions: on the one hand the more ecumenical
vision of world-history represented by Hodgson; on the other
hand a profounder appreciation of Judeo-Christian heresy, the
alternatives eliminated by that triumph of orthodoxy which Hegel regards, as he regards all world-historical triumphs, as the
triumph of God. *Victrix causa deis placuit sed victa Catoni.*

Taking an ecumenical view, appreciating a little better the
symbiotic rivalry between "first worlds" and "third worlds," and
that "law of uneven development" which makes yesterday's
"backward" tomorrow's challengers, we begin to see Arabia and
Mecca in the seventh century C.E. as the dynamic frontier and link
between, and refuge from, two superannuated empires, Roman
and Sasanian. We begin to see the Transjordanian cultural matrix
in which Islam was born as a refuge for the preservation of a
variety of saving remnants from the Judeo-Christian tradition.
There were on the one hand Jewish (including Samaritan) and
Jewish Christian (Ebionite) refugees from the destruction of Jerusalem and later persecutions; on the other hand "heretical"
Christian deviations from conciliar orthodoxy and the Constan-
tinian compromise: Monophysites, Nestorians, Jacobites; and

more elusive, perhaps more pervasive, remnants of "Gnostic" Christianity. In the Transjordanian alembic these saving remnants of the Judeo-Christian tradition interacted with bedouin resistance to imperialism to produce Islam. And not only the Judeo-Christian tradition took refuge in the desert from the triumph of Caesaropapism—also another essential element in the subsequent dialogue between Islam and Western Civilization: Greek philosophy. "When Justinian, in the year 529, closed the schools of philosophy through anxiety for the Christian doctrine, he did not realize that if he had let them continue, the anti-Christian philosophy would not have been in the least dangerous, because it would have perished of itself, but being compelled to emigrate toward the Orient, it would, centuries afterwards, exercise an influence upon Christian thought more powerful than he had ever feared."[6] The death of Justinian brings us to the birth of the Prophet (c. 570 C.E.).

In Islam is fulfilled the prophecy of Matthew 21:42–43: "The stone which the builders rejected, the same was made the head of the corner; this was from the Lord, and it is marvellous in our eyes. Therefore say I unto you, the kingdom of God shall be taken away from you, and shall be given to a nation bringing forth the fruits thereof." At this point a necessary and wonderful guide appears, to purify and elevate our understanding of the relation between Islam and Christianity, and to break through the wall of orthodox prejudice that has blocked our understanding of the middle term, Gnostic Judaeo-Christian heresy, the stone which the builders rejected. Henri Corbin picks up Harnack's proposed definition of Islam as "a transformation on Arab soil of a Jewish religion that had itself been transformed by Gnostic Judaeo-Christianity."[7] A special role was played by that "heresy" which struggled to avoid the catastrophic rupture between Christianity and Judaism, "Jewish Christianity" or "Ebionism." The authoritative expert on Jewish Christianity, H.-J. Schoeps, substantiates Harnack's judgment and draws out the world-historical implications:

The Arabian Christianity which Mohammed found at the beginning of his public activity was not the state religion of Byzantium but a schismatic Christianity characterized by Ebionite and Monophysite views. . . . Thus we have a paradox of world-historical proportions, viz., the fact that Jewish Christianity indeed disappeared within the Christian church, but was preserved in Islam and thereby extended some of its basic ideas even to our own day. According to Islamic doctrine, the Ebionite combination of Moses and Jesus found its fulfillment in Mohammed; the two elements, through the agency of Jewish Christianity, were, in Hegelian terms, "taken up" in Islam.[8]

Islam is to be envisaged as dialectical evolution, or evolutionary mutation, in the prophetic tradition, in response to the limitations built into the structure of orthodox Christianity by its historic compromise with Roman imperialism; by its commitment to scriptural canon, creedal orthodoxy, and episcopal hierarchy; and by its consequent scandalous history of schism and persecution (duly noted in the Koran). To begin to envisage the prophetic tradition in truly world-historical terms, in which we can situate Blake—even as he situated himself—the following hazardous generalizations are offered as preliminary orientation.

Islam picks up and extends the notion, already present in Jewish (Ebionite) Christianity, of the unity of the prophetic spirit: *Christus aeternus, verus propheta ab initio mundi per saeculum currens*; the one true prophet, from age to age, from the beginning of the world; Adam, Noah, Abraham, Moses, Christ, Muhammad. The later prophet comes to reiterate the Eternal and Everlasting Gospel—the "seim anew," *Lex mosaica per Jesum prophetam reformata*, the mosaic law reformed by Jesus the prophet. The tradition gets de-formed and has to be re-formed. Thus "true Christianity" is identical with "true Judaism"; H.-J. Schoeps speaks of Ebionite "federal theology," according to which just as Moses was the teacher of the Jews, so Jesus was the teacher of the Gentiles. Compare Blake: "The Religions of all Nations are derived from each Nation's different reception of the Poetic Genius, which is every where call'd the Spirit of Prophecy."[9] Schoeps points out the implications with respect to religious toleration. In the same spirit the Koran says, in the passage recited by Sadat in his speech to the Knesset, "Say: We believe in God and that which was revealed unto us, and that which was revealed unto Abraham, and Ismaïl, and Isaac, and Jacob, and the tribes, and that which Moses and Jesus received, and that which the Prophets received from their Lord. We make no distinctions between any of them, and unto Him we surrender."[10]

Islam represents a return to the original Mosaic theocratic or theopolitical idea.[11] The kingdom of God is a real kingdom on earth. The dualism between temporal and spiritual regimen is rejected; the concessions to Caesar (or Constantine) are abrogated. Prophetic revelation has to replace Roman law with its own law: "The Law, which is the constitution of the Community, cannot be other than the Will of God, revealed through the Prophet."[12] The prophetic movement then has to be a political revolution: Muhammad is the prophet armed; Islam is committed by the hegira and the takeover of Medina to the seizure of power. At the same time the Mosaic theocratic idea is freed from its national (ethnic) limitations and given new and revolutionary content as a program for instituting theocratic world government. The glorious idealism of Dante's *De Monarchia*, book I, is pure Islam: "Of all things ordained for our happiness, the greatest is universal peace"; "To achieve this state of universal well-being a single world-government is necessary"; "Since any particular institution needs unity of direction, mankind as a whole must also need it"; "Human government is but a part of that single world-administration which has its unity in God"; "Man is by nature in God's likeness and therefore should, like God, be one"; "At the root of what it means to be good is being one; thus we can see what sin is: it is to scorn unity and hence to proceed to multiplicity."[13] But whereas Dante in Book II proceeds to declare that the Roman Empire existed by right, and in Book III to differentiate papal and imperial power, Muhammad toward the end of his life called on the empires of the world to submit to the rule of God.[14] Prophet against empire: but Prophet armed.

There is in Islamic tradition an attempt to unify the opposites which in the West gives us Dante on the one hand and Machiavelli on the other. To apply the overworked word "revolution," "revolutionary" to the politics of Islam is to suggest that the origins of modern radical politics lie in the transformation of prophetic radicalism into a political movement prepared to seize power ("The Revolution of the Saints"); and that Islam pioneered this modern development, in the seventh century c.e. The failures of Islam are also part of the story. We are just beginning to be able to see the internecine struggles of the tenth, eleventh, twelfth centuries, which left Islam exhausted and divided, as desperate attempts to salvage, from the corruption of the times, the original prophetic dream of theocratic social reconstruction. Three centuries of intransigent, polymorphously inventive, revolutionary politics; not enough studied by Marxists or Muslims.[15]

Shariah ("Law") on the one hand, and Tariqah, the spiritual path, the mystic way ("Sufism") on the other; the two great symbols of Islamic aspiration and achievement. Islam is a fundamental critique of Christianity not only as a theopolitical idea but also as a path to "enlightenment" or "salvation."

Islam is first of all a reduction of the prophetic tradition to its pure essence as revelation, discarding the element of sacramental magic common to both conciliar Christianity and the mystery religions of late classical antiquity. By discarding sacramental and sacerdotal magic Islam prepares the way for Dante and Blake: the only miracle is the book: and the book authenticates itself as miracle. At the same time it is a return to that emphasis on cognition, visionary cognition, which orthodox Christianity condemned and condemns as Gnosticism.

Islam discards the Trinitarian mythology: "Say not Three; He is One; He begetteth not; Surely they are unbelievers who say God is the Messiah, son of Mary."[16] Islam discards the notion of vicarious atonement: there is no world-historical drama of original sin and sacrificial redemption; no "Death of God"; no Oedipal drama (old Nobodaddy), no sacrifice of the Son to appease the wrath of the Father; compare Blake: "Speaking of the Atonement in the ordinary Calvinistic sense, he said 'It is a horrible doctrine; if another pay your debt, I do not forgive it.' "[17] "Mohammedanism, true to its anti-Christian character, ignores the doctrine that without the shedding of blood there is no remission of sins."[18] (In Islam there is sacrifice, but it is commemorative and eucharistic, not expiatory.) In Islam there are no theurgic sacraments; no priesthood, no sacerdotal (ecclesiastical) organization administering the means of grace.

Islam discards the notion of an Incarnate Son of God and, Ebionite fashion, clings to prophecy as the essential mode of miraculous conjunction between the *lahut* and *nasut*, the divine nature and the human or created condition. "The Prophet possessed eminently both the human (*nasut*) and spiritual (*lahut*) natures. Yet, there was never an incarnation of the *lahut* into the *nasut*, a perspective which Islam does not accept."[19] The prophet is not an incarnation but a revelation, a theophany. "His knowledge marks a direct intervention of the Divine in the human order, an intervention which is not, from the Islamic point of view, an incarnation but a theophany (*tajalli*)."[20] It is in terms of prophecy, not incarnation, and therefore in terms of theophany or epiphany that Islam envisages the Divine Humanity: "Islam without in any way overlooking the limited and weak aspect of human nature does not consider man in his aspect as a perverted will but essentially as a theomorphic being who as the vicegerent (*khalifah*) of God on earth is the central theophany (*tajalli*) of God's Names and Qualities."[21] Corbin defines the theological position of mystic Islam as follows: "If the experience of the Prophet has been meditated and relived as the prototype of mystical experience, it is because of the exemplary character of the conjunction of *lahut* and *nasut* in his person. But this conjunction is conceived not as a hypostatic union of two natures (after the manner of the Christology of the Church Councils), but as a theophanic union, that is, as the union of a divine Name and of the sensible form, or appearance, in which this Name *becomes visible*."[22]

To make the Name or Names visible: Theophany, *hic labor, hoc opus est*. It is not a datum given to the natural man; or conferred by supernatural sacraments; it is the work of the Creative Imagination.

The initial idea of Ibn 'Arabī's mystic theosophy and of all related theosophies is that the Creation is essentially a *theophany* (*tajallī*). As such, creation is an act of the divine imaginative power: this divine creative imagination is essentially a theophanic Imagination. The Active Imagination in the gnostic is likewise a theophanic Imagination. . . . The God whom it "creates," far from being an unreal product of our fantasy, is also a theophany, for man's Active Imagination is merely the organ of the absolute theophanic Imagination (*takhayyul mutlaq*).[23]

All my Blakean life I have been awed by the stunning heterodoxy of Blake's central theological affirmation:

> Prayer is the Study of Art.
> Praise is the Practise of Art.
> Fasting &c., all relate to Art.
> The outward Ceremony is Antichrist.
> The Eternal Body of Man is The Imagination, that is,
> God himself } יש[ו]ע, Jesus: we are his Members.
> The Divine Body }
> It manifests itself in his Works of Art (In Eternity All is Vision).[24]

In his Works of Art the divine Names become Visible. In Eternity all is Vision. Corbin's title is *Creative Imagination in the Sufism of Ibn Arabi*. The message of this essay is that Blake's theology must be glossed by the light of Ibn Arabi and with the help of Corbin; an ecumenical, world-historical, i.e., prophetic interpretation of the prophet Blake.

Corbin is aware of the correspondences between Ibn Arabi and modern theosophy (Paracelsus, Boehme, Swedenborg are mentioned). But his great contribution is to enable us to see this whole tradition world-historically by connecting it with the Christian, more specifically Gnostic, heresy of Docetism; in so doing correcting millennia of misunderstanding about Gnosticism and early Christianity.[25]

The conventional definition of Docetism is "the theological error of those who deny the material reality of the body of Christ":

Docetism is the heresy which teaches that Christ had no real material body and human nature, but only an apparent body, a phantasm of humanity. . . . It may seem strange that Docetism should thus be the earliest of all heresies. One would have thought that the first and second Christian generations would at any rate have had no doubt about our Lord's real manhood. The explanation is that Docetism did not develop by a perverse process from the gospel and the Christian system, but came to Christianity from without. Already, before the time of Christ, the philosophy of dualism (*q.v.*) was in possession in Greek and Jewish schools. The concept of the universe as the battle-ground between two worlds—a good world of spirit and a bad world of matter—had a large number of adherents when the Christian gospel was first preached. Dualistic philosophies, then, combining with the Christian faith, produced the long chain of heresies that we class together as Gnosticism and Manichaeism. . . . Docetism is a corollary of Gnostic dualism. All these combinations of the old Persian philosophy with the new religion took from the gospel at least the name of Jesus Christ as the leading champion of the good world of spirit, if not a final emanation from God its creator and protector. It followed, then, that He could not be Himself polluted by matter. He had come down to redeem men's souls by freeing them from matter; He Himself must be pure spirit.[26]

The truth is that Docetism is an alternative to the Incarnationism inherent in Christianity from the start, an undercurrent which became the mainstream in Islam, which is not inspired by the idea that the flesh is evil and that salvation consists in evading the consequences of having a body. Incarnationism has not saved orthodox Christianity from the tendency to equate world and flesh with the Devil, but there is no monkery in Islam. Docetism, as the Greek root of the word indicates, is devotion to appearances, to apparitions, to visionary experience, to vision. In Eternity all is Vision. It is not disparagement of the body but glorification of the imagination that makes the Docetic Gnostic say that the Divine body is imaginary: "Mental Things are alone Real; what is call'd Corporeal, Nobody Knows of its Dwelling Place."[27] Or, in Blake's fullest apologia for art as the organ of the theophanic imagination:

The connoisseurs and artists who have made objections to Mr. B.'s mode of representing spirits with real bodies, would do well to consider that the Venus, the Minerva, the Jupiter, the Apollo, which they admire in Greek statues are all of them representations of spiritual existences, of Gods immortal, to the mortal perishing organ of sight; and yet they are embodied and organized in solid marble. Mr. B. requires the same latitude, and all is well. The Prophets describe what they saw in Vision as real and existing men, whom they saw with their imaginative and immortal organs; the Apostles the same; the clearer the organ the more distinct the object. A Spirit and a Vision are not, as the modern philosophy supposes, a cloudy vapour, or a nothing: they are organized and minutely articulated beyond all that the mortal and perishing nature can produce. He who does not imagine in stronger and better lineaments, and in stronger and better light than his perishing and mortal eye can see, does not imagine at all.[28]

Corbin begins his most esoteric, most essential exposition of "The Metamorphosis of Theophanic Visions" as follows:

In the Acts of Peter, a book belonging to those so-called "apocryphal" collections which were particularly esteemed and meditated upon in Gnostic and Manichaean circles, we read a narrative that provides an exemplary illustration of theophanic vision. Before a gathering of people the apostle Peter refers to the scene of the Transfiguration that he had witnessed on Mount Tabor. And essentially all he can say is this: *Talem eum vidi qualem capere potui* ("I saw him in such a form as I was able to take in"). Now in this gathering there are several widows, afflicted at once with physical blindness and incredulity of heart. The apostle speaks to them in a tone of urgency: "Perceive in your mind that which ye see not with your eyes." The assemblage begins to pray, and thereupon the hall is filled with a resplendent light; it does not resemble the light of day, but is an ineffable, *invisible* light such as no man can describe. And this radiant "invisible light" shines into the eyes of these women, who alone are standing in the midst of the prostrate assemblage. Afterward, when they are asked what they have *seen*, some have seen an old man, others a youth; still others a little child who lightly touched their eyes and made them open. Each one has seen in a different form, appropriate to the capacity of her being; each one may say: *Talem eum vidi qualem capere potui.*[29]

Docetism is a meditation on Transfiguration; it is no accident that traditional translations avoid the word given us in the text, *metamorphosis*: "his face shone like the sun and his clothes became as white as the light." "The mystery of the Transfiguration, Francis de Sales and Cajetan tell us, was no miracle; it was the suspension of a miracle."[30] In other words the light body was his "real" body, and his ordinary body—what shall we say?—a phantasm. The Transfiguration is the inexpungeable Docetic moment in our canonical gospels.

As Northrop Frye said a long time ago, if *esse est percipi*, then *esse est percipere* as well.[31] To see God is to be God, in the only way possible in Gnostic, Docetic, Theophanic theology. It is another Transfiguration; after the manner of a mirror (cf. 2 Corinthians 3:18—a Gnostic thought in Paul!): "But we all, with unveiled face beholding as in a mirror the glory of the Lord, are transformed into the same image from glory to glory, even as from the Lord the Spirit." They Become what they Behold. The Gnostic Gospel is pure Blake. It is also pure Sufism. "In fact, the Sufi masters have over the ages defined Sufism by the well-known *Hadith* of the Prophet who when asked about the definition of *ihsan* said: '*Ihsan* is to adore Allah as though thou didst see him.' "[32] Corbin is fond of quoting the statement attributed to the First Imam: "I should never worship a God I did not see."[33]

For Docetism, Transfiguration = Metamorphosis is central. The Docetic view of the Crucifixion is a scandal. "The blood of Christ was still fresh in Judaea," says Jerome, "when His body was said to be a phantasm." The Gnostic Basilides, as reported in orthodox polemics, "says it was not Jesus who suffered; He had no real body and so could not be held by His enemies, but was able, whenever He wished, to ascend to God. At the Crucifixion He stood by, invisible, and watched Simon of Cyrene crucified in His stead, and He laughed His cheated adversaries to scorn. It is therefore wrong to confess Christ as 'the Crucified'; we should rather confess Him who was believed to be crucified."[34] The same position is taken in Nag Hammadi Gnostic texts.[35] The same position is taken in the Koran 4:156–158 (trans. Pickthall):

And because of their disbelief and of their speaking against Mary a tremendous calumny; and because of their saying: We slew the

Messiah Jesus son of Mary, Allah's messenger—They slew him not nor crucified, but it appeared so unto them; and lo! those who disagree concerning it are in doubt thereof; they have no knowledge thereof save pursuit of a conjecture; they slew him not for certain, but Allah took him up unto Himself. Allah was ever Mighty, Wise.

Arberry's version:

> and for their unbelief, and their uttering
> against Mary a mighty calumny,
> and for their saying, "We slew the Messiah,
> Jesus son of Mary, the Messenger of God"—
> yet they did not slay him, neither crucified him,
> only a likeness of that was shown to them.
> Those who are at variance concerning him surely
> are in doubt regarding him; they have no knowledge
> of him, except the following of surmise;
> and they slew him not of a certainty—
> no indeed; God raised him up to Him; God is
> All-mighty, All-wise.

Or, "he was counterfeited for them"; "it was caused to appear to them that way." Or, "they have been caught in the trap of the assimilation committed by themselves"; or, "the trap of their own imagination." *Talem eum vidi qualem capere potui.* Every Eye Sees differently. As the Eye, Such the Object.[36]

The fundamental issue is vicarious atonement and sacramental history. For the orthodox, without the shedding of blood there is no remission of sins (Hebrews 9:22, Leviticus 17:11). The blood must be real—and what do they mean by "real"? They mean that it is a literal, i.e., historical fact. The atonement takes place in historical time, $\kappa\alpha\tau\grave{\alpha}\ \tau\grave{\eta}\nu\ \tau o\hat{\upsilon}\ \chi\rho\acute{o}\nu o\upsilon\ \tau\acute{\alpha}\xi\iota\nu$; they give justice and reparation to each other "according to the ordinance of time" (Anaximander). In Blake's decisive antithesis, sacramental efficacy is a structure of memory ("rotten rags") and not of the imagination. For the Gnostic, "Mental Things are alone Real; what is call'd Corporeal, Nobody Knows of its dwelling Place" ("Vision of the Last Judgement"). "The Eternal Body of Man is The Imagination, that is, God himself. The Divine Body, Jesus" ("The Laocoön"). The Crucifixion is not a literal or historical fact but a suprahistorical reality, an eternal truth. Corbin points

to the definitive statement in the Apocryphal (and Gnostic) Acts
of John:

> Perhaps we shall find the key to these visions, the basis of their
> reality and their variations, in a few striking pages of these same Acts
> of John. On the evening of Good Friday the Angel Christos, while
> the multitude below, in Jerusalem, imagines that it is crucifying him,
> causes the apostle John to go up the Mount of Olives and into the
> grotto illumined by his presence; and there the angel reveals to John
> the mystery of the "Cross of Light." This cross is called sometimes
> Word, sometimes Mind, sometimes Jesus and sometimes Christ,
> sometimes Door, sometimes Way, sometimes Son, Father, Spirit,
> sometimes Life, and sometimes Truth. It separates the things on high
> that *are* from the things below that *become* (the things of birth and
> of death), and at the same time, being one, streams forth into all
> things. "This is not the cross of wood which thou wilt see when thou
> goest down hence: neither am I he that is on the cross, whom now
> thou seest not, but only hearest his voice. I was reckoned to be that
> which I am not, not being what I was unto many others. . . . Thou
> hearest that I suffered, yet I did not suffer; that I suffered not, yet
> did I suffer; . . . and in a word, what they say of me, that befell me
> not. But what they say not, that did I suffer."[37]

Corbin has produced a text of Sejestani, the (Ismailian) Shiite
Gnostic master of the tenth century, in which the esoteric meaning of the Shahada (the Islamic profession of faith, "There is no
god but God and Muhammad is His Prophet") is identified with
the esoteric meaning of the Christian Cross, and the transition
from the Cross of Wood to the Cross of Light is identified with
the apocalyptic Resurrection. The cruciform quaternity at the
heart of Being is based on the dialectical dynamics of negation,
and negation of the negation, inherent in the Shahada and in the
contradiction between Appearance and Reality, between *Deus
Absconditus* and Revelation (prophecy).[38] Compare Pascal and
Lucien Goldmann, *Le Dieu Caché*.

In Gnostic Docetic Ebionite Christianity, and in Islam, Christ
is an angelic or angelomorphic reality. Docetism is the belief in
angels, not the repudiation of the flesh; and the belief in angels
is no pagan intrusion but an integral part of the prophetic tradition from Abraham's entertainment of strangers—some have

entertained angels unawares (Hebrews 13:2)—in Genesis 18
down to the Book of Mormon.[39] As Corbin says, a docetic Christology is an angel Christology. Tertullian says of the Ebionites
that they make of Christ a mere man "though more glorious than
the prophets in that they say an angel was in him."[40] Schoeps
explains that they held the adoptionist view that the Christ, who
entered Jesus "from above" at baptism, was an angelic being, the
apocalyptic angelic figure of the Son of Man who comes down
from heaven, inaugurates the era of salvation, and will come
again in the Day of Judgment.[41] In Islam the privilege of being
close to God is shared by Jesus with the angels: but however
sublime both they and he remain created beings.[42] The Koran
differs from Ebionite Christology in making Jesus a supernatural
being from miraculous birth to miraculous assumption from the
cross; with extra miraculous episodes in his childhood, not found
in our canonical gospels, but in the spirit of some (Gnostic) apoc-
rypha. Based on an obscure Koranic text which connects Jesus
with the Final Hour, Islamic tradition includes a belief in the
second coming of Christ associated or identified with the
Mahdi.[43]

Peter Pan said—Do you believe in angels? The Necessary Angel? Or are you afraid? *Jeder Engel ist schrecklich.* Corbin speaks
of "fear of the Angel" in the collapse of Latin Avicennism and
the rise of orthodox Western scholasticism. Corbin says every
theophany is an angelophany: "One does not encounter, one
does not see the Divine Essence; for it is itself the Temple, the
Mystery of the heart; into which the mystic penetrates when,
having achieved the microcosmic plenitude of the Perfect Man,
he *encounters* the 'Form of God' which is that of 'His Angels,'
that is to say, the theophany constitutive of his being."[44] It was
from reading Corbin that Charles Olson, at the Harbor, October
23 and 24, 1961, learned that

> Paradise is a person. Come into this world.
> The soul is a magnificent Angel.[45]

while at the same time making out of the Greek word *apophain-
esthai* an incantation to evoke a theophany of Ocean.[46]

Incarnationist Christology inevitably led to the withering away of angels in its version of the prophetic tradition. Who takes Pseudo-Dionysius on the *Celestial Hierarchies* seriously today? Angels are the vehicles for the continuing operation of the Spirit, moving in our hearts again, and for fresh revelations—Again He speaks. All the dangers of enthusiasm. The canny considerations governing the Roman Catholic "synthesis" can be discerned between the lines of Cardinal Danielou's formulations:

> Pseudo-Dionysius obviously likes to emphasize the permanence of the angels' mediation after the coming of Jesus. The older Fathers, on the contrary, after St. Paul, stressed the passing of this mediation. Actually, these are merely two aspects of one mystery. On the one hand, it is true that the older economy was transmitted much more directly through the ministry of angels and that this mediation ceased with Christ, who is Himself the "Angel" of the New Covenant. That, since he minimizes the history of salvation, Pseudo-Dionysius failed to recognize. But, on the other hand, it is also true that, even though the angels no longer play the role of mediator, they remain the ministers of Him who is the sole Mediator, and consequently their ministry continues after the coming of Christ.[47]

Orthodox Protestantism characteristically lays the axe to the root of the tree and eliminates the Celestial Hierarchies of Pseudo-Dionysius as sheer Gnostic heresy; which they are.[48]

Angels are alive and well in Islam. The angelic Christos lives more freely and more abundantly in Islam than in Christianity. Rilke himself says, "The angel of the *Elegies* has nothing to do with the angel of the Christian heaven (rather with the angelic figures of Islam)."[49] In Sufism Jesus became the model of the pilgrims, the "imam of the wanderers," the inspiration of the saint and mystic. Ibn Arabi said, "Muhammad is the Seal of the Prophets and Jesus is the Seal of the Saints."[50] The angelology of Pseudo-Dionysius, which Catholic Christianity left to wither and Protestant Christianity cut down, was developed and put on an altogether new plane in the work of Avicenna and Ibn Arabi. Their theoretical work enfranchised and legitimated the individual search for visionary experience, for the Angel, on a mass scale, thus laying the basis for both Shiite Gnosis and (Sunni)

Sufism in all their multifarious variety of spiritual ways, corresponding to the variety of individual gifts and bents—*talem eum vidi qualem capere potui.*[51]

"Would to God that all the Lord's people were Prophets"—that agonized cry of Moses at the beginning of the prophetic tradition and repeated by Blake toward its close (?).[52] It would be wrong to imply that Islam has resolved the tension between the authority of the past and the authenticity of present experience, between individual autonomy and authoritative guidance: indeed these issues sustain the ever-living tension between Sunni and Sufi, between Sunni and Shiite, between *shariah* (Law) and *tariqah* (spiritual way). Islam is the boldest attempt to affirm both poles of this dilemma inherent in the prophetic tradition, to remain radically open to visionary experience. Ghazali, the supreme theologian of Islamic consensus, recognizes a universal call to prophecy, each according to his ability; prophetic authority can only be recognized by a touch of the prophetic spirit (*spiritus per spiritum intellegitur*).[53] For the supreme Sufi poet Rumi there is an angelic Christos in all of us, waiting to be born—"Nothing can be accomplished without pain as the guide. The body is like our Lady Mariam (on whom be peace), for everyone of us has a Jesus within himself who without pain will never be born, but will return whence he came, by the same secret pathway, leaving us bereft." New Nazareths in us.[54]

In the mature structure of Islam the continuing presence of angels balances the voice of the Prophet. Muhammad is "the Seal of the Prophets."

After him there will be no new *Shari'ah* or Divine Law brought into the world until the end of time. There are to be no revelations (*wahy*) after him, for he marks the termination of the prophetic cycle (*da'irat al-nubuwwah*). It may on the surface appear as a great tragedy that man seems to be thus left without any possibility of renewing the truths of the revelation through new contact with the source of the truth. But in reality the termination of the prophetic cycle does not mean that all possibility of contact with the Divine order has ceased. Whereas revelation (*wahy*) is no longer possible, inspiration (*ilham*) remains always as a latent possibility. Whereas the cycle of prophecy (*da'irat al-nubuwwah*) has come to an end, the cycle of *wilayat* (*da'irat al-wilayah*), which for want of a better term may be translated as the 'cycle of initiation' and also sanctity, continues.[55]

These are Shiite formulations: the cycle of *wilayat* begins with Ali, the First Imam. In Shiite Islam, as Corbin has demonstrated once and for all, the Gnostic religion had a new birth.

The prophetic Genius of Muhammad (and specifically the Koran), is still grossly and grotesquely slighted in the West. The line from Jesus to Blake goes through Muhammad. In its sublime and mysterious manner the Koran seems to declare that Muhammad is a transitional figure. Muhammad is the last, the "Seal" of the Prophets. Miracles are heaped upon the figure of Jesus; the only miracle Muhammad claims is the Book. (His followers after him were not so restrained.) Angelic status is attributed to Jesus; Muhammad says firmly and clearly, "I say not unto you: Lo! I am an angel." In a sublime, apparently ironic, soliloquy the Koran repudiates angelomorphic status for the Prophet as well as hocus-pocus, "sorcery," (e.g., golden plates) about the provenance of the Book:

> Had We sent down on thee a Book on parchment
> and so they touched it with their hands, yet
> the unbelievers would have said, "This is naught
>   but manifest sorcery."
> "Why has an angel not been sent down on him?"
> they say; yet had We sent down an angel, the matter
> would have been determined, and then no respite
>   would be given them.
> And had We made him an angel, yet assuredly
> We would have made him a man, and confused
> for them the thing which they themselves
>   are confusing.[56]

With the mystique of the Book Islam moves into modernity: "Reader! *lover* of books! *lover* of heaven" (*Jerusalem*, pl. 1). The Logos is not made flesh; it is a Book. The central mystery is the Descent of the Heavenly Book, dictated by the Archangel Gabriel, the bearer of the Annunciation in Christianity. "The Word of God in Islam is the Quran; in Christianity it is Christ. The vehicle of the Divine Message in Christianity is the Virgin Mary; in Islam it is the soul of the Prophet. The Prophet must be un-lettered for the same reason that the Virgin Mary must be vir-gin. . . . The Quran, being the Word of God, therefore corre-sponds to Christ in Christianity and the form of this book, which like the content is determined by the dictum of heaven, corre-sponds in a sense to the body of Christ."[57]

Muhammad is not an angel but, like Blake, receives dictation from the Angel. He also has overwhelming visionary experiences in which he sees the Angel. Shiite theosophical speculation de-velops the idea that Muhammad is the last to experience the Angel in his "real," i.e., supernatural form:

The Koran verses (53:3–4; 81:19–29) preserve the memory of the first grandiose visions when the Prophet, emerging from his tent, con-templated the majesty of the Angel whose outspread wings covered the whole horizon. In certain traditions invoked by the commentators these sumptuous angelophanies even recalled by contrast the memory of the refusal suffered by Moses on Mount Sinai when he asked to be favored with a direct vision and the Lord answered: "Thou shalt not see me" (lan tarānī). Mohammed also expresses the fervent desire to see the Angel in his real form. Although warned, he insists. The vision is not refused him, but he is thrown into a swoon by the beauty and majesty of the Angel in his superhuman form of Glory; henceforth a terrestrial human Form will be the epiphanic figure (mazhar) of the Angel.[58]

"Henceforth a terrestrial human Form will be the epiphanic fig-ure of the Angel." The way is open that leads to La Vita Nuova. The epiphany of the angel in the form of Beatrice is anticipated in the poetry and mystical meditations of Ibn Arabi (1165–1240 C.E.), who says:

We can typify Him and take Him as an object of our contemplation, not only in our innermost hearts but also before our eyes and in our imagination, as though we saw Him, or better still, so that we really see Him. . . . It is He who in every beloved being is manifested to the gaze of each lover . . . and none other than He is adored, for it is impossible to adore a being without conceiving the Godhead in that being. . . . So it is with love: a being does not truly love anyone other than his Creator.[59]

"Love God as if you saw Him." To see God is to see the Angel, is to see Beauty. "Ibn Arabī and Jalāluddīn Rūmī made the 'conspiration' of the sensible and the spiritual the cornerstone of their Islam." "One of the greatest masters of this way was Rūzbehān Baqlī of Shīrāz (d. 1209): Beauty is perceived as a hierophany only if divine love (*'ishq rabbānī*) is experienced in a human love (*'ishq insānī*) which it transfigures. Ibn Arabī went to considerable length in explaining his favorite symbols: ruins, encampments, Magi, gardens, meadows, mansions, flowers, clouds, lightning flashes, zephirs, hills, copses, paths, friends, idols, women who rise like suns (*Dhakhā'ir*, p. 5). 'All the things I have just mentioned, or all the things that resemble them, are, if you understand them, mysteries, high and sublime illuminations which the Lord of the heavens sent to my heart.' "[60] Hierophanies everywhere. "Beauty is the theophany par excellence: God is a beautiful being who loves beauty." Returning to Blake's *Laocoön* for the last time: Blake says it manifests itself in his Works of Art: "Prayer is the Study of Art." Corbin says Prayer is the highest form, the supreme act of the Creative Imagination.[61]

NOTES

1. M. Hodgson, *The Venture of Islam*, 3 vols. (Chicago, 1974). Cf. E. Burke, III, "Islamic History as World History: Marshall Hodgson, 'The Venture of Islam,' " *Int. J. Middle East Studies* 10 (1979): 241–264.

2. Cf. J. Ellul, *The Meaning of the City* (Grand Rapids, 1970); J. Ellul, *The Technological Society* (New York, 1964); H. Schneidau, *Sacred Discontent: The Bible and Western Tradition* (Baton Rouge, 1976).

3. S. H. Nasr, *Ideals and Realities of Islam* (Boston, 1972), 33.

4. E. L. Fackenheim, *The Religious Dimension in Hegel's Thought* (Bloomington, Ind., 1967), 154n.

5. The latest example illustrates in an ominous way the politics of Orientalism: P. Crone and M. Cook, *Hagarism: The Making of the Islamic World* (New York and Cambridge, 1977). The Western tradition of urbane condescension has degenerated into aggressive, unscrupulous even, calumny; cf. the review by O. Grabar in *Speculum* 53 (1978): 795–799. Islam is barbarism armed with a travesty of Judaism; with a fundamentalist hostility to high civilization, Greco-Roman, Iranian, and the Western synthesis of all that's best. The learned authors make no

reference to Hodgson's work in any of its many forms; it is as if the secret animus in Crone and Cook is to counter Hodgson, to provide an alternative world-historical interpretation of Islam. They say that theirs is a book written by infidels for infidels; charity and hope are also lacking. Hodgson prefixes a quotation from John Woolman: "To consider mankind otherwise than brethren, to think favours are peculiar to one nation and exclude others, plainly supposes a darkness in the understanding." *Hic Rhodus, hic salta.*

6. J. W. Sweetman, *Islam and Christian Theology* (London, 1945), 1:85. Cf. Schoeps, *Jewish Christianity* (Philadelphia, 1969), 22–27.

7. H. Corbin, *Creative Imagination in the Sufism of Ibn Arabi* (Princeton, 1969); "Divine Epiphany and Spiritual Birth in Ismailian Gnosis," *Papers from the Eranos Yearbooks*, vol. 5, *Man and Transformation*, 69–160. The quotation is from "Divine Epiphany," 76.

8. Schoeps, *Jewish Christianity*, 137, 140.

9. W. Blake, "All Religions are One," in *Blake: Complete Writings with Variant Readings*, ed. G. Keynes (London, Oxford U. Press, 1966), 98. All references to Blake are to the Keynes edition.

10. Schoeps, *Jewish Christianity*, 40, 67, 70–71. Koran 2:136.

11. In these days when the word *theocracy* is being used in vulgar polemics to discredit Islamic revolutionaries, it is essential to realize that the entire prophetic tradition, in fact our entire political tradition, is inextricably linked with the idea of theocracy. Cf. B. Spinoza, *Tractatus Theologico-Politicus*, chapter 17; M. Buber, *Moses*; E. Voegelin, *Israel and Revelation*.

12. Santillana, quoted in H. A. R. Gibb, *Mohammedanism* (Oxford, 1962), 99.

13. *De Monarchia*, trans. H. Schneider (New York, 1957), 7, 8, 9, 11, 10, 21 (quotes occur in the order of pages).

14. A. Guillaume, trans., *The Life of Muhammad, A Translation of Ibn Ishaq's Sirat Rasul Allah* (Oxford, 1955), 653–659. The sceptical Western authorities underestimate the scope of the Prophet's vision. See Gibb, *Mohammedanism*, 31.

15. On mystical-revolutionary politics in the Shiite tradition Hodgson, Quaker and Marxist, is indispensable: *The Order of Assassins: The Struggle of the Early Nizari Ismailis Against the Islamic World* (The Hague, 1955); "The Ismaili State," *Cambridge History of Iran*, vol. 5, chapter 5. Corbin, indispensable in other ways, refuses to see any political dimension whatsoever: compare, for example, his treatment of the crucial turning point in the history of the Assassins, "Divine Epiphany," 127, with Hodgson, *Assassins*, 160–184.

16. Koran 4:169; 5:19, 112.

17. H. C. Robinson, *Diary Account of Blake*, ed. E. J. Morley (New York, 1967), 26.

18. Hughes, *Dictionary of Islam*, s.v. "Sacrifice."

19. Nasr, *Ideals and Realities*, 90.

20. Ibid, 84.

21. Ibid, 18.

22. Corbin, *Creative Imagination*, 120.

23. Ibid, 182–183. Corbin's theosophical formulation is substantially identical with Coleridge's *Biographia Literaria*, chapter 13: "The primary Imagination I hold to be the living power and prime agent of all human perception, and as a repetition in the finite mind of the eternal act of creation in the infinite I AM."

24. Blake, "The Laocoön," 776.

25. Millennia of misunderstanding not really corrected by E. Pagels, *The Gnostic Gospels* (New York, 1979). Pagels ignores Islam and Corbin.

26. Hastings' *Encyclopedia of Religion and Ethics*; cf. *Catholic Encyclopedia*, s.v. "Docetism."

27. Blake, "Vision of the Last Judgement," 617.

28. Blake, "Descriptive Catalogue," 576.

29. Corbin, "Divine Epiphany," 69.

30. P. Miquel O. S. B., "The Mystery of the Transfiguration," *Theology Digest* II (1963): 163.

31. N. Frye, *Fearful Symmetry* (Princeton, 1969), 18.

32. Nasr, *Ideals and Realities*, 134.

33. Corbin, *Creative Imagination*, 335.

34. A. Nygren, *Agape and Eros* (Philadelphia, 1953), 312.

35. J. M. Robinson, ed., *The Nag Hammadi Library* (New York, 1977), 245, 344, 332.

36. Blake, "Annotations to Reynolds: Discourse II," 456. Orthodox Christian apologists shuffle the (abundant) Koranic texts about Jesus in order to leave the impression that Muhammad's theology is simpleminded, inconsistent and confused; cf. R. C. Zaehner, *At Sundry Times* (London, 1958), 210–214; E. G. Parrinder, *Jesus in the Qur'an* (Oxford, 1977), 108–121.

37. Corbin, "Divine Epiphany," 70.

38. H. Corbin, "L'Ismaélisme et le Symbole de la Croix," *La Table Ronde* (December 1957).

39. R. N. Longenecker, *The Christology of Early Jewish Christianity* (London, 1970), 26–28.

40. Corbin, *Creative Imagination*, 141.

41. Schoeps, *Jewish Christianity*, 63–64.

42. *Encyclopedia of Islam*, s.v. "Isa."

43. Cf. Koran 4:170; 43:61.

44. Corbin, *Creative Imagination*, 281; cf. 10–11.

45. C. Olson, *Maximus Poems* IV, V, VI (London, 1968).

46. Compare Corbin, "Divine Epiphany," 83, 123, 132, 139, and passim.

47. J. Danielou, *The Angels and Their Mission* (Westminster, 1957), 30.

48. Nygren, *Agape and Eros*, 576–593.

49. Rilke in J. B. Greene and M. D. Herter Norton, *Letters of Rainer Maria Rilke* (New York, 1947), 2:375; I owe this reference to Jay Cantor.

50. Parrinder, *Jesus in the Qur'an*, 40. Cf. *Encyclopedia of Islam*, s.v. "Isa."

51. Cf. H. Corbin, *Avicenna and the Visionary Recital* (New York, 1960).

52. Numbers 11:29; Blake, *Milton*, pl. I (p. 481).

53. Cf. Hodgson, *The Venture of Islam* 2:180–192; F. Jabre, *La Notion de Certitude Selon Ghazali, Etudes Musulmanes* (Paris, 1958), 6:272.

54. Peter Lamborn Wilson in *Labrys*, no. 4 (February 1979), 27. Cf. Hopkins, "The Blessed Virgin Compared to the Air We Breathe."

55. Nasr, *Ideals and Realities*, 87.

56. Koran 6:7–9 (trans. Arberry); cf. 6:50.

57. Nasr, *Ideals and Realities*, 43–44.

58. Corbin, "Divine Epiphany," 84.

59. Corbin, *Creative Imagination*, 146.

60. Corbin, *Creative Imagination*, 322–323.

61. Corbin, *Creative Imagination*, 248; cf. 155, 163, 355.

6

The Apocalypse of Islam

We can read the Bhagavad Gita in translation, and Confucius; we cannot read the Koran. Carlyle has perfectly articulated the response of every honest Englishman: "I must say, it is as toilsome reading as I ever undertook. A wearisome confused jumble, crude, incondite; endless iterations, long-windedness, entanglement; most crude, incondite;—insupportable stupidity, in short! Nothing but a sense of duty could carry any European through the Koran. . . . With every allowance, one feels it difficult to see how any mortal ever could consider this Koran as a Book written in Heaven, too good for the Earth; as a well-written book, or indeed as a *book* at all."

In the twentieth century the work of syncretism is beginning to change the picture: the work above all of Louis Massignon, the mystically minded Roman Catholic, and Henri Corbin, the mystically minded Protestant. Louis Massignon called sura 18 the apocalypse of Islam. The solemn recitation of sura 18 every Friday is all that Islam has in the way of weekly liturgy corresponding to the Christian Eucharist. In Islam the Body is the Book, and the part that represents the whole is sura 18.[1]

SURA 18—THE CAVE
REVEALED AT MECCA

In the name of Allah, the Beneficent, the Merciful.

Lecture for the Facing Apocalypse Conference, Salve Regina College, Newport, R.I., June 1983. Published in *Social Text*, no. 8 (Winter 1983–1984), 155–170. Also in V. Andrews, R. Bosnak, and K. W. Goodwin, eds., *Facing Apocalypse* (Dallas, 1987), 137–162. Reprinted by permission of Spring Publications.

1. Praise be to Allah Who hath revealed the Scripture unto His slave, and hath not placed therein any crookedness.

2. (But hath made it) straight, to give warning of stern punishment from Him, and to bring unto the believers who do good works the news that theirs will be a fair reward.

3. Wherein they will abide for ever;

4. And to warn those who say: Allah hath chosen a son,

5. (A thing) whereof they have no knowledge, nor (had) their fathers. Dreadful is the word that cometh out of their mouths. They speak naught but a lie.

6. Yet it may be, if they believe not in this statement, that thou (Muhammad) wilt torment thy soul with grief over their footsteps.

7. Lo! We have placed all that is in the earth as an ornament thereof that we may try them: which of them is best in conduct.

8. And lo! We shall make all that is therein a barren mound.

9. Or deemest thou that the People of the Cave and the Inscription are a wonder among Our portents?

10. When the young men fled for refuge to the Cave and said: Our Lord! Give us mercy from Thy presence, and shape for us right conduct in our plight.

11. Then We sealed up their hearing in the Cave for a number of years.

12. And afterward We raised them up that We might know which of the two parties would best calculate the time that they had tarried.

13. We narrate unto thee their story with truth. Lo! they were young men who believed in their Lord, and We increased them in guidance.

14. And We made firm their hearts when they stood forth and said: Our Lord is the Lord of the heavens and the earth. We cry unto no god beside Him, for then should we utter an enormity.

15. These, our people, have chosen (other) gods beside Him though they bring no clear warrant (vouchsafed) to them. And who doth greater wrong than he who inventeth a lie concerning Allah?

16. And when ye withdraw from them and that which they worship except Allah, then seek refuge in the Cave; your Lord will spread for you of His mercy and will prepare for you a pillow in your plight.

17. And thou mightest have seen the sun when it rose move away from their cave to the right, and when it set go past them on the left, and they were in the cleft thereof. That was (one) of the portents of Allah. He whom Allah guideth, he indeed is led aright,

and he whom He sendeth astray, for him thou wilt not find a guiding friend.

18. And thou wouldst have deemed them waking though they were asleep, and we caused them to turn over to the right and the left, and their dog stretching out his paws on the threshold.

19. If thou hadst observed them closely thou hadst assuredly turned away from them in flight, and hadst been filled with awe of them.

20. And in like manner We awakened them that they might question one another. A speaker from among them said: How long have ye tarried? They said: We have tarried a day or some part of a day, (Others) said: Your Lord best knoweth what ye have tarried. Now send one of you with this your silver coin unto the city, and let him see what food is purest there and bring you a supply thereof. Let him be courteous and let no man know of you.

21. For they, if they should come to know of you, will stone you or turn you back to their religion; then ye will never prosper.

22. And in like manner We disclosed them (to the people of the city) that they might know that the promise of Allah is true, and that, as for the Hour, there is no doubt concerning it. When (the people of the city) disputed of their case among themselves, they said: Build over them a building; their Lord knoweth best concerning them. Those who won their point said: We verily shall build a place of worship over them.

23. (Some) will say: They were three, their dog the fourth, and (some) say: Five, their dog the sixth, guessing at random; and (some) say: Seven, and their dog eighth. Say (O Muhammad): My Lord is best aware of their number. None knoweth them save a few. So contend not concerning them except with an outward contending, and ask not any of them to pronounce concerning them.

24. And say not of anything: Lo! I shall do that tomorrow.

25. Except if Allah will. And remember thy Lord when thou forgettest, and say: It may be that my Lord guideth me unto a nearer way of truth than this.

26. And (it is said) they tarried in their Cave three hundred years and add nine.

27. Say: Allah is best aware how long they tarried. His is the invisible of the heavens and the earth. How clear of sight is He and keen of hearing! They have no protecting friend beside Him, and He maketh none to share in His government.

28. And recite that which hath been revealed unto thee of the Scripture of thy Lord. There is none who can change His words, and thou wilt find no refuge beside Him.

29. Restrain thyself along with those who cry unto their Lord at morn and evening, seeking His countenance; and let not thine eyes overlook them, desiring the pomp of the life of the world; and obey not him whose heart We have made heedless of Our remembrance, who followeth his own lust and whose case hath been abandoned.

30. Say: (It is) the truth from the Lord of you (all). Then whosoever will, let him believe, and whosoever will, let him disbelieve. Lo! We have prepared for disbelievers Fire. Its tent encloseth them. If they ask for showers, they will be showered with water like to molten lead which burneth the faces. Calamitous the drink and ill the resting-place!

31. Lo! as for those who believe and do good works—Lo! We suffer not the reward of one whose work is goodly to be lost.

32. As for such, theirs will be Gardens of Eden, wherein rivers flow beneath them; therein they will be given armlets of gold and will wear green robes of finest silk and gold embroidery, reclining upon thrones therein. Blest the reward, and fair the resting-place!

33. Coin for them a similitude: Two men, unto one of whom We had assigned two gardens of grapes, and We had surrounded both with date-palms and had put between them tillage.

34. Each of the gardens gave its fruit and withheld naught thereof. And We caused a river to gush forth therein.

35. And he had fruit. And he said unto his comrade, when he spake with him: I am more than thee in wealth, and stronger in respect of men.

36. And he went into his garden, while he (thus) wronged himself. He said: I think not that all this will ever perish.

37. I think not that the Hour will ever come, and if indeed I am brought back unto my Lord I surely shall find better than this as a resort.

38. And his comrade, while he disputed with him, exclaimed: Disbelievest thou in Him Who created thee of dust, then of a drop (of seed), and then fashioned thee a man?

39. But He is Allah, my Lord, and I ascribe unto my Lord no partner.

40. If only, when thou enteredst thy garden, thou hadst said: That which Allah willeth (will come to pass)! There is no strength save in Allah! Though thou seest me as less than thee in wealth and children.

41. Yet it may be that my Lord will give me better than thy garden, and will send on it a bolt from heaven, and some morning it will be a smooth hillside,

42. Or some morning the water thereof will be lost in the earth so that thou canst not make search for it.

43. And his fruit was beset (with destruction). Then began he to wring his hands for all that he had spent upon it, when (now) it was all ruined on its trellises, and to say: Would that I had ascribed no partner to my Lord!

44. And he had no troop of men to help him as against Allah, nor could he save himself.

45. In this case is protection only from Allah, the True. He is best for reward, and best for consequence.

46. And coin for them the similitude of the life of the world as water which We send down from the sky, and the vegetation of the earth mingleth with it and then becometh dry twigs that the winds scatter. Allah is Able to do all things.

47. Wealth and children are an ornament of life of the world. But the good deeds which endure are better in thy Lord's sight for reward, and better in respect of hope.

48. And (bethink you of) the Day when We remove the hills and ye see the earth emerging, and We gather them together so as to leave not one of them behind.

49. And they are set before thy Lord in ranks (and it is said unto them): Now verily have ye come unto Us as We created you at the first. But ye thought that We had set no tryst for you.

50. And the Book is placed, and thou seest the guilty fearful of that which is therein, and they say: What kind of a book is this that leaveth not a small thing nor a great thing but hath counted it! And they find all that they did confronting them, and thy Lord wrongeth no one.

51. And (remember) when We said unto the angels: Fall prostrate before Adam, and they fell prostrate, all save Iblis. He was of the Jinn, so he rebelled against his Lord's command. Will ye choose him and his seed for your protecting friends instead of Me, when they are an enemy unto you? Calamitous is the exchange for evil-doers!

52. I made them not to witness the creation of the heavens and the earth, nor their own creation; nor choose I misleaders for (My) helpers.

53. And (be mindful of) the Day when He will say: Call those partners of Mine whom ye pretended. Then they will cry unto them, but they will not hear their prayer, and We shall set a gulf of doom between them.

54. And the guilty behold the Fire and know that they are about to fall therein, and they find no way of escape thence.

55. And verily We have displayed for mankind in this Qur'an all manner of similitudes, but man is more than anything contentious.

56. And naught hindereth mankind from believing when the guidance cometh unto them, and from asking forgiveness of their Lord, unless (it be that they wish) that the judgement of the men of old should come upon them or (that) they should be confronted with the Doom.

57. We send not the messengers save as bearers of good news and warners. Those who disbelieve contend with falsehood in order to refute the Truth thereby. And they take Our revelations and that wherewith they are threatened as a jest.

58. And who doth greater wrong than he who hath been reminded of the revelations of his Lord, yet turneth away from them and forgetteth what his hands send forward (to the Judgement)? Lo! on their hearts We have placed coverings so that they understand not, and in their ears a deafness. And though thou call them to the guidance, in that case they can never be led aright.

59. Thy Lord is the Forgiver, Full of Mercy. If He took them to task (now) for what they earn, He would hasten on the doom for them; but theirs is an appointed term from which they will find no escape.

60. And (all) those townships! We destroyed them when they did wrong, and We appointed a fixed time for their destruction.

61. And when Moses said unto his servant: I will not give up until I reach the point where the two rivers meet, though I march on for ages.

62. And when they reached the point where the two met, they forgot their fish, and it took its way into the waters, being free.

63. And when they had gone further, he said unto his servant: Bring us our breakfast. Verily we have found fatigue in this our journey.

64. He said: Didst thou see, when we took refuge on the rock, and I forgot the fish—and none but Satan caused me to forget to mention it—it took its way into the waters by a marvel.

65. He said: This is that which we have been seeking. So they retraced their steps again.

66. Then found they one of Our slaves, unto whom We had given mercy from Us, and had taught him knowledge from Our presence.

67. Moses said unto him: May I follow thee, to the end that thou mayst teach me right conduct of that which thou hast been taught?

68. He said: Lo! thou canst not bear with me.

69. How canst thou bear with that whereof thou canst not compass any knowledge?

70. He said: Allah willing, thou shalt find me patient and I shall not in aught gainsay thee.

71. He said: Well, if thou go with me, ask me not concerning aught till I myself mention of it unto thee.

72. So the twain set out till, when they were in the ship, he made a hole therein. (Moses) said: Hast thou made a hole therein to drown the folk thereof? Thou verily hast done a dreadful thing.

73. He said: Did I not tell thee thou couldst not bear with me?

74. (Moses) said: Be not wroth with me that I forgot, and be not hard upon me for my fault.

75. So the twain journeyed on till, when they met a lad, he slew him. (Moses) said: What! Hast thou slain an innocent soul who hath slain no man? Verily thou hast done a horrid thing.

76. He said: Did I not tell thee that thou couldst not bear with me?

77. (Moses) said: If I ask thee after this concerning aught, keep not company with me. Thou hast received an excuse from me.

78. So they twain journeyed on till, when they came unto the folk of a certain township, they asked its folk for food, but they refused to make them guests. And they found therein a wall upon the point of falling into ruin, and he repaired it. (Moses) said: If thou hadst wished, thou couldst have taken payment for it.

79. He said: This is the parting between thee and me! I will announce unto thee the interpretation of that thou couldst not bear with patience.

80. As for the ship, it belonged to poor people working on the river, and I wished to mar it, for there was a king behind them who is taking every ship by force.

81. And as for the lad, his parents were believers and We feared lest he should oppress them by rebellion and disbelief.

82. And We intended that their Lord should change him for them for one better in purity and nearer to mercy.

83. And as for the wall, it belonged to two orphan boys in the city, and there was beneath it a treasure belonging to them, and their father had been righteous, and thy Lord intended that they should come to their full strength and should bring forth their treasure as a mercy from their Lord; and I did it not upon my own command. Such is the interpretation of that wherewith thou couldst not bear.

84. They will ask thee of Dhu'l-Qarneyn. Say: I shall recite unto you a remembrance of him.

85. Lo! We made him strong in the land and gave him unto every thing a road.

86. And he followed a road

87. Till, when he reached the setting-place of the sun, he found it setting in a muddy spring, and found a people thereabout: We said: O Dhu'l-Qarneyn! Either punish or show them kindness.

88. He said: As for him who doeth wrong, we shall punish him, and then he will be brought back unto his Lord, who will punish him with awful punishment!

89. But as for him who believeth and doeth right, good will be his reward, and We shall speak unto him a mild command.

90. Then he followed a road

91. Till, when he reached the rising-place of the sun, he found it rising on a people for whom We had appointed no shelter therefrom.

92. So (it was). And We knew all concerning him.

93. Then he followed a road

94. Till, when he came between the two mountains, he found upon their hither side a folk that scarce could understand a saying.

95. They said: O Dhu'l-Qarneyn! Lo! Gog and Magog are spoiling the land. So may we pay thee tribute on condition that thou set a barrier between us and them?

96. He said: That wherein my Lord hath established me is better (than your tribute). Do but help me with strength (of men), I will set between you and them a bank.

97. Give me pieces of iron—till, when he had levelled up (the gap) between the cliffs, he said: Blow!—till, when he had made it a fire, he said: Bring me molten copper to pour thereon.

98. And (Gog and Magog) were not able to surmount, nor could they pierce (it).

99. He said: This is a mercy from my Lord; but when the promise of my Lord cometh to pass, He will lay it low, for the promise of my Lord is true.

100. And on that day We shall let some of them surge against others, and the Trumpet will be blown. Then We shall gather them together in one gathering.

101. On that day We shall present hell to the disbelievers, plain to view,

102. Those whose eyes were hoodwinked from My reminder, and who could not bear to hear.

103. Do the disbelievers reckon that they can choose My bondmen as protecting friends beside Me? Lo! We have prepared hell as a welcome for the disbelievers.

104. Say: Shall We inform you who will be the greatest losers by their works?

105. Those whose effort goeth astray in the life of the world, and yet they reckon that they do good work.

106. Those are they who disbelieve in the revelations of their Lord and in the meeting with Him. Therefore their works are vain, and on the Day of Resurrection We assign no weight to them.

107. That is their reward: hell, because they disbelieved, and made a jest of Our revelations and Our messengers.

108. Lo! those who believe and do good works, theirs are the Gardens of Paradise for welcome,

109. Wherein they will abide, with no desire to be removed from thence.

110. Say: Though the sea became ink for the Words of my Lord, verily the sea would be used up before the Words of my Lord were exhausted, even though We brought the like thereof to help.

111. Say: I am only a mortal like you. My Lord inspireth in me that your God is only One God. And whoever hopeth for the meeting with his Lord, let him do righteous work, and make none sharer of the worship due unto his Lord.

২৯

In the farrago of sura 18 the bewildered Western mind discerns and fastens onto three mysterious episodes—one cannot call them narratives—(1) The Sleepers in the Cave (vs. 9–26), (2) Moses' journey (vs. 61–83), and (3) Dhu'l-Qarneyn's wall against Gog and Magog (vs. 84–99).

The Sleepers in the Cave:

ASHAB al-KAHF, "those of the cave." This is the name given in the Kur'an, and in later Arabic literature, to the youths who in the Christian Occident are usually called the "Seven Sleepers of Ephesus." According to the legend, in the time of the Christian persecution under the Emperor Decius (249–51), seven Christian youths fled into a cave near Ephesus and there sank into a miraculous sleep for centuries, awoke under the Christian Emperor Theodosius (c. 437 A.D.), were discovered and then went to sleep for ever. Their resting place and grave was considered, at any rate since the beginnings of the 6th century A.D., as a place of worship.[2]

Dhu'l-Qarneyn, literally the "two-horned," is Alexander the Great, as in Syriac legend of the sixth century A.D., in which

Alexander says to God: "I know that thou hast caused horns to
grow upon my head, so that I may crush the kingdoms of the
world with them." In late classical antiquity—in between Christ
and Muhammad—apocalyptic syncretism, Judeo-Christian-Hel-
lenistic, expanding on lines laid down in the biblical books of
Daniel and Revelation, absorbed the figure of Alexander into its
sequence of world conquerors. Gog and Magog are biblical figures of eschatological terror. In Ezekiel 38 and 39, Gog and Magog represent peoples of the north who are let loose against the
peaceful land of Israel, unwalled and undefended, with a great
army of countless troops. In Revelation 20:7, "When the thousand years are over, Satan will be let loose from his prison and
will come out to seduce the nations in the four quarters of the
earth and to muster them for battle, yes, the hosts of Gog and
Magog." Koranic commentary, in the spirit of the modern historian W. W. Tarn, sees in Alexander a prophet of the unity of
mankind as well as a world conqueror, and thus a prefiguration
of Muhammad himself. Early Christian tradition, and Jewish tradition as early as Josephus, identified Gog and Magog with bar-
barian peoples to the north, locked away behind iron gates at the
Caspian Sea by Alexander the Great, but destined to break loose
at the end of time.[3]

The episodes of the Sleepers in the Cave and Dhu'l-Qarneyn's
Wall palpably allude to preexistent legends. The episode of
Moses' journey is more complex. The most bafflingly elliptical of
the three episodes, and the centerpiece of the sura, introduces a
new Moses, a Moses who like Gilgamesh and Alexander is committed to the quest for the Fountain of Life: "I will not give up
until I reach the point where the two rivers meet" (v. 61). The
new Moses, having become a seeker, submits to spiritual direction by a mysterious master who bewilders Moses through a
series of Zen-like absurd actions, finally justified by his privy
knowledge of the secrets of predestination.

Again we have to do with preexistent materials, but here the
action is positive confusion. To begin with, confusion between
Moses and Alexander; not the historical but the mythical Alexander of the Alexander Romance, a complex literary production,

completed about 300 C.E., giving voice to eschatological dreams close to the heart of late classical antiquity. Alexander goes in quest of the Fountain of Life. By the merest chance his cook discovers the fountain: he was preparing a dried fish by cleaning it in a fountain; the fish came to life again and swam away. The cook jumps in and gains immortality. He tells Alexander the story, but they cannot find the fountain again.

The Koran, with its creative confusion of Moses and Alexander, in a characteristically abrupt and monumental gesture, breaks with Judaic ethnocentrism and reprojects the prophetic tradition on a new transcultural, universal, world-historical plane. At the same time, by making Moses a seeker on the same plane as the pagan Alexander, the Koran defines a limitation in Moses and in the Halakhic Judaism of which he is the author: he lacks eternal life. In so doing the passage mobilizes, without naming, the powerful contrast, latent in Jewish tradition, between Moses and Elijah—Elijah the most popular figure in the legendary world of postbiblical Judaism: Elijah who did not, like Moses, die in sight of the Promised Land but who never died, being caught up to heaven in a chariot of fire; Elijah the omnipresent Comforter-Spirit present at every Jewish circumcision ceremony and every Jewish Passover; Elijah the herald and helper of the Messiah at the time of the return; Elijah, who knows the secrets of heaven and is claimed as the direct source of revelation by Jewish mystics including Kabbalists. The Koran sends Moses to Elijah's school—"it was taught in Elijah's school," Jewish mystics say.[4]

To represent what Moses learned in Elijah's school, the Koran has recourse to a folktale, type no. 759 in Aarne and Thompson's *Types of the Folktale*: "God's Justice vindicated." Thompson's paradigm is the Christian story of the angel and the hermit, very popular among Oriental Christians about the middle of the fifth century: "An angel takes a hermit with him and does many seemingly unjust things (repays hospitality by stealing a cup; inhospitality by giving a cup; hospitality by throwing his host's servant from a bridge and by killing the host's son). The angel shows the hermit why each of these was just." Just as the Koran transplants the Christian legend of the Seven Sleepers and the Hellenistic legend of Alexander into a new Koranic context, so it is drawing here on the vast ocean of traditional Talmudic Midrashic Haggadic wisdom.

First of all the story of Rabbi Akiba, who was often made to feel the truth of his favorite maxim: "Whatever God does He does for the best." Once he was compelled to pass the night outside the town walls because he was refused any hospitality in the town. Without a murmur he resigned himself to this hardship, and even when a lion devoured his ass, a cat killed his cock, and the wind extinguished his candle he only said: "Gam Zu Letovah" (This, too, must be for a good purpose). When morning dawned R. Akiba learned how true his words were. A band of robbers had attacked the town and carried its inhabitants into captivity, but he had escaped. Thus the fact of getting no accommodation in the town, as well as the killing of his ass and cock, turned out to be a blessing from God, otherwise the ass or the cock could easily have betrayed his whereabouts.[5]

Conventional Western commentators, who are quite sure there is nothing new in the Koran, assume without hesitation that the folktale is to be taken literally and that all that is going on in the passage is the transmission of conventional Haggadic piety. A detailed study of the Jewish and Muslim theodicy legends by Haim Schwarzbaum shows that sura 18, taken literally, offers nothing new to justify the ways of God to men. What is new is the sura's promotion of Haggadic folklore material to the status of revelation, its transgression or confusion of the boundary separating Haggadah and Torah. The Koran, with characteristic monumentality, reduces the folktale to its archetypal essence and makes evident its folktale form, thereby alerting the intelligence to the problem of interpretation. Folktales, like dreams, are not to be interpreted literally. And the content of the folktale—the episodes of the ship, the youth, and the wall—tells us in the most literal, even crude way, three times reiterated, that there is a distinction between "what actually happened," events as seen by the eye of historical materialism, and "what is really going on," events sub specie aeternitatis, as seen by the inward, clairvoyant eye, the second sight. The form and the content of the folktale oblige us, as they have obliged all subsequent Islamic culture, to make the distinction between literal meaning and something beyond—in Islamic terminology between *zahir* and *batin*, between outer (exoteric) and inner (esoteric); between external-visible-patent and internal-invisible-latent; between materialist and spiritual meanings.[6]

Sura 18 is the apocalypse of Islam: the heart of its message, not displayed on the surface, is the distinction between surface and substance, between *zahir* and *batin*. The context in which the folktale is embedded contains further paradoxical revelations for those who have eyes to see and are alert to read between the lines as well as in them. The context obliges us to identify prophecy (the prophet Moses) with the literal or external view of events (the ship, the youth, the wall) and to attribute the deeper view into the hidden reality to a mysterious other servant of God; not a prophet, or a prophet of the Elijah type as opposed to the Moses type. The context also obliges us to associate the mysterious other with the water of life—or where the two waters meet, the water of life and the water of death.

Sura 18 opens up, silently, majestically, in the heart of the Koran the question, What lies beyond or after the Koran? For Muhammad, like Moses, is a prophet. Muhammad is the seal of prophecy; what comes after prophecy? Prophecy is delivered in the form of a book, a scripture. But everything including the Book has an exterior (*zahir*) and an interior (*batin*). Especially the Book, according to the Prophet himself. Of Ibn Abbas, one of the most respected sources of Hadith (traditions about the Prophet), it is said: "One day while standing on Mt. Arafat he made an allusion to the verse 'Allah it is who hath created seven heavens, and of the earth the like thereof' (65:12) and turned to the people saying 'O men! if I were to comment before you on this verse as I heard it commented upon by the Prophet himself you would stone me.' " There is therefore a basic distinction between *ta'wil*, the symbolic and hermeneutic interpretation of the inner meaning, and *tafsir*, the literal explanation of the external aspect of the Book.[7] In the subsequent history of Islam, sura 18 became the basis for the elaboration of a distinction between prophecy and another transcendent or esoteric kind of wisdom; a kind of wisdom which in the fullness of time came to be most notoriously represented by, on the one hand, the Sufi master (*pir*) and, on the other, the Shiite imam. Whereas the cycle of prophecy is over (Muhammad is the seal of prophecy), the cycle of *wilayat* continues, which Seyyed Hossein Nasr tells us, for want of a better term, may be translated as the "cycle of initiation" and also "sanctity."[8] For want of a better term: the translation has to be in terms of Western Judeo-Christian religious experience. "Initiation" is closer to Shiite notions: Sufi masters are often more like Christian saints. The Shiite imam represents a principle of authoritative guidance in interpretation of the revelation; the Sufi *pir* represents a principle of mystic illumination which supplements the legislative or imperative mood of prophecy.

The text of sura 18 leaves us with a riddle: who is the mysterious other to whom Moses turns for guidance, "one of Our slaves, unto whom We had given mercy from Us, and had taught him knowledge from Our presence" (v. 66). Although he is like Elijah, he is not exactly Elijah; the Koran with a characteristically majestic gesture leaves him unnamed. The Koran leaves us with a riddle, or an assignment, to find him. The ellipses in the Koran are pregnant with the future. Very soon, within the first century, Muslim traditions and commentary on the Koran had given a name to the "Servant of God" who initiates Moses—al-Khadir, or Khidr, the Green (the sacred color of Islam), or Evergreen; taking their cue not from the reminiscence of Elijah but from the bold Koranic association of the servant with the Fountain of Life in the Alexander Romance. The name, the Evergreen, while naming, preserves his unnamable, unhistorical or suprahistorical, archetypal or folkloristic essence. In traditional Muslim piety, Khidr, like Elijah, enjoys eternal life and invisible omnipresence. Like Elijah he participates in the small rituals of domestic life and in the great public liturgies. Every Friday he prays in five different places—Mecca, Medina, Jerusalem, Quba (southeast of Medina), and Tur Sina (Sinai). For the annual fast of Ramadan he is in Jerusalem; for the hajj (pilgrimage) he is always in Mecca. The eternal protector of the community will appear at the Return at the head of the armies of the Mahdi, who will fill the earth with justice even as it is now full of injustice.[9] In Islam the umbilical cord which connects "popular superstition" with avant-garde esoteric, theosophic speculation has not been cut; and Khidr is that cord. The Sufis attribute their illuminations to the inspiration of Khidr: Corbin's book on Ibn Arabi, the mastermind of Sufistic theosophy, *Creative Imagination in the Sufism of Ibn Arabi*, is organized around the two questions—Who is Khidr? What does it mean to be a disciple of Khidr? The rendezvous of Moses and Khidr becomes the prototype of all those later mystic voyages in the company of a spiritual guide; including, when Western Civilization becomes strong enough to absorb into its own system some of the strong medicine of Islam, Dante under the guidance of Virgil and Beatrice. The visionary journey of the *Divine Comedy* is an appropriation of the Islamic *miraj*, the Ascension of the Prophet; the poet inherits the prophetic task of rescuing the Eternal Gospel from ecclesiastical deformations.[10]

The postbiblical Haggadah shows the efforts of Jewish orthodoxy to reduce Elijah's stature and to counter the excessive veneration accorded to him in apocalyptic Jewish sectarianism and Christian circles. It was denied that Elijah had ever gone up to heaven, biblical evidence to the contrary notwithstanding. Elijah's habit of revealing divine secrets to pious mortals once earned him a severe punishment of sixty lashes of fire. The Koran goes the other way. Without impairing its veneration for Moses as a prophetic figure, it endorses the eschatological longings and mystic revelations associated with the figure of Elijah, without naming him. But the orthodox Sunni *ulama* regress to the posture of Halakhic Judaism. The official theologians of Islam, we are told, are and always have been averse to these excesses of the popular Khidr belief; even as the Talmudic rabbis tried to put down the popularity of Elijah. "There are two things I hate about the orthodox canonists," says the mystic master Shadhili. "They say that Khidr is dead and that Hallaj was an infidel"—Hallaj the martyred prototype of Sufi mysticism, the subject of Massignon's masterpiece. Who is Khidr? How much does he know? These are questions neoorthodox Sunni Islam can do without. The great

Egyptian modernist, or neofundamentalist, Islamic reformer
Rashid Rida attacked the Friday liturgy of sura 18 as a degenerate innovation (*bida*), a departure from the original Sunna, the
hallowed practice of primitive Islam. Rashid Rida also condemns
as subjective interpretation all *ta'wil* which claims to find a hidden sense beyond the literal, and he restricts Koranic exegesis to
simple literalist commentary, *tafsir*.[11]

The controversy between literalism and mysticism in the interpretation of the Koran is aboriginal in Islam, and reaches into
the split in the core of the Prophet's followers over the succession
to his leadership. The rejected leader Ali is to be identified not
simply with the principle of hereditary legitimacy, but also with
the assertion of charismatic authority after the Prophet, and with
inspired interpretation after the Koran. Sura 18 is pregnant with
the Sunni-Shiite split and the whole subsequent history of Islam.

The Koran is pregnant with the future. It is only in the light
of later developments that we can find the riddle, the question—
Who is Khidr?—in sura 18. Later Islamic traditions linked the
occult spirit of Khidr with the Seven Sleepers and with Dhu'l-
Qarneyn's wall. Khidr is the Director of the Seven Sleepers, their
watchdog; together they form a community of apotropaic or in-
tercessory saints whose virtue saves the city, like those ten just
men for whose sake the Lord would have, at Abraham's inter-
cession, spared Sodom. They repair breaches in the wall against
Gog and Magog that Dhu'l-Qarneyn built. The weekly liturgical
recitation of sura 18 is to invoke the spirit of Khidr and join the
communion of saints in their action of repairing that wall. The
fight (*jihad*) against Gog and Magog is an eschatological reality,
but not in the future. In the Islamic sense of time we are always
in the last days.

The interpenetration works both ways: Khidr is assimilated to
the Seven Sleepers: he is an anchorite who has to flee from persecution and lives, exempt from death, having found the Fountain of Life, concealed in a remote island; like Kevin, of increate
God the servant, in *Finnegans Wake*. The melting or merging—
"confusion"—of Khidr and the Seven Sleepers generates mystical—i.e., nonliteral—interpretations of that sleep. The literalists,

Christian or Islamic, cite the story as "proof" of the resurrection, literally understood as life after death. Seen with the inward eye, to be immured alive in a cave is an image of saintly or eremite withdrawal from the world, taking refuge with Allah; and sleep the image of that extinction of self, that condition of being lost in God which characterizes the saint (*wali*) as distinct from the prophet (*nabi*); in the Night of Unction, the Night of the Heavenly Ascension, the blessed Night, the Night of Enshrouding which is also the Night of Power; the Dark Night of the Soul which is also the Night of *Finnegans Wake*.[12]

The spirit of Khidr is eschatological as well as mystical. The Sleepers Awake at the end of time, to figure together with Khidr in the Return of the Mahdi. History becomes a night, or seven nights. And everything is their sleep: The Seven Sleepers can represent the seven prophets who periodize world history—Adam, Idris, Noah, Abraham, Moses, Jesus, and Muhammad. The text explicitly provokes millenarian calculations: "which of the two parties would best calculate the time that they had tarried"; "it is said they tarried in their Cave three hundred years and add nine"; "say: Allah is best aware how long they tarried" (vs. 12, 26–27).

It is Shiite exegesis that has made the most elaborate eschatological interpretations of sura 18. The Sleepers hidden in the cave are the Koranic authority for the Shiite notion of the *ghayba*, or occultation, of the Hidden Imam. In the Ithna'ashari, or Twelver Shiites, the occultation becomes the principle on which they base their periodization of the whole of post-Koranic history. We are living in the occultation, which began with the disappearance, or sleep, of the Twelfth Imam in 874 c.e. and will last till his reappearance, or reawakening, with the Mahdi at the end of time. Modern times are divided into the lesser occultation, which lasted from 874–941 c.e., in which the imam, although invisible, was still in regular touch with visible representatives of his authority; and the greater occultation, which began in 941 c.e. and is still our present condition, in which communication with the imam is irregular, rare, unpredictable, miraculous. In this vision of history modernity means the disappearance of authority (authoritative guidance in the interpretation of scripture). The Shiite notion of the Hidden Imam is to be understood in analogy with folktale no. D1960.2. in Stith Thompson's index: Barbarossa, king asleep in a mountain, will awake one day to succor his people. Thus interpreted, the legend of the Seven Sleepers contains the perpetual threat of an eschatological outbreak. For example, the Seven Sleepers are seven imams of the Ismaili Shiites hidden in the cave, the womb of Fatima, and guarded over by their watchdog, Ali. The great Shiite insurrection (resurrection) on behalf of social justice in the ninth and tenth centuries C.E., which succeeded in establishing the Fatimid anticaliphate in Egypt, was commenced in the 309th year of the Hegira, as prophesied in sura 18:26.[13]

Massignon calls Sura 18 the apocalypse of Islam. But sura 18 is a résumé, epitome of the whole Koran. The Koran is not like the Bible, historical, running from Genesis to Apocalypse. The Koran is altogether apocalyptic. The Koran backs off from that linear organization of time, revelation, and history which became the backbone of orthodox Christianity and remains the backbone of the Western culture after the death of God. Islam is wholly apocalyptic or eschatological, and its eschatology is not teleology. The moment of decision, the Hour of Judgment, is not reached at the end of a line, nor by a predestined cycle of cosmic recurrence; eschatology can break out at any moment. Koran 16:77: "To Allah belong the secrets of the heavens and the earth, and the matter of the Hour is as the twinkling of an eye, or it is nearer still." In fully developed Islamic theology only the moment is real. There is no necessary connection between cause and effect. The world is made up of atomic space-time points, among which the only continuity is the utterly inscrutable will of God, who creates every atomic point anew at every moment.[14] And the Islamic mosque discards the orientation toward time essential to a Christian church: "The space," says Titus Burckhardt, "is as if reabsorbed into the ubiquity of the present moment; it does not beckon the eye in a specific direction; it suggests no tension or antinomy between the here below and the beyond, or between earth and heaven; it possesses all its fullness in every place."[15]

The rejection of linearity involves a rejection of narrative. There is only one decent narrative in the Koran: sura 12, "Joseph," acclaimed by condescending Western Orientalists: for once Muhammad overcame his temperamental incoherence and managed to do it right. The strict sect of the Kharidjis, on this point and on others the voice of rigorous Islamic consistency, condemned sura 12 on the ground that narrative has no place in revelation.[16] The Koran breaks decisively with that alliance between the prophetic tradition and materialistic historicism— "what actually happened"—which set in with the materialistically historical triumph of Christianity. Hence the strangely abortive and incoherent character of the pseudonarratives in sura 18. Something happened, but this strange revelation manages not to reveal what or why. In fact the impossibility of history as "what actually happened" becomes the theme of an abrupt interruption in the narrative at vs. 23–25: the Sleepers; how many were there? The Lord only knows.

"Recalls of former times" are an integral component of Koranic revelation, but as Massignon's Muslim disciple Nwyia says in his indispensable study of the mystic tradition of Koranic exegesis, "recalls of former times" does not mean history:

Schooled in the Koran, Muslim consciousness is spontaneously ahistorical, that is to say mythic. It takes up events of the past in approximately the same way as the apocryphal gospels adapt the gospel narratives. When Muslim consciousness takes up for its own ends an event borrowed from the Bible or Judeo-Christian hagiography, it in most cases cannot resist effecting a transvaluation by introducing fabulous details or otherwise transforming the meaning. Passing from one hand to another in a chain of Muslim transmission the historical event evaporates and all that is left is a vague memory submerged in a story which has become mythic.[17]

The use of the term *mythic*, with its Hellenic origins and overtones, may be questionable. At any rate apocryphal: not obsessed with the question, what really happened; willing to surrender to the fiction that is more real. Gibbon delighted in the irony that the Immaculate Conception of the Virgin, the Dogma of 1854, is first offered as a salvific image in the Koran (3:35–36). The Koran, with its angels and jinns, is pregnant also with the *Arabian Nights*; and with Rumi's *Masnavi*, that synthesis of Koranic inspiration and *Arabian Nights* imagination.[18]

In sura 18, in the Koran, there is a mysterious regression to a more primitive stratum, archetypal, folkloristic, fabulous, apocryphal. Historical material is fragmented into its archetypal constituents and then subjected to displacement and condensation, as in dreams. It is a rebirth of images, as in Revelation, or *Finnegans Wake*. In becoming unhistorical, it becomes elliptical: "And they forgot their fish; and it took its way into the waters, being free." The fish appears suddenly from nowhere, as in dreams; no causal explanation, no narrative coherence. The fish becomes a symbolic, or the archetypal, fish, the same one you see on California bumper-stickers; or in the mediaeval jingle *piscis assus Christus passus*. Moses and Elijah meet; Moses and Alexander merge, or "reamalgamerge" (*Finnegans Wake*, 49), not on the plane of materialistic historicism—what actually happened—but in the world of archetypal images, that world in which Moses and Alexander meet because they are both two-horned. In sura 19:25–26, Mary giving birth under a palm tree on the desert is also Agar the wife of Abraham; and in sura 3 Mary is also Miriam the sister of Moses. In this condensation Western scholarship sees only confusion—who is who when everybody is somebody else; as in *Finnegans Wake*. Massignon speaks of transhistorical, or metahistorical, telescoping; systematic anachronism. Islam is committed by the Koran to project a metahistorical plane on which the eternal meaning of historical events is disclosed. It is that plane on which Moses and Elijah are seen conversing with Jesus in Matthew 17; that plane on which Dante's *Divine Comedy* unfolds; and Blake's prophetic books; and *Finnegans Wake*. History sub specie aeternitatis.[19]

There is an apocalyptic or eschatological style: every sura is an epiphany and a portent; a warning, "plain tokens that haply we may take heed" (24:1). The apocalyptic style is *totum simul*, simultaneous totality: the whole in every part. Marshall Hodgson, in *The Venture of Islam*—still the outstanding and only ecumenical Western history—says of the Koran, "Almost every element which goes to make up its message is somehow present in any given passage." Simultaneous totality, as in *Finnegans Wake*. Or, more generally, what Umberto Eco calls "The Poetics of the Open Work": "We can see it as an infinite contained within finiteness. The work therefore has infinite aspects, because each of them, and any moment of it, contains the totality of the work." Eco is trying to characterize a revolution in the aesthetic sensibility of the West: we are the first generation in the West able to read the Koran, if we are able to read *Finnegans Wake*. In fact Carlyle's reaction to the Koran—"a wearisome confused jumble, crude, incondite; endless iterations, long-windedness, entanglement"—is exactly our first reaction to *Finnegans Wake*. The affinity between this most recalcitrant of sacred texts and this most avant-garde of literary experiments is a sign of our times. Joyce was fully aware of the connection, as Atherton shows in the most exciting chapter of *The Books at the Wake*; I particularly like his discovery in the *Wake* of the titles of 111 of the 114 suras.[20]

In both the Koran and *Finnegans Wake* this effect of simultaneous totality involves systematic violation of the classic rules of unity, propriety and harmony; bewildering changes of subject; abrupt juxtaposition of incongruities. Sura 18 is a good example. In addition to the melange of pseudonarratives, there are two intrusive parables ("similitudes," vs. 33 and 46) to remind us of the Day of Judgment; intrusive allusions to the current circumstances of the Prophet (his grief, v. 6; his lack of children, v. 40); and one intrusive pointer on pious decorum or etiquette in speech (vs. 24–25). Like *Finnegans Wake* the Koran rudely insists on indecent conjunctions. The Sura on Light (14), in the words of Hodgson, contains the most ethereal passage of visionary mysticism juxtaposed with what might seem the most sordid, dealing with matters of etiquette, with sexual decency, and in particular with an accusation of infidelity levied against a wife of the Prophet. The whole texture is one of interruption (Joyce's "enterruption"); collision (Joyce's "collideorscape"); abrupt collage, or bricolage, of disconnected ejaculations, *disjecta membra*, miscellaneous fragments. The widely accepted tradition is that the

Koran was collected, after the death of the Prophet, not only from the "hearts of men" but also from pieces of parchment or papyrus, flat stones, palm leaves, shoulderblades and ribs of animals, pieces of leather and wooden boards. In the words of *Finnegans Wake*, "A bone, a pebble, a ramskin; chip them, chap them, cut them up allways; leave them to terracook in the muttering pot" (*FW*, 20).[21]

Hence, it does not matter in what order you read the Koran: it is all there all the time; and it is supposed to be all there all the time in your mind or at the back of your mind, memorized and available for appropriate quotation and collage into your conversation or your writing, or your action. Hence the beautiful inconsequentiality of the arrangement of the suras: from the longest to the shortest. In this respect the Koran is more avant-garde than *Finnegans Wake*, in which the overall organization is entangled in both the linear and the cyclical patterns the novel is trying to transcend.

Every sura is an epiphany and a portent; and therefore not beautiful but sublime. Again He speaks in thunder and in fire! What the thunder said. Dumbfounding. Wonderstruck us at a thunder, yunder. Well, all be dumbed! (*FW*, 47, 262). In the Koran as in *Finnegans Wake* there is a destruction of human language. To quote Seyyed Hossein Nasr:

Many people, especially non-Muslims, who read the Quran for the first time are struck by what appears as a kind of incoherence from the human point of view. It is neither like a highly mystical text nor a manual of Aristotelian logic, though it contains both mysticism and logic. It is not just poetry although it contains the most powerful poetry. The text of the Quran reveals human language crushed by the power of the Divine Word. It is as if human language were scattered into a thousand fragments like a wave scattered into drops against the rocks at sea. One feels through the shattering effect left upon the language of the Quran, the power of the Divine whence it originated. The Quran displays human language with all the weakness inherent in it becoming suddenly the recipient of the Divine Word and displaying its frailty before a power which is infinitely greater than man can imagine.[22]

In Islamic apologetics the miracle is not the incarnation of God, but a book. The miraculous character of the Koran is self-evident in the immediate effect of its style, its *idjaz*, literally "the rendering incapable, powerless"; the overwhelming experience of manifest transcendence, compelling surrender to a new world vision.[23] The bewilderment is part of the message: "Through the windr of a wondr in a wildr is a weltr as a wirbl of a warbl is a world" (*FW*, 597).

How do you start a new civilization—in the seventh or the twentieth century c.e., with all that history weighing like an Alp on the brains of the living? Out of the rubble of the old; there is no other way. "He dumptied the wholeborrow of rubbages on to soil here" (*FW*, 17). Massignon speaks of the farrago of folklore (*fatras folkloriste*) in the Koran. First you trash or junk the old, as in *Finnegans Wake*, or the Koran; reducing preexistent traditions to rubble. Muslim piety, for whom the Koran is the supra-historical word of God, is troubled by the question of the relation of the Koran to preexistent traditions. Western historicism, with its well-honed methods of source criticism—*Quellenforsch-ung*—is only too delighted to lose itself in tracing the Koran to its sources, with the usual nihilistic result: the Koran is reduced to a meaningless confusion. Meaning is attributed to the original sources, but in sura 18 it has been "mutilated almost beyond recognition" and mechanically combined "in a most artificial and clumsy manner." Schwarzbaum refers to Muhammad as making a brave show with "borrowed trappings."[24] The notion that Mu-hammad was a charlatan, who stole from the treasury of Western Civilization and passed off his plagiarisms on his unsophisticated bedouin audience as the voice of God, is still very much alive at the back of Western minds.

Muslim piety need not be so troubled, nor Western scholar-ship so complacent and condescending. Sura 18 with its imperi-ous restructuring of Christian Hellenistic and Judaic tradition is not troubled. It is a prototypical model of Islamic syncretism. The Koran is not an operation of high cultural continuity, the *trans-latio* of the legacy of Greece and Rome (or Jerusalem), or the appropriation of the jewels of Egypt as we make our Exodus, as in Augustine's *De Civitate Dei*. To start a new civilization is not to introduce some new refinement in higher culture but to change the imagination of the masses, the folk who shape and are shaped by folklore and folktales. Prophecy is an operation in what Vico called vulgar metaphysics. The Islamic imagination, Massignon has written, should be seen as the product of a desperate regression back to the primitive, the eternal pagan substrate of all religions—that proteiform cubehouse the Ka'ba—as well as to a primitive pre-Mosaic monotheism of Abraham. The Dome is built on the Rock. Islam stays with the dream-life of the masses, the eschatological imagination of the lowly and oppressed. The dream-life of the masses, discarded by the elite of the Enlightenment as superstition—the stone which the builders rejected—becomes in the twentieth century the Golden Bough for the return to the archetypal unconscious, *quod semper, quod ubique, quod ab omnibus*. Here Comes Everybody.[25]

Sura 18, and the Koran as a whole, like *Finnegans Wake*, shows us preexistent traditions, Jewish, Christian, Hellenistic, pulverized into condensed atoms or etyms of meaning: the abnihilisation of the etym (*FW*, 353). Out of this dust the world is to be made new. We are once amore as babes awondering in a wold made fresh where with the hen in the storyaboot we start from scratch (*FW*, 336). In the words of Muhammad Iqbal in his *Javid-nama*—that syncretistic (*West-östlich*) resumption of the Koranic, Dantesque, Faustian journey through all worlds and all history—

> the Koran—
> a hundred new worlds lie within its verses,
> whole centuries are involved in its moments. . . .
> A believing servant himself is a sign of God,
> every world to his breast is as a garment;
> and when one world grows old upon his bosom,
> the Koran gives him another world!

The Koran is not responsible for the way Islam developed into a closed system and for the drily rational spirit of the Sunni *ulama* who turned all the luxuriant cosmic imagery of the Koran into legalistic prose. In the tragic view of history taken by the Shiites, things went wrong from the moment the Prophet died. The problem is, What comes after the prophet? The question is, Who is Khidr? And, What does it mean to be a disciple of Khidr?—the question at the heart of Sura 18. Pursuing that question, Ibn Arabi said that he had plunged into an ocean on whose shore the prophets remained behind standing.[26]

NOTES

1. L. Massignon, *Opera Minora*, 3 vols. (Paris, 1969): "L'Homme Parfait en Islam et Son Originalité Eschatologique," 1:107–125; "Elie et Son Rôle Transhistorique, Khadiriya, en Islam," 1:142–161; "Le Temps dans la Pensée Islamique," 2:606–612; "Les 'Sept Dormants' Apocalypse de l'Islam," 3:104–118; "Le Culte Liturgique et Populaire des Sept Dormants Martyres d'Ephèse (Ahl al-Kahf): Trait d'Union Orient-Occident Entre l'Islam et la Chrétienté," 3:119–180. The translation is that of M. M. Pickthall, *The Meaning of the Glorious Koran* (London: George Allen and Unwin).

2. *Encyclopedia of Islam*, s.v. "Ashab al Kahf." A juicier account of this "insipid legend of ecclesiastical history," which is often retaled early in bed and later in life down through all Christian and also Muslim minstrelsy, is Gibbon, *Decline and Fall*, chapter 33, *sub fin.*

3. *Encyclopedia of Islam*, s.v. "al-Khadir." *Encyclopedia Judaica*, s.v. "Gog and Magog." G. Cary, *The Medieval Alexander* (Cambridge, 1956), 130. Cf. F. Pfister, *Kleine Schriften zum Alexanderroman* (Meisenheim, 1976), 143–150.

4. *Encyclopedia Judaica*, s.v. "Elijah."

5. H. Schwarzbaum, "The Jewish and Moslem Versions of Some Theodicy Legends," *Fabula* 3 (1959–1960): 127.

6. S. H. Nasr, *Ideals and Realities of Islam* (Boston, 1972), 58. I. Goldziher, *Die Richtungen der islamischen Koranauslegung* (Leiden, 1920), 182.

7. Nasr, *Ideals and Realities*, 58–59.

8. Ibid., 87.

9. Massingnon, *Opera Minora* 1:151–152.

10. W. Anderson, *Dante the Maker* (New York, 1982), 277.

11. *Encyclopedia Judaica*, s.v. "Elijah." *Hastings Encyclopedia of Religion and Ethics*, s.v. "Khidr," 695. Massignon, *Opera Minora*

1:148. Goldziher, *Richtungen*, 335. *Encyclopedia of Islam*, s.v. "Islah," 147.

12. Koran 44:3; 92:1; 97:1. Massignon, *Opera Minora* 2:354; 3:104–118. H. Ritter, *Das Meer der Seele* (Leiden, 1955), 588–589.

13. Massignon, *Opera Minora* 3:104–118. *Encyclopedia of Islam*, s.v. "Ghayba," "Ithna'ashari."

14. M. G. S. Hodgson, *The Venture of Islam* (Chicago, 1974), 1:443. Massignon, *Opera Minora* 1:108; 2:606.

15. T. Burckhardt, *Art of Islam: Language and Meaning* (London, 1976), 19.

16. W. M. Watt, *Bell's Introduction to the Qur'an* (Edinburgh, 1977), 46.

17. P. Nwyia, *Exégèse Coranique et Langage Mystique* (Beirut, 1970), 74.

18. Cf. Massignon, "Le Folklore chez les Mystiques Musulmanes," *Opera Minora* 2:345–352.

19. Massignon, *Opera Minora* 1:109; cf. 1:143 and 3:143.

20. M. G. S. Hodgson, "A Comparison of Islam and Christianity as Framework for Religious Life," *Diogenes* 32 (1960): 61. U. Eco, *The Role of the Reader* (Bloomington, Ind., 1979), 63. J. S. Atherton, *The Books at the Wake* (Carbondale, Ill., 1974), chapter 12.

21. Hodgson, "A Comparison," 62. Watt, *Bell's Introduction*, 32.

22. Nasr, *Ideals and Realities*, 47–48.

23. *Encyclopedia of Islam*, s.v. "Idjaz."

24. *Hastings Encyclopedia of Religion and Ethics*, s.v. "Khidr," 694. Schwarzbaum, "Theodicy Legends," 135.

25. Massignon, *Opera Minora* 1:158–159, 162–163; 3:128, 143.

26. M. Iqbal, *Javid-nama*, trans. A. J. Arberry (London, 1966), ll. 1132–1140. Hodgson, *Venture of Islam* 1:392. Goldziher, *Richtungen*, 217.

7

Philosophy and Prophecy
Spinoza's Hermeneutics

The philosopher who in the *Ethics* celebrates the pure life of theoretical contemplation in the *Tractatus Theologico-Politicus* (like Plato's philosopher coming back down into the cave) faces the complex and muddy problems involved in the relation between philosophy and the nonphilosophic real world. Philosophy has to come to terms with two predominant nonphilosophical institutions: political power and positive religion. In the "Preface" Spinoza reviews the tendency for religion to degenerate into superstition and political power to degenerate into tyranny; superstition and tyranny threaten the very existence of philosophic freedom. The *Tractatus* is not an exercise in pure cognition but a model of practical reason in action, or even a political act: "I have not written with a view to introducing (intellectual) novelties, but in order to correct abuses."[1]

The political act undertaken in the *Tractacus* is mediation—to regulate the relations among positive religion, political power, and philosophic freedom: to lay the basis for their peaceful coexistence. The aim is not another broadside in the old war between reason and revelation (or even freedom and tyranny), but peace. "Reason, though Hobbes thinks otherwise, is always on the side of peace."[2] In order to function as peacemaker, philosophy can no longer function simply as philosophy. The *Tractatus* is not a pure product of philosophic thought but a hybrid: moving in the terrain between philosophy, political power, and pos-

Printed in *Political Theory*, 14, no. 2 (May 1986), 195–214.

itive religion; mediating among these institutions in order to make peace.

To mediate among these institutions means to establish principles for making their several languages mutually comprehensible. Spinoza already exists in the modern world: there is the distinct language of political power, articulated by Machiavelli and Hobbes; there is the scriptural language of traditional religion; and there is the new language of philosophy, Descartes and Spinoza. These several languages need to be interpreted each to the other. In the *Tractatus Theologico-Politicus* the philosopher comes forward to play the role of interpreter. In order to become practically and politically effective, to advance the cause of peace and freedom in the real world, philosophy transforms itself into hermeneutics. Although Spinoza says his aim is not to introduce intellectual novelties but to correct abuses, there is one decisive intellectual novelty in the *Tractatus Theologico-Politicus*: "I determined to examine the Bible afresh in a careful, impartial, and free spirit, making no assumptions concerning it, and attributing to it no doctrines, which I did not find most clearly therein set down. With these precautions I constructed a method of Scriptural interpretation."[3]

By what authority does Spinoza introduce a new method of scriptural interpretation? By the power that inspired the Cartesian revolution, the free spirit taking a fresh look and subjecting everything to skeptical examination: in a word, the power of reason. Into the strife of contending principles of authority a new voice is injected which acknowledges no authority. After the Cartesian revolution, as developed in Spinoza's *Ethics*, to be rational means to be free; to know one's own mind; to depend on no external authority for knowledge of God or knowledge of right and wrong. The *Tractatus Theologico-Politicus*, as a rational or scientific investigation of the nature of authority, has to be the rational investigation of the principle of irrationality in human affairs. It is reason examining its own opposite, faith; it is philosophy confronting its own opposite, prophecy, and recognizing in prophecy the fundamental form of the principle of authority in human affairs. "I constructed a method of Scriptural interpretation and thus equipped proceeded first of all to ask—What is prophecy? A prophet is one who interprets the revelations of God to those who are unable to attain sure knowledge of the things revealed by God, and therefore can only apprehend them by simple faith . . . and whose belief relies only on the prophet's authority and their faith in him."[4]

Philosophy has to transform itself into scriptural hermeneutics in order to investigate the nature of authority; that is to say, the scientific investigation of the nature of authority takes the form of an interpretation of history. Strictly speaking, philosophy has direct knowledge of God and his eternal laws and has no need of Scripture. But in order to challenge traditional authority, philosophy has to become an interpretation of tradition. Being in itself a fresh start with the slate wiped clean, philosophy must examine the way the slate is actually inscribed with the legacy of the past. Philosophical hermeneutics is historical hermeneutics. The legacy of the past is a history of prophecy. Prophecy transmits itself from generation to generation in the form of historical narratives (Spinoza's word is "histories"); Spinoza defines his own task as "synthesizing the history of prophecy" (*historiam prophetiae concinnare*).[5] Historical hermeneutics is an exercise of natural reason, but it is natural reason recognizing the authority of the past and seeking to arrive at the essence of prophecy in its own terms: hence the basic rule that "our understanding of Scripture must be totally derived from Scripture only."[6]

Natural reason so operating on Scripture cannot produce philosophy but only an interpretation. But interpretation is per se prophecy—a prophet is "one who interprets the revelations of God to those who are unable to attain sure knowledge by themselves." Scriptural hermeneutics is a hybrid form, or mask, that enables philosophy to enter the political arena disguised as the modern form of prophecy, the form of prophecy in an age in which there are no longer any living prophets.[7] In form and texture the *Tractatus Theologico-Politicus* is not philosophy but prophecy, not theoretical science but practical wisdom, affording (as Spinoza says) not mathematical but only moral certainty.[8] It is an exercise in persuasion involving Spinoza's creative imagi-

nation and operating on productions of the human imagination—the original legacy of prophecy and the subsequent contending interpretations.

Historical hermeneutics is philosophic enlightenment coming
to understand itself as emancipation from the authority of the
past and therefore understanding itself as historically emergent.
Spinoza's historical method is therefore genealogical. Prophecy is
the archetype or origin from which the three contending institutions in the modern world—political power, positive religion,
and philosophic freedom—are all derived, the common notion in
terms of which they can arrive at mutual understanding. History
is the history of the human race's release from self-incurred
tutelage—Kant's definition of enlightenment. Kant's definition of
tutelage—"man's inability to make use of his understanding
without direction from another"—exactly corresponds to Spinoza's definition of prophecy: a prophet is a tutor for those who are
unable to attain cognitive autonomy and must therefore rely on
external authority.

The evolution of humanity inevitably begins with prophecy,
even as tutelage is inevitable for children. Historical hermeneutics
teaches us not to look for pure doctrines of philosophic wisdom
in the Mosaic dispensation, but for elementary social discipline
appropriate (Spinoza's term is "accommodated") to a rude and
uncivilized state:

In truth, it is hardly likely that men accustomed to the superstitions
of Egypt, uncultivated and sunk in most abject slavery, should have
held any sound notions about the Deity, or that Moses should have
taught them anything beyond a rule of right living; inculcating it not
like a philosopher, as the result of freedom, but like a lawgiver
compelling them to be moral by legal authority. Thus the rule of
right living, the worship and love of God, was to them rather a
bondage than the true liberty, the gift and grace of the Deity. Moses
bid them love God and keep His law, because they had in the past
received benefits from Him (such as the deliverance from slavery in
Egypt), and further terrified them with threats if they transgressed
His commands, holding out many promises of good if they should
observe them; thus treating them as parents treat irrational children.[9]

History, which is the history of prophecy, goes from Moses in the wilderness to the great modern city of Amsterdam, which "reaps the fruit of freedom in its own great prosperity."[10] At the other end of history is civilized toleration, in which "we have the rare happiness of living in a republic, where everyone's judgment is free and unshackled, where each may worship God as his conscience dictates, and where freedom is esteemed before all things dear and precious."[11]

Philosophic freedom emerges as humanity outgrows the need for authority; philosophy itself is a new and more enlightened chapter in the history of prophecy. Spinoza's historical perspective contradicts the usual view of philosophy as a legacy of Greek rationality distinct from and opposed to the Hebraic legacy of prophecy. Spinoza contemptuously dismisses the speculations of Platonists and Aristotelians. Philosophy is defined as knowledge of God and His eternal laws revealed by the natural light of reason common to all: philosophy is equated with natural religion. And natural religion emerged from the mutation in the prophetic tradition that is recorded in the transition from the Old Testament to the New. The archetypal philosopher is not Socrates but Jesus Christ. The historical mutation in the prophetic tradition is crystallized in the antithesis between Moses and Christ. The prophets who preached religion before Christ preached it as a national law in virtue of the covenant entered into in the time of Moses, whereas the Apostles preached it as the universal, or catholic, religion for all.[12]

Mosaic prophecy includes the foundation of a particular state and positive laws to sustain it; its method is constraint rather than instruction, and it promises temporal prosperity. Christ's mission was to teach universal moral precepts, and for this reason he promises a spiritual rather than a temporal reward.[13] Christ reduced the prophetic religion to its essence, and in formulating the Golden Rule—to love God above all things and one's neighbor as oneself—transcended the prophetic principle of obedience to the law and prefigured the philosophic religion of love.[14] In line with the fundamental distinction he draws between (philosophic) mind and (prophetic) imagination, Spinoza goes out of his way to differentiate Christ from Moses in epistemological terms. Christ was unique in the prophetic tradition in communicating with God without the intervention of imaginary appearances such as Moses' voice, but directly mind to mind, with clear and distinct ideas, so that Christ was not so much a prophet as the mouth of God; that is, in Christ the wisdom of God took upon itself human nature.[15]

The mutation represented by Christ is the nodal point in a long-range tendency in the historical process (the prophetic tradition) in the direction of rationality. The universal religion, which we now can apprehend as a precept of reason in philosophic form, had first to be introduced in the form of prophetic revelation.[16] After Christ the Apostolic epistles, especially Paul's, represent a further advance over the Gospels in the direction of rational form; didactic and argumentative rather than prophetic (or fabulous) narrative. "Paul teaches exactly the same as ourselves."[17] Old Testament prophecy, notably Isaiah, shows a long-range tendency to transform prophetic revelation into universal, or catholic, religion for the entire human race; to discard ceremonial laws in favor of a simple rule of charity and the upright heart; and, above all, to supersede the external covenant of God, written in ink or on tables of stone, with the true original covenant inscribed by the Spirit on the human heart, on the fleshy tables of the heart (2 Corinthians 3:3); stamped with his own seal, that is, the idea of God himself in the image of his Godhead.[18] Spinoza interprets "the Word of God written in our hearts" as the equivalent, in biblical language, of what philosophy formulates as the natural light of reason that is common to all. Thus, rationality was at work even though it was not understood as such (i.e., philosophically). The paradoxical situation is expounded by Spinoza in biblical language: "It was in the world," as John the Evangelist says, "and the world knew it not."[19]

Spinoza's *Tractatus Theologico-Politicus* takes up where his *Ethics* left off. If philosophy is going to contribute to the improvement of the human condition (Spinoza's program in the treatise *On the Improvement of the Understanding*), it must find a basis for mediating between the antinomies left static and absolute in the *Ethics*: the antinomies between reason and imagination, freedom and bondage, theory and practice. Translated into the world of political realities, these philosophical antinomies become the polarity between prophecy and philosophy, between (political and religious) authority and philosophic freedom. There is a need for mediation not only between philosophy and the real world outside but also inside the philosophic system itself. A static and absolute antinomy between reason and imagination is inconsistent with the epistemological premise of the *Ethics*, the coherence of truth, and the overriding metaphysical principle of unity: truth is a unity; the function of reason is to make it all cohere. "Reason (though Hobbes thinks otherwise) is always on the side of peace."[20] Philosophy, to vindicate itself, must establish peace between reason and revelation. Already in his early *Metaphysical Meditations* Spinoza had asserted that sacred Scripture teaches the same doctrines as natural reason, for "truth cannot be at war with truth" (*veritas veritati non repugnat*).[21] The historical hermeneutics developed in the *Tractatus* is the middle term the whole system cries out for.

It is an essential corollary of the principle of coherence, and the whole system of the *Ethics*, to discriminate different degrees or levels of truth, power, and perfection. All our practical problems arise from the fact that all humans are not perfectly rational. But all are endowed with the natural light of reason; both the human individual and the human collectivity must be seen as in transition from a lesser to a greater degree of what Spinoza calls perfection. Morality, ethics, our whole duty individually and collectively lies in the *improvement* of the human mind: all our actions and thoughts must be directed to one end; namely, to attain the greatest possible human perfection.[22]

From the doctrine of degrees or levels of truth and perfection it also follows that error can never be absolute, but must always be a matter of having relatively incomplete (inadequate) knowledge. Mediation between reason and imagination cannot take place if the polarity remains static; it is set in motion by a dynamic nisus toward perfection. Philosophy needs the plane of history in order to unfold as enlightenment: then prophecy can be seen as *praeparatio philosophandi*, preparing the way for philosophy. The power that sets in motion the civilizational process, the progress toward perfection, is not philosophy but prophecy, not reason but imagination. "Prophets were not endowed with more perfect minds, but rather with the power of a more vivid imagination."[23] In the *Ethics* Spinoza spoke only of the limitations of the imagination as compared with the clear and distinct ideas of pure geometric reasoning; in the *Tractatus* we see the positive and creative power of the imagination. Prophecy is imagination in action: it produces the first form of human society and the first form of the knowledge of God. With it humankind emerges from the state of nature into the state of religion and law. Prophecy is perfected as it becomes more rational and moves toward a conjunction with philosophy, with Jesus Christ as the turning point.

The end of the process is historical hermeneutics, which is the perfection of both prophecy and philosophy. To perfect prophecy in hermeneutics, philosophy has to transform itself from the pure pursuit of knowledge for its own sake into something practically and politically effective in the real world. In Spinoza's *Ethics* power and perfection are equated, and "the more perfection a thing possesses, the more it acts and the less it suffers; the more it acts the more perfect it is."[24] Philosophy cannot rest impotent in the divorce of theory from practice. The philosopher is not and cannot become king, but he can inherit the prophetic function of speaking truth to kings and raise his voice on behalf of peace.

There is an instructive analogy in Islamic philosophy: coming to terms with the prophet Muhammad. According to al-Farabi, philosophy is prior to religion, and religion is an "imitation" of philosophy. Religion is an imitation of philosophy inasmuch as while both give an account of the ultimate principles of being, religion supplies an imaginative account of things whereof philosophy possesses direct and demonstrative knowledge. Nevertheless, a purely theoretical perfection is an incomplete perfection: the perfect philosopher is also the supreme ruler and lawgiver; he must have the capacity to teach the community and to form character so that everyone is enabled to achieve the perfection of which he is capable. For this purpose the philosopher will need religion, defined as the assent, secured by persuasion rather than demonstration, to an imaginative account of reality appropriate, accommodated, to the nonphilosophic multitude. Thus, the perfect human is both philosopher and prophet, combining theoretical knowledge with mastery of the arts of rhetoric and poetry. Muhammad is an actual embodiment of that excellence given literary portrayal in the writings of Plato.[25] Mediation between prophecy and philosophy is the central problem in Islamic philosophy. Spinoza inherits this tradition via Maimonides.

ᴥ

In order to become practical, philosophy has to become hermeneutics and master the problem of language—the refraction of the light of the One into the diversity of tongues, times, and places. The term the *Tractatus* uses to articulate the problem is "accommodation." Historical hermeneutics shows how religion is always accommodated to the intellectual level and imaginative complexion of both the prophets and the people in different historical circumstances, "accommodated to the prejudices of each age."[26] Hermeneutics gives us a pragmatic understanding of the limits of the possible and thus equips us for historical action. It also gives us psychological understanding of the variety of human opinion and thus lays the basis for toleration.

Spinoza's first programmatic manifesto, *On the Improvement of the Understanding*, had laid down as the first rule guiding the practical life of the philosopher to accommodate his language to the capacity of the vulgar, or, as we might say, to ordinary language.[27] The passage is misinterpreted and mistranslated in the current English translation, "to speak in a manner intelligible to the multitude." The Latin is *ad captum vulgi loqui*; comparison with the *Tractatus* shows that this is a shorthand phrase to refer to the principle of accommodation.[28] The programmatic treatise *On the Improvement of the Understanding* presents philosophy as a private and personal pursuit of self-perfection, which then joins "together with other individuals if possible, insofar as it is necessary to form a social order conducive to the attainment of self-perfection by the greatest possible number."[29] It is as if there was a primary philosophic activity of self-perfection that could be pursued in solitary self-sufficiency, and the problem of the relation of philosophy to ordinary language only arose when the philosopher reached out to collaborate with other individuals, "if possible," in the practical task of improving society. The underlying epistemological assumption is the Spinozistic separation of reason from imagination: the art (or science) of language is relegated to the sphere of the imagination; the connection between the two is "accommodation." It is only in the *Tractatus* that Spinoza deals directly with what is meant by accommodation. Thus, the *Tractatus* (as hermeneutics) is the key to Spinoza's use of language, even in the *Ethics*.

Accommodation is precisely what distinguishes prophecy from philosophy. "Scripture does not teach philosophy but only piety, and all that it contains has been accommodated to the capacity and preconceived opinions of the vulgar."[30] The maxim or rule *ad captum vulgi loqui* that Spinoza imposes on himself is derived not from the nature of philosophy but from the prophetic tradition, and it assimilates Spinoza's public utterances to prophetic speech. Spinoza wants to keep the theoretical distinction between two spheres—reason and imagination, philosophy and theology: "The sphere of reason is, as we have said, truth and wisdom: the sphere of theology is piety and obedience."[31] But the real world of practical politics belongs ultimately to theology. The social order depends on obedience, but the power of reason does not extend so far as to establish the principle of obedience. Therefore, revelation was necessary; and revelation is essentially a combination of reason and imagination (i.e., essentially involves accommodation). Hence, on one hand Scripture must not be ₂ commodated to reason, nor reason to Scripture; on the other hand scriptural hermeneutics, which is the way the prophetic tradition stays alive in a postprophetic age, is both the study of accommodation as exemplified in the biblical record and itself an exercise in accommodation.

The principle of accommodation enables us to understand the refraction of the One into the variety of human imagination, and thus establishes the difference between dogmatic uniformity and pluralistic concord (toleration). The more flexible and pragmatic understanding of the nature of religion ("true religion") introduced by historical hermeneutics reduces religion to its essence, the fundamental dogmas of religion universal to the whole human race. Nevertheless, these bare bones must be fleshed out by the obligatory practice of accommodation:

> Every man is bound to accommodate these dogmas to his own way of thinking, and to interpret them according as he feels that he can give them his fullest and most unhesitating assent, so that he may the more easily obey God with his whole heart. Such was the manner, as we have already pointed out, in which the faith was in old time revealed and written, in accordance with the understanding and opinions of the prophets and people of the period; so, in like fashion, every man is bound to accommodate it to his own opinions, so that he may accept it without any hesitation or mental repugnance.[32]

Accommodation necessarily involves a sacrifice of the Cartesian ideal of clear and distinct ideas. Clear and distinct ideas make clear distinctions: they will never teach us, as Spinoza does in the *Tractatus*, that "it makes no difference whether religion be apprehended by our natural faculties or by revelation. . . . Religion is one and the same and is equally revealed by God, whatever be the manner in which it becomes known to men."[33] Accommodation needs ambiguity, equivocation ("to express oneself in terms that admit of different interpretations"), prevarication (the basic metaphor is from straddling, with one's legs apart). The equivocation or prevarication in the *Tractatus* enables us to recognize the supreme equivocation in the *Ethics—Deus sive Natura*.

In his initial and basic terminological arrangements Spinoza allows prophecy and philosophy to share the idea of God. Prophecy, or revelation, is "certain knowledge revealed by God to man"; natural knowledge, knowledge revealed by the natural light of reason, is also prophecy, as it "depends entirely on knowledge of God and his eternal decrees."[34] If prophecy (as seen by philosophy) were dismissed as mere error or mere superstition, or if philosophy (as seen by theology) turned out to be atheistic, then the whole project of mediation would collapse. Hence, religion has to be one and the same, and "equally revealed by God, whatever be the manner in which it becomes known to men."

Similar equivocation or prevarication occurs with "divine law." Spinoza first identifies divine law with laws derived from (philosophic) true knowledge and love of God. The rest are human laws, which have a different aim, "unless they have been sanctioned by revelation," "for from this point of view also things are referred to God"; so that the law of Moses, "although not universal and very largely accommodated to the particular preservation of a single people, may nevertheless be called law of God or divine law inasmuch as we believe it to have been sanctioned by the light of prophecy."[35] These are not clear and distinct ideas. In formulating the "universal religion," the fundamental dogmas of the whole of Scripture, language is strained to accommodate (i.e., reduce) the gap between the prophetic religion of obedience, rewards, and punishments and the philosophic religion of love; to effect a compromise.[36]

Strictly speaking, some evasion is involved, some masking (*larvatus prodeo*), some disguise. The philosopher is not speaking with his own voice but is instead "adopting the language of John"; or "I affirm with Paul."[37] Spinoza achieves unspoken (persuasive) effects by manipulating discourses that are not his own; for example, juxtaposing his version of the social contract theory of origins (chapter 16) with the biblical account of the Mosaic covenant (chapter 17), letting the analogy speak for itself.

In Spinoza's philosophy, accommodation is not prudent dissimulation, as Leo Strauss takes it, but an active effort to promote tolerant concord—in a word, charity. Toleration is not a maxim of mutual indifference laid down by raison d'état (Hobbes and Locke), a negative limit to a rational requirement of conformity: it is mutual understanding based on recognition of the variety of the human imagination; that is, charity made scientific by the new science of hermeneutics. Without equivocation, no toleration. Accommodation without equivocation is the hegemonic assertion of uniformity or conformity, the one-sided domination of philosophy over theology or theology over philosophy. Toleration is based not on rational uniformity but on sentimental concord, located in the heart, the heart that has its reasons that reason does not know.

Accommodation is equivocation. Equivocation is justified by faith—the substance of things hoped for, the evidence of things unseen—faith in the existence of a hidden or preestablished harmony; a hidden harmony transcending verbal disagreement; a hidden harmony in spite of the contradictory facts of linguistic variety, sectarian discord, the Tower of Babel. It is the faith that in spite of the contradictory facts, the patent contradiction between the philosophic few and the superstitious multitude, there is, hidden in the human breast, the natural light of reason common to all human beings as such. "It is no accident," says Spinoza, that "the word of God in the prophets is in entire agreement with the very word of God which speaks inside of us" (as prefigured in Christ, who was not so much a prophet as the mouth of God, in whom the wisdom of God manifested itself in human form.)[38] It is the prophetic faith, invoked five times in the *Tractatus*, that religion, first imparted to the human race in the form of an external code of law written down, is now inscribed in God's own handwriting, in the form of the idea of himself and the very image of his Godhead, on the fleshy tables of the human heart.[39] It is no accident that this, the central proposition in the *Tractatus*, relies on prophetic rhetoric for its persuasive force: Spinoza cites Deuteronomy (30:6), Jeremiah (31:33), and 2 Corinthians (3:3). And what it asserts is equivalence or equivocation between the voice of reason and the voice of imagination.

፨

Philosophy transforms the prophetic faith in hidden harmony into philosophic knowledge (of the Unity: that it all coheres), and transforms the prophetic ethic of charity into the intellectual love of God.

Divine laws appear to us as laws or positive commandments only so long as we are ignorant of their cause; as soon as their cause is known they cease to be laws and we embrace them not as laws but as eternal truths; that is to say obedience passes over into love, which emanates from true knowledge as necessarily as light emanates from the sun.[40]

The intellectual love of God transforms, perfects, and finally transcends the prophetic religion.

Obedientia in amorem transit: obedience passes over into love. There is a dialectical mutation, prefigured in the dialectical mutation from the Old to the New Testament. Like Jesus, philosophy can say, "I came not to destroy the law and the prophets, but to fulfill." It is a mystic transcendence: the *Tractatus* illuminates the controversial mysteries of the *Ethics*. To pass over beyond prophecy is to pass over beyond words and images: "Inasmuch as God revealed Himself to Christ, or to Christ's mind, immediately, and not as to the prophets through words and images, we must suppose that Christ truly perceived or understood what was revealed; for a thing is understood when it is perceived purely by the mind beyond words and images."[41] It is only at this point—when we pass beyond words and images—that we can discard equivocation.

The intellectual effort in the *Tractatus* is to transcend the dualisms from which it begins. "Although natural knowledge is divine, its propagators cannot be called prophets":

[A prophet] interprets [i.e., mediates] the decrees of God revealed to him to others who have received no revelation, and whose belief therefore relies merely on the authority of the prophet and faith reposed in him. If it were otherwise, and all who listen to prophets became prophets themselves, as all who listen to philosophers become philosophers, a prophet would no longer be the interpreter of the divine decrees, inasmuch as the listeners would no longer rely on the prophet's testimony and authority but on actual revelation and inward testimony.[42]

Philosophy is here presented as a dialectical transcendence of prophecy, both perfecting it and superseding it. Prophecy would be perfected if all became prophets; but at this point quantity passes over into quality: reliance on external authority falls away; the inner light that had privileged the prophet passes over into the natural light common to all; we are in the realm of freedom and philosophy.

Prophetic theology passes over into philosophical theology. On the political side the point at which dualism is transcended is democracy. Spinoza says his chief purpose in the *Tractatus* is to exhibit the fundamental principles of democracy as being the most natural form of rule and the most consistent with individual liberty.[43] The argument takes the form of expounding an (equivocal) concordance between social contract theory (chapter 16) and the scriptural history of the Mosaic covenant (chapter 17).

In the language of social contract theory, as against Hobbes, Spinoza insists on the theoretical possibility of democracy:

A society can be formed without any contradiction of natural rights, and the compact can be entirely and eternally kept with the utmost fidelity, if each individual hands over all the power he has to society; society will then have sole possession of natural rights over all things; that is, it will have supreme sovereignty, and everyone will be bound to obey, either as a free choice or by fear of punishment. Such a constitution of society is called a democracy, which accordingly is defined as a collective body which collegially exercises unlimited sovereign rights.[44]

Democracy is the natural outcome of a rational understanding of the social contract on which society is based: another passage says that in a democracy all agree with common consent to live according to the dictates of reason.[45]

But at the same time Spinoza insists on the religious dimension of the social contract. Obedience is not a rational but a theological principle, and therefore society has to begin with prophetic revelation.[46] Society is brought into existence not by rational fear and the rational instinct of self-preservation, as in Hobbes, but by the prophetic indoctrination with the idea of God: Moses introduced a religion so that the people might do their duty willingly, with fidelity and constancy, from devotion, and not from fear.[47] The social contract was essentially a covenant, including an oath, whereby humans agreed to obey God in all things, as it were surrendering their natural liberty and transferring their rights to God.[48] Political organization is intrinsically theocratic.

It is intrinsically theocratic, but there are degrees of perfection and truth to be distinguished. In the childhood of the human race, given the fickle and irrational disposition of the multitude, the regime of authority and obedience that makes possible the transition from barbarism to civilization reflects fictions and distortions that are necessary concessions to the demands of the human imagination. The institution of divine kingship depends on "the belief that kingship is sacred and plays the part of God on earth, that it has been instituted by God, not by the suffrage and consent of men."[49] Spinoza cites instances from pagan history, such as Alexander and Augustus, and then like Machiavelli lets us infer that Moses was not so different: "Moses, not by fraud, but by divine virtue, gained such a hold on the popular judgement that he was thought to be divine, and divinely inspired in all his words and actions."[50] In the institution of divine kingship the interpreter of God (i.e., the prophet) takes the place of God. In his initial and basic definition of prophet as interpreter of God, Spinoza cites Exodus 6:1, in which God says to Moses, "See I have made thee a god to Pharaoh, and Aaron thy brother shall be thy prophet"; glossing the text Spinoza says, "Since in interpreting Moses' words to Pharaoh Aaron acted the part of a prophet, Moses would be to Pharaoh *quasi Deus*, as it were God; or as acting in the place of God, *vicem Dei agit*."[51] Spinoza has incorporated into the *Tractatus* the doctrine of Hobbes in Part III of the *Leviathan*: the Kingdom of God is a real, not a metaphorical Kingdom; the Kingdom of God is a Civil Commonwealth, in which God himself is Sovereign, wherein he reigneth by his Vicar, Vicegerent, Lieutenant, Sovereign Prophet, or Representative. Exactly so Spinoza reiterates that those who actually exercise sovereign power (*imperium*) are the interpreters and therefore masters of all law, both civil and religious; religion acquires the force of law only from the command of sovereign rulers. God has no special kingdom on earth except through those who actually exercise sovereign power.[52] The construction of civil society according to the pattern of the human imagination requires not only an idolatrous usurpation of divine status by human kings, but also the anthropomorphic representation of God as sovereign potentate, king, legislator, in direct violation of Spinoza's warning in the *Ethics* that it is essential to avoid any confusion between the power of God and the human power and rights of kings.[53]

The history of the Hebrew republic shows us a better way, a better form of theocracy. That government is best, the most natural, in which dependence on prophetic authority is transcended by all together being their own prophets, as is the case in the theoretical ideal of democracy. Spinoza cites, as Milton did before him and Blake did after him, Moses' own exclamation in Numbers 11:29—"Would to God that all the Lord's people were prophets"—and comments, "that is, would to God that the right of consulting God resulted in power being in the hands of the people."[54] Democracy is the most perfect form of theocracy, the only true theocracy: all the Lord's people being their own prophets would mean transcending the idolatrous worship of God's earthly vicegerent and discovering the one and only true God, the very image of his Godhead inscribed in the fleshy tables of the human heart, which is the natural light of reason common to all human beings, by virtue of which all are equal.

Spinoza fleshes out this theoretical possibility with his own (prophetic) interpretation of the events on Sinai (Exodus 20; Deuteronomy 5). The original contract was between God and all the people together, "as in a democracy," but the experience of God speaking out of the fire was so terrifying that the people asked Moses to be the mediator, interpreter, or prophet, saying, "Go thou near, and hear all that the Lord our God shall say, and speak then unto us all that the Lord our God shall speak unto thee; and we will hear it and do it" (Deuteronomy 5:27).[55] "God alone held sovereignty over the Hebrews; by virtue of the covenant or compact their state was called God's kingdom. . . . There was no distinction between civil and religious law; inasmuch as the citizens were bound only by law directly revealed by God, the state could be called a theocracy."[56]

Although all states, by virtue of the fundamental nature of the social contract, are theocratic, the Hebrew republic is theocratic par excellence and represents the perfection of the theocratic principle; and it is theocratic par excellence by being democratic. In Spinoza's interpretation of Hebrew history the theocracy comes to an end with the institution of kingship, when the people break with God's rule ("divine right") and ask for a king like the Gentiles have (1 Samuel 8).[57] In Spinoza's extraordinary and still unsurpassed interpretation of Hebrew history, the change over to kingship is the final fall, but there was a fatal seed of corruption in the Mosaic constitution: the separate Levitic priesthood instead of the universal priesthood of the firstborn in every family, as originally intended by God until the people's defection to the Golden Calf.[58] That God should have ordered the introduction of a fatal flaw marring his own revelation of the perfect theocratic constitution draws from Spinoza a daring recall of Tacitus' epigram: God's concern at that time was not human well-being but punishment. The effect of this Machiavellian use of Tacitean irony is to liberate the theological imagination from bondage to the letter. To find the perfect theocratic constitution we have to go back to God's "original intention": "If the state had been formed according to the original intention, the rights and honour of all the tribes would have been equal, and everything would have rested on a firm basis."[59] The theopolitical premise of perfect democratic or republican equality is the priesthood of all believers, or at least of every paterfamilias.

But for this flaw (the separate Levitic priesthood) the Hebrew republic might have been immortal, eternal (*aeternum*).[60] An "immortal commonwealth," a republic made exempt from the cycle of degeneration by mixing and balancing, as in Polybius' theory, monarchical aristocratic and democratic elements. The *Tractatus*, as a venture in mediation, in hybrid or mixed or "impure" thought, reaches here its most advanced point. Spinoza is effecting a conjunction between prophetic history and the most advanced speculations of contemporary republicanism, based on classical political theory as modernized by Machiavelli.[61] Chapter 17 of the *Tractatus Theologico-Politicus* shows that a model of republican stability, such as James Harrington had projected in his utopian scheme *Oceana* (1656), is enshrined in the early Hebrew commonwealth, which (Spinoza says) although "it would be impossible to imitate today," nevertheless "possessed many excellent features which should be brought to our attention and perhaps imitated with advantage."[62]

Spinoza's analysis conforms to Harringtonian principles. Moses, who himself exercised sovereign power, did not establish a successor with sovereign power, but distributed his prerogatives and divided his powers, separating the high priesthood and the interpretation of the laws (Aaron) from the executive power and military command (Joshua) and even distributing the military command according to a federal (tribal) principle, as in the United States of the Netherlands. As in Harrington, the checks and balances which, Spinoza says, "so effectively kept within bounds both rulers and ruled" are sustained by a patriotic civic consciousness based on freehold tenure of equal lots of land, universal possession of arms, and systematic instruction in the holy book of law. The result is an armed popular commonwealth, in Spinoza's words, the rule of the people, *regnum populi*, defended by the ardent patriotism of free citizen-soldiers. The civic consciousness that animates the whole is saturated with religion; the checks and balances that cancel out the predominance of human agencies leave God as the center of political life.

After the death of Moses no one man wielded all the power of a sovereign; as affairs were not at all managed by one man, nor by a single council, nor by the popular vote, but partly by one tribe, partly by the rest in equal shares, it is most evident that the government, after the death of Moses, was neither monarchic, nor aristocratic, nor popular, but as we have said, Theocratic. The reasons for applying this term are: I. Because the royal seat of government was the Temple, and in respect to it alone, as we have shown, all the tribes were fellow-citizens. II. Because all the people owed allegiance to God, their supreme Judge, to whom only they had promised implicit obedience in all things. III. Because the general-in-chief or dictator, when there was need of such, was elected by none save God alone.[63]

Even so Harrington—like Spinoza, a strong defender of religious freedom and enemy of priestly power—maintained that the Mosaic commonwealth had been a true classical republic; that Oceana, the restored republic, is both a new Israel and a new Rome; and that a republic is a theocracy. Harrington reaches for the same point of transcendence at which reason and revelation coincide: "A commonwealth is a monarchy: to her God is king, in as much as reason, his dictat, is her soverain power."[64]

NOTES

1. TTP 189 (3:76). (References to the *Tractatus Theologico-Politicus* are to Benedict de Spinoza, *A Theologico-Political Treatise and a Political Treatise*, trans. R. H. M. Elwes [New York, 1951], followed by the corresponding page of the Latin edition by C. Gebhardt, *Spinoza Opera*, 4 vols. [Heidelberg, 1971]. I have frequently made my own corrections to the Elwes translation.)

2. TTP 276 (3:263).

3. TTP 8 (3:9).

4. TTP 13 (3:15).

5. TTP 96 (3:95).

6. TTP 100 (3:99).

7. No longer any prophets; see TTP 14 (3:16) and TTP 256 (3:238).

8. See TTP 195–196 (3:185).

9. TTP 38–39 (3:40–41).

10. TTP 264 (3:245–246).

11. TTP 6 (3:7).

12. See TTP 160 (3:154); TTP 170 (3:163).

13. See TTP 64 (3:64); TTP 70–71 (3:70–71).

14. See TTP 172 (3:165).

15. See TTP 19 (3:21); TTP 64 (3:64).

16. See TTP 248 (3:231).

17. TTP 53 (3:54); see TTP 160–163 (3:154–157).

18. See TTP 165 (3:158); TTP 197 (3:186); TTP 237 (3:221).

19. TTP 170 (3:163).

20. TTP 276 (3:263).

21. *Cogitata Metaphysica*, part 2, chapter 8 (Gebhardt 1:265).

22. *Tractatus de Intellectus Emendatione* (Gebhardt 2:9).

24. *Ethics*, part 5, prop. 40.

25. M. Mahdi, *Alfarabi's Philosophy of Plato and Aristotle* (New York, 1962), 6–7.

26. TTP 106 (3:104).

27. See Gebhardt 2:9.

28. See L. Strauss, *Persecution and the Art of Writing* (New York, 1952), 178–180. I am indebted to, and contending with, Strauss's essay "How to Study Spinoza's *Theologico-Political Treatise*," in *Persecution*, 142–201.

29. See Gebhardt 2:8–9.

30. TTP 190 (3:180).

31. TTP 194–195 (3:184–185).

32. TTP 188 (3:178).

33. TTP 247 (3:230).

34. TTP 13 (3:15).

35. TTP 61 (3:61).

36. TTP 186–187 (3:177–178).

37. TTP 186 (3:176); TTP 53 (3:54).

38. TTP 197 (3:186).

39. See TTP 165 (3:158); TTP 169 (3:162); TTP 192 (3:182); TTP 197 (3:186); TTP 237 (3:221).

40. TTP 277 (3:264).

41. TTP 64 (3:64–65).

42. TTP 269 (3:251).

43. See TTP 207 (3:195); TTP 263 (3:245).

44. TTP 205 (3:193).

45. TTP 247 (3:230).

46. See TTP 194–195 (3:184–185).

47. See TTP 75 (3:75); TTP 216 (3:203).

48. See TTP 210 (3:198); TTP 219 (3:205).

49. TTP 218 (3:205).

50. TTP 257 (3:239).

51. TTP 13 (3:15).

52. See TTP 245 (3:228); TTP 248 (3:231).

53. *Ethics*, part 2, prop. 3, note.

54. TTP 277 (3:265).

55. TTP 220 (3:206–207); see TTP 247 (3:230).

56. TTP 219–220 (3:206).

57. TTP 235 (3:219).

58. TTP 232–233 (3:218).

59. TTP 233 (3:218).

60. TTP 236, 237 (3:220, 221).

61. See C. Blitzer, *An Immortal Commonwealth: The Political Thought of James Harrington* (New Haven, 1960); J. G. A. Pocock, *The Machiavellian Moment: Florentine Political Thought and the Atlantic Republican Tradition* (Princeton, 1975), 388.

62. TTP 237 (3:221).

63. TTP 225–226 (3:211). See chapter 17, passim; "regnum populi," TTP 240 (3:224).

64. Pocock, *Machiavellian Moment*, 398, note 116.

8

The Turn to Spinoza

PART I: THE MESSAGE FROM PARIS

A highly stimulating article by Etienne Balibar in *Les Temps Modernes*, with the provocative title "Spinoza, Anti-Orwell: The Fear of the Masses,"[1] proposes to persuade us that a new interpretation of Spinoza, an interpretation which emphasizes his political thought even to the point of making it the key to his metaphysics, is "indispensable for us today." The "we" who need it are no doubt the world, but more particularly intellectuals "on the Left," and even more particularly those intellectuals on the Left for whom Marxism has been a vital point of reference.

In effect Balibar's article signals a dialectical mutation in the intellectual movement in France, especially associated with the name of Althusser, to modernize Marxism by casting out the spirit of Hegel. It is as if the effort to exorcise the ghost of the nineteenth century led back to the seventeenth century, to a more fundamental reconsideration of the intellectual premises of modernity. Althusser himself, especially in his *Autocritique*, had pointed to Spinoza. Balibar's fellow Althusserian Pierre Macherey wrote a book with the title *Hegel or Spinoza*, which presents Spinoza as the way to avoid Hegelian teleology. But, as Balibar acknowledges, the qualitative leap in the Marxist interpretation of Spinoza was made by Antonio Negri, the philosopher accused by the Italian government of complicity in the conspiracies of the Red Brigades, in a book signed as having been written in the prisons of Rovigo, Rebibbia, Fossombrone, Palmi, and Trani, April 7, 1979–April 7, 1980: *Anomalia Selvaggia, Saggio su Po*

Written in 1986; revised in 1989.

tere e Potenza in Baruch Spinoza; the enigmatic title translated into French as *L'Anomalie Sauvage, Puissance et Pouvoir chez Spinoza*. I don't know how to translate the distinction between *puissance* and *pouvoir* (*potenza* and *potere*) into English. Negri's book is a brilliant Promethean venture, to steal Spinoza from the academics and the tradition of cloistered contemplation and install him in the revolutionary pantheon as the last of the bourgeois Renaissance pantheists and the first to anticipate the revolt of the masses (or at least the advent of mass politics); in both directions out of joint with his environment, an "uncouth anomaly."

Negri's book—in spite of or because of its enthusiastic overstatement, it needs to be available in English translation—accomplishes three things. First, it more successfully than any other book relates Spinoza's thought to the vital historical currents of his time and place. In the second half of the seventeenth century, Holland sheltered survivals of Renaissance utopianism, not only philosophical but also religious and political, after England and France had made the transition from revolutionary disturbance to absolutist order. Negri is here drawing on a large array of modern historical work, the most important for him being the early work of L. Kolakowski (in French translation, *Chrétiens sans Eglise: La Conscience Religieuse et le Lien Confessionel au XVIIe Siècle*); the effect is to take Spinoza out of the academic cloister and put him in the seventeenth-century revolutionary ferment in which the foundations of the modern world were laid. The first phase of Spinoza's thought, after his expulsion from the synagogue in 1656, is anchored in retreat to Rijnsburg, near Leiden, supported by a circle of illuminati, radical free-thinking pietists whose commitment and project, the reconciliation of reason and religion, remains the central theme of Spinoza's masterworks, the *Ethics* and the *Tractatus Theologico-Politicus*.

The second great thing that Negri accomplishes is to show Spinoza's thought as living thought, growing thought, changing his mind. "For the actualization of mind is life"—the motto, from Aristotle's *Metaphysics*, that Werner Jaeger chose for his classic book on how Aristotle grew from Platonist to Aristotelian. In Negri's view Spinoza evolves from contemplative Renaissance idealist, bent on reforming his own mind (*Treatise on the Emendation of the Intellect*, 1662) to a primary concern with politics. Negri's hypothesis of a crisis or caesura in Spinoza's development makes new meaning out of well-known facts in the meager biographical record. In 1663 Spinoza abandoned the Rijnsburg retreat and moved to Voorburg, a suburb of The Hague. He had already written the first part of the *Ethics*, but nevertheless he set this work aside and devoted the years 1665–1670 to the *Tractatus Theologico-Politicus*, the *Ethics* not being completed till 1675. For Negri the move to The Hague reflects a determination in Spinoza to confront his maturing ontology with social and political reality, with power. The publication of the *Tractatus Theologico-Politicus*—"an instrument forged in hell by a renegade Jew and issued with the knowledge of Mr. Jan de Witt," in the words of one of many denunciators—was a radical political act. In Negri's perspective the *Tractatus Theologico-Politicus* is also the crux in the evolution of Spinoza's metaphysical thought, which takes final shape only in the years 1670–1675. The *Tractatus Theologico-Politicus* demonstrates that the ontological sphere of the imagination, which is the sphere of both religion and politics, cannot be understood by the methods of rational theology or philosophy, but needs in addition a new empirical method of historical hermeneutics. (See Chapter 7 in this book.) Thus through his work on the *Tractatus Theologico-Politicus* power-political reality and historical concreteness are absorbed into the texture of Spinoza's mind and then are reflected again in the sophisticated doctrine of the mass imagination which Negri discerns in the final version of the *Ethics* and in Spinoza's last, unfinished work, the *Tractatus Politicus*.

Negri's new perspective—and this is his third contribution—for the first time makes sense out of Spinoza's last, unfinished, unrevised, and unsutured text, the *Tractatus Politicus*. For many years an admirer of the *Tractatus Theologico-Politicus*, I could not see what the later treatise was trying to add to the earlier one, or why Spinoza, after completing the *Ethics*, should in the final few years of his fatally stricken life, "apply my mind to politics," in spite of the promise, in the *Ethics*, of a further treatise on epistemology.[2] In Negri's perspective the whole evolution of Spinoza's life is from the religious to the political: the personal forays into political actions toward the end of his life fall into place. In the conventional view, Spinoza (Spinoza!) just lost his head. A typical comment: "The shameful massacre of the brothers De Witt by an infatuated mob brought Spinoza into close and painful contact with the passions seething around him. For once his philosophic calm was broken: he was only by force prevented from rushing forth into the streets at the peril of his life, and proclaiming his abhorrence of the crime."

There is also something political left undone in the realm of theory, which Spinoza started to do in the *Tractatus Politicus*. The metaphysics of the *Ethics*, distilled from the historical studies of the *Tractatus Theologico-Politicus*, needs to be translated into a physics of politics, a physics robust enough to overthrow the giant of absolutism, Thomas Hobbes. Through the sometimes uncertain wandering of Spinoza's text Negri has discerned the main drift. Spinoza develops his thought in the Machiavellian mode of historical reflection, transposing Machiavellian realism and materialism into Spinozistic terms: taking men as they are and not as philosophers would like them to be, "neither to mock, lament, or denounce, but to understand." Spinoza takes from Hobbes the concept and word *multitude*: "The essence of the Commonwealth is One Person, of whose Acts a great Multitude, by mutual covenants one with another, have made themselves every one the Author." But whereas in Hobbes the multitude appears on stage only for a moment, immediately to abdicate in favor of the absolutist state in return for the gift of peace and order, in Spinoza the multitude, the consent of the masses and their potential revolt, remains the ultimate, permanent, and problematical reality in all politics and in all constitutions. "For the right [*jus*] of the state is determined by the power of the multitude which is led as it were by one mind." "If there be any absolute sovereignty [*imperium absolutum*], it is in fact that which is held by the multitude as a whole." The consent of the masses, and their political revolt. A specter is haunting politics;

Spinoza cites a Tacitean epigram, "The mob is fearsome when it is not afraid." Absolutism is constrained by the fear of the fear it inspires in the citizens turning into indignation, and consequently reducing civil society to a state of war. As against the virtually universal assumption that the freedom which Spinoza espouses in all his writings is individual freedom, Negri convincingly shows that in this his last writing Spinoza is exploring the enigmatic notion of a "free multitude."[3] The subject of the last chapter, left unfinished and confused, is democracy, "the most perfect (absolute) form of sovereignty." The text breaks off with Spinoza excluding women from the citizenship not only on grounds of their natural inferiority but also because of their disturbing effect on male rationality. As Balibar observes, the fear of women is the same as fear of the masses; Spinoza cannot solve the problem. The thought is aporetic through and through.

Negri's book, written in the jails of Italy, reasserts the validity of an "uncouth," refractory, dissenting, and intransigent tradition of radical materialism, going from Machiavelli to Spinoza to Marx, as against the main line of bourgeois ideology going, as he sees it, from Hobbes to Rousseau, Kant, and Hegel. It is as if critical thought, detaching itself from the Hegelian-Marxist "locomotive of history," has to regress in order to find ground to stand on, either (with Colletti) to the bourgeois liberalism of Kant, or (with Negri) in a desperate leap, to escape embourgeoisement, to the more uncompromisingly radical utopianism of Spinoza, seen as uncouth anomaly or heroic freak. It is as if Marxism has an opportunity to find its soul in this its moment of historical defeat, to discard its erroneous attachment to Hegelian notions of historical evolution and triumphal progress, to discover its suprahistorical utopian principles, perhaps even the Spinozistic principle that "it is of the nature of reason to perceive things under a certain aspect of eternity."[4]

The texture of Balibar's article is quite different. Balibar allows himself to be jolted by Negri's book out of the rut of neo-Marxist scholasticism into radically new territory: an open-ended exploration of how political thought, making a fresh start from Spinozistic premises, might encompass twentieth-century political realities ("Spinoza, Anti-Orwell"). Marxism is not repudiated; but neither is it found, as occasionally in Negri, to be an indispensable corrective supplement to inadequacies in Spinoza; it is simply suspended. The (musical) key to Balibar's discourse is the word *aporia*: (from Greek *aporos*, without a passage, at a loss) "*Rhet.* a professing to be at a loss what course to pursue, to be in doubt." Balibar begins with the assertion that Spinoza's political thought is indispensable for us because of its fundamentally aporetic texture. In thinking through Spinoza's aporia we can get to know our own. Thus, Balibar's article reflects the crisis in the tradition which Negri defiantly vindicates. A subsequent book by Balibar (*Spinoza et la Politique*) seems more resigned to the conventional parameters of bourgeois political thought. But Spinoza's aporia is our aporia: the search for an adequate theory of mass politics. The step backward from Hegel to Spinoza, a fresh start from Spinozistic premises, enables Balibar to let the concept of mass or masses entirely push aside the concept of class or classes, the classic Marxist notion that "the history of all hitherto existing society is the history of class struggles." (This is the Balibar who in the 1976 Congress of the French Communist Party fought and lost the fight for the retention of the idea of the dictatorship of the proletariat.)

Looking at Balibar's article as an outcome in the evolution of the Althusserian effort at Marxist revisionism: the turn to Spinoza puts in abeyance the Marxist notion of class; it also activates at a new and qualitatively higher level the Althusserian involvement with Freudian and post-Freudian, specifically Lacanian, psychoanalysis. In Althusser's project of Marxism as scientific structuralism, infusions from the Lacanian version of psychoanalysis were essential: the primacy of language as an analytical model for the structure of psychological and social reality; the dissipation of all human subjectivity, the disintegration of the ego or self in "decentered" impersonal, collective structures and processes. Althusserian structuralism can be seen as a move from a "class" to a "mass" line (hence the attraction of Maoism for some members of the school), with the aid of Lacanian psychoanalysis. In Balibar's eclectic and experimental inventory of what there is for us today in Spinoza, Spinoza is interpreted as if he had been trying to write something that could be called "Mass Psychology and Analysis of the Ego" (Freud's title erroneously translated as "Group Psychology"). It is as if we need something like the Spinozistic metaphysics, or rather physics, in order to carry through the critique of the individual ego inherent in Althusserian sociology and Lacanian psychoanalysis.

PART II: SPINOZA THE COMMUNIST

Spinoza says, "Whatever things conduce to the communization of human society [*ad hominum communem societatem conducunt*], or cause men to live in concord [*concorditer*], are useful." Mrs. Thatcher says that there is no such thing as society, only individuals and their families. Roger Scruton is right in recognizing Spinoza as the antagonist: "If we were to describe the world objectively, from no point of view within it, the 'self' and all its mysteries would vanish—as it vanishes from the impersonal metaphysics of Spinoza."[5] The present social order depends upon a notion of the individual self, the individual soul, the individual person, that is scientifically and philosophically untenable. Descartes is the philosopher of modernity: with *Cogito ergo sum* he made the ego the starting-point and posited its substantial reality. Spinoza is the philosopher of the future because right at the beginning of modernity he saw that the Cartesian metaphysic would not work, and by systematic exposure of its internal self-contradictions he was able, in a supreme effort of intellectual abstraction, to arrive at the alternative.

The notion of the individual self, soul, or person as a substantial reality, philosophically defensible or not, is what is implied by our economic structure (private enterprise), our political institutions (the social contract with individual rights), our morality (individual responsibility), and even (so Roger Scruton) the popular mythology, or mystique, of individual love (*Amo ergo sum*). Individualism, pluralism, and lofty idealism on the subjective side; monism and materialism on the objective side: an irrevocable commitment to material development, opening up the infinite world of interacting energy in the physical universe and the infinite world of expanding desire in the human universe (Hobbes's "perpetuall and restless desire of Power after power, that ceaseth only in Death"). Bourgeois are those philosophers, beginning with Descartes, who affirmed the compatibility of individualism and idealism on the subjective side with the commitment to materialism on the objective side. Descartes saw what had to be done: the individual self or soul had to be separated from the world of matter; the autonomy of the soul had to be rescued from the automatism of the body (the mechanical world of matter from which the human body cannot be separated). In this way we arrive at, and are stuck with, Cartesian dualism: soul and body as two heterogeneous, substantially distinct, realities. To explain what the autonomous soul is doing in the mechanized body, to supply "meaning" and "purpose," normative support for the cognitive and moral activity of the soul, we need to posit a third, transcendental, supernatural reality, God. And in civil society we need a sovereign to keep the peace between individuals who have nothing in common with each other. Bourgeois philosophy after Descartes is given its final reformulation by Kant, who on the one hand reiterated that our attachment to individualized morality presupposed the metaphysical belief in an immaterial self and a transcendental God, while on the other hand recognizing that these metaphysical beliefs were philosophically untenable: they are to be retained as transcendental, necessary, and therefore "well-founded" illusions.

Spinoza is the first of the great dissenters: Spinoza, Marx, Nietzsche, Freud. Dissenters and realists, they all say that the bourgeois synthesis is a house built on illusion that cannot stand. They all in different ways expose the deceptions and contradictions in the ideology of individualism. Spinoza, the self-conscious antithesis of Descartes, goes to the metaphysical root of the matter; he becomes the philosopher of the future by becoming the philosopher of monism. No matter what "common sense" or "ordinary language"—i.e., the existing social order—disposes us to believe, mind and body are interconnected: two dimensions of one substance; two complementary aspects of one and the same reality. Individuals (existing as minds-and-bodies) are not independent (self-contained, self-subsistent, self-explanatory) substances but "modes," modifications (complex events) occurring in one underlying substance (reality, process). A social order which depends on a mythology conferring unreal reality and privileged status to human individuals, "souls," "persons," "selves," is at variance with what Spinoza calls the eternal laws of nature, or God: "Most persons who have written about the emotions and man's conduct of life seem to discuss, not the natural things which follow the common laws of Nature, but things which are outside her. They seem indeed to consider man in Nature as a kingdom within a kingdom. For they believe that man disturbs rather than follows her order, that he has an absolute power over his own actions, and that he is altogether self-determined."[6]

Thus, Spinoza is committed by his metaphysical principles to radical criticism of the established social order and the conventional morality. The aim is to produce a new ethics, to bring the human universe and the social order into line with universal principles governing the relations of parts to whole in the one process. The crux is the notion of human individuality. Individuation (existence as minds-and-bodies) is for Spinoza not a human privilege but a universal characteristic of all process, with lower and higher grades of individuality and complexity of organization. As in Whitehead's philosophy of organism, everything is "animate," although in different degrees.[7] At every level and in every part the process manifests itself in two dimensions, corresponding to mind and body in the human individual: a dimension of physical action and reaction, and a dimension of mutual "perception." (Unlike Whitehead, who reduces events to the one dimension of "perception.") There is no essential difference, but only a difference in degree of complexity, between human and animal individuality, or even between animate and inanimate nature.

This perspective can only be monist, monist in both directions: the unity of the mind and the body in every individual, and the unity of individuals with each other as parts of the whole, the process. The two directions imply each other: the function of the illusion of the soul separate from the body is to keep us (body-and-soul) separate from each other, to give the individual a separate reality. In this philosophy of organismic materialism the idea of purpose is replaced by the idea of process (immanent necessity), the idea of a self-expressive totality (God = Nature) expressing itself by self-differentiating individuation. Individuals have no independent, substantial existence; to realize the real potentialities of any individual thing is to activate it as a partial expression of the whole. Individual existence means to interact with the rest of existence in a flux of communicative exchange (the process). At every level individuality is constituted by being a whole composed of constituent individuals, itself in turn a constituent part of a larger whole. There are different levels of organism reflecting different degrees of what Spinoza calls reality, power, or perfection.

We thus see in what manner a composite individual can be affected in many ways and yet retain its nature. Up to this point we have conceived an individual to be composed merely of bodies which are distinguished from one another solely by motion and rest, speed and slowness, that is to say, to be composed of the most simple bodies. If we now consider an individual of another kind, composed of many individuals of diverse natures, we shall discover that it may be affected in many other ways, its nature nevertheless being preserved. For since each of its parts is composed of a number of bodies, each part (by the preceding Lemma), without any change of its nature, can move more slowly or more quickly, and consequently can communicate its motion more quickly or more slowly to the rest. If we now imagine a third kind of individual composed of these of the second kind, we shall discover that it can be affected in many other ways without any change of form. Thus, if we advance *ad infinitum*, we may easily conceive the whole of nature to be one individual whose parts, that is to say all bodies, differ in infinite ways without any change of the whole individual.[8]

No man is an island: "The human body needs for its preservation many other bodies, by which it is, as it were, continually regenerated." Again, from Postulate 4, Part 2,

It follows that we can never free ourselves from the need of something outside us for the preservation of our being, and that we can never live in such a manner as to have no intercourse with objects which are outside us. Indeed, so far as the mind is concerned, our intellect would be less perfect if the mind were alone and understood nothing but itself. There are many things, therefore, outside us which are useful to us, and which, therefore, are to be sought. Of all these, none more excellent can be discovered than those which exactly agree with our nature. If for example, two individuals of exactly the same nature are joined together, they compose a single individual, twice as powerful as each alone. Nothing, therefore, is more useful to man than man. Men can desire, I say, nothing more excellent for the preservation of their being than that all should so agree in all things that the minds and bodies of all should compose, as it were, one mind and one body; that all should together endeavor as much as possible to preserve their being, and that all should together seek the common good of all.

"Above all things it is profitable to men to form communities and to unite themselves to one another by bonds which may make out of all of them one thing," *de se omnibus unum.*[9]

In Spinoza the Nietzschean recognition of the death of God— that God who by arbitrary fiat established human beings as a "kingdom within a kingdom," giving them a free will which set them apart from the rest of nature—becomes the basis for a Nietzschean transvaluation of all values, beyond (bourgeois) morality with its alternatives of (utilitarian) egoism and (Kantian) obligations, to a (liberated) ethic of power and empowerment. But while Nietzsche dreams once more the Cartesian dream of the liberated and all-powerful individual (Superman), Spinoza, like Marx, sees that the road to empowerment is through the fusion of individuals to form one collective body.

At this turning point in history (1989), we are trying to read Spinoza's profound diagnosis of the sick flaw, the disease, in modernity—*das Unbehagen in der Kultur*—and it is not easy. *Omnia praeclara tam difficilia quam rara.* His materialism, his rejection of all mind-body dualism, has always appealed to that "progressive" segment of modern thought which pinned its hope on scientific enlightenment and economic development. In my generation Stuart Hampshire's book on Spinoza has been the classic statement of this point of view. The problem is what to make of his monism; or rather, what to make of the combination of monism and materialism. Liberal individualists (Stuart Hampshire) interpret the monism, reduced to the aphoristic equation God = Nature, as a moment of mystic feeling, a philosophic or rather quasi-religious posture of "identification with the whole of Nature," a purely mental act in the mind of the isolated and purely contemplative philosopher.[10] It is not difficult to see a contradiction between Spinoza's monism, so interpreted, and his materialism. And even if there were no contradiction, Spinoza's monism would then have no more hold on us than Einstein's or Oppenheimer's private mystical or "oceanic" feelings.

It is no accident that Spinozists such as Stuart Hampshire, seeking to maximize Spinoza's affinity with modernity as they understand it, make no use of the previously quoted passages, in which the communist implications of his thought are disclosed. "Men can desire . . . nothing more excellent for the preservation of their being than that all should so agree in all things that the minds and bodies of all should compose, as it were, one mind and one body." Spinoza's monism has been interpreted mystically. But if we interpret it politically, it can be seen as setting the historical agenda for us today: to rectify the flaw in modernity; to arrive at one world; to reorganize the gigantic material processes of intercommunication released by modernity into a coherent unity; call it Love's Body.

The power and perfection of the mind (or soul) can only be the power and perfection of the body: "Since the essence of the mind consists in its affirmation of the actual existence of its body, and since we understand by perfection the essence itself of the thing, it follows that the mind passes to a greater or less perfection when it is able to affirm of its body, or some part of it, something which involves a greater or less reality than before." And the power and perfection of the human body can only be its capacity for polymorphous communicative interaction with other bodies. "The human mind is adapted to the perception of very many things, and its aptitude increases in proportion to the number of ways in which its body can be disposed." "If anything increases, diminishes, helps or represses (*coercet*) our body's power of action, the idea of that thing increases, diminishes, helps or represses our mind's power of thought." "That which so disposes the human body that it can be affected in very many ways, or which adapts it towards affecting external bodies in very many ways, is useful to man; and the more the body is adapted towards affecting other bodies or being affected in very many ways, the more useful it is; on the other hand that which diminishes the body's aptitude for these things is harmful." "He who has a body with very many aptitudes, has a mind of which the great part is eternal." If Hegel is the philosopher who envisioned the eternal realm of Absolute (perfected) Spirit, Spinoza is his opposite who envisioned eternity (like Nietzsche) as dependent upon the perfection of the body. "It pertains to the nature of mind to conceive the essence of the body under the aspect of eternity."[11]

The reality of our life, the reality of which we are ignorant, the reality which we do not want to accept, is our fluid membership and causal interdependence in the intercommunicating world of bodies. "The human mind, when it perceives things in the common order of nature, has no adequate knowledge of itself, or of its own body, or of external bodies, but only a confused and mutilated knowledge." The crux in our ordinary commonsense misconception of ourselves is a false idea of freedom, a childish notion of free will: "They think themselves free and the sole reason for thinking so is that they are conscious of their actions and ignorant of the causes by which those actions are determined." This childish notion of free will is elaborated into a childish (grandiose) delusion of human independence from the interconnected body of nature (human nature as "a kingdom within a kingdom"). The delusion of free will is the illusion of independence of the part from the whole. But what we think of as "our" "emotions," but which are better called *affects*, are traces of, or habits built up by, the interaction of our body with other bodies, in the past or present, and present to the mind in the form of images. The result is a confused and mutilated form of self-consciousness which Spinoza calls the imagination. By virtue of this trace of the past upon the present, imagination is the power to contemplate things which do not exist as though they were present. Hence, though in itself no defect but rather a positive virtue (advantage, power), it is the source of error: "The mind is not in error because it imagines, but only in so far as it is considered as lacking the idea which excludes the existence of these things which it imagines as present." It is the imagination which represents our actual intersubjectivity to us in the form of an illusory subjectivity. We cannot escape the reality of our bodily intersubjectivity—"Nothing can happen in the body which is not perceived by the mind"—all those interactions with other bodies of whose existence, nature, and causal impact on ourselves we are ignorant are nevertheless deposited and preserved in the structure of the human imagination, in the character structure we call our "self," in the form of an image of self-subsistent identity attached to the emotion or affect of the moment.[12]

"No man is an island, we are all part of the main." The trouble is we are both. "It is impossible that a man should not be a part of nature, and that he should suffer no changes except those which can be understood through his own nature alone, and of which he is the adequate cause." In the common order or nature, as individuals, as finite parts, we passively allow ourselves to be led by things outside ourselves. Passivity in the emotions (affects) corresponds to impotence in the body and ignorance (inadequate, confused ideas) in the mind. Passivity is the consequence of finitude and individuality, of being a part which by itself and without other parts cannot be clearly and distinctly perceived. The consequences of passivity are fortuitous inconsistency, dissonance, and contrariety. "Men can diverge in nature in so far as they are conflicted by affects which are passive, and in so far as one and the same man is variable and inconstant." "In so far as men are conflicted by affects which are passive, they can be contrary to one another." And insofar as we are passive, we are driven, determined, by forces of which we are unconscious. "From what has been said it is plain that we are agitated by external causes in a number of ways, and that, like waves of the sea agitated by contrary winds, we fluctuate in ignorance of our future and our fate."[13]

At the opposite pole to our passive life in the common order of nature is "the concatenation of ideas which takes place according to the order of the intellect." Becoming conscious of the realities of the human condition we have the power to reorganize our lives. "So long as we are not conflicted by affects which are contrary to our nature, we have the power of ordering and concatenating the affections of the body according to the order of the intellect." As opposed to the idiosyncrasies of the individual imagination, the confused mixture produced by fortuitous interaction with the external bodies, the order of the intellect is based on common notions. Common notions are notions based on that which is common to all bodies as such; they constitute a nucleus of adequate ideas, clearly and distinctly perceived; the foundations of our reasoning, the source of our deliverance from error. In Spinoza as in Heraclitus, we are saved by commonalty: "Therefore we should be guided by the communal, the conjoint; the communal is the conjoint; but although reason (Logos) is conjoint, the many live as if the mind were a private (individual, idiosyncratic) thing." "Don't listen to me but listen to Logos, and agree that all things are one."[14]

"So far as men live according to the guidance of reason, so far only do they always necessarily agree in nature." The guidance of reason points toward a communist, or communal, organization of society: "Whatever conduces to a communal [*communis*] society of men, or causes men to live in concord, is good." What is common is not simply the foundation of our reasoning, as common notions; communism is good for us, or it is the good: "Nothing can be evil through what it has in common with our nature"; "In so far as a thing agrees with our nature it is necessarily good." Agreement, coming together, in Latin *convenire*, is unequivocally good because it is the only way to an expansion of power, of being, of reality, the only good. "Things which are said to agree in nature are understood to agree in power, and not in impotence or negation." Agreement is coexistent affirmation of being by beings of the same nature. And coexistent affirmation of being by two beings of the same nature makes out of them one being, twice as strong as each alone. "Composition," fusion, takes place. "I consider things as parts of some one whole, in so far as their natures are mutually accommodated so that as far as possible they are in accord among themselves [*consentiant*]." Liberal individualists have seized upon Spinoza's *conatus in suo esse perseverandi*, "the effort by which each thing endeavors to persevere in its being," as if it corresponded to their own (and Hobbes's) assumption of universal selfishness. They ignore the statement in the basic definition of individuality that "if several individuals so concur in one action that altogether they are the cause of one effect, I consider them all, to that extent as one individual thing." That is why in the explanation of the *conatus*, "the effort by which each thing endeavors to persevere in its own being," Spinoza includes the effort by which it *either alone or with others*, endeavors to do something. If it "does it with others," they join forces and reinforce each other; fusion takes place, and to that extent they constitute one individual thing.[15]

Whether in the passive life of the common order of nature, or reorganized according to the order of the intellect, we are in any case, and whether we know it or not, in one body. In the passive life of the common order of nature we are mixed up with each other in a "confused and mutilated" and unconscious way. Starting not from individual but from a mass psychology, Spinoza posits a natural tendency toward communication, an impersonal law of mutual attraction or interpenetration between bodies of a similar nature, which at the lowest level takes the form of imitation leading to identification: "If the nature of the external body is like the nature of our body, then the idea of the external body which we imagine will involve an affection of our body like the affection of the external body. Consequently, if we imagine someone like ourselves to be affected with some affect, this imagination will express an affection of our body like this affect. And so, from the fact that we imagine a thing like us to be affected with an affect, we are affected with a like affect." That is why, says Spinoza, children, because their bodies are continually as it were in a state of equilibrium, laugh or cry simply because they see others laugh and cry. At the lowest level, identification is not free from ambivalence: Spinoza's term is "fluctuation of the mind," which he says arises from two contrary affects (emotions) and which is related to affect as doubt is to the imagination. It is the task of intellect to remove the doubt, to straighten out the confusion, to remove the ambivalence, to make a more perfect union, to make it all cohere. "To make it all cohere" is not to arrive at some purely mental state of purely mental intellectual understanding. There is no such thing as a purely mental state: "The order and connection of ideas is the same as the order and connection of things," the radical touchstone of genuine Spinozism. The physical correlate, in the order and connection of things, of the common notions which reflect human agreement, is composition, or fusion. Therefore, "men can desire . . . nothing more excellent for the preservation of their being than that all should so agree in all things that the minds and bodies of all should compose, as it were, one mind and one body."[16] Q.E.D.

"All should in all things so come together that the minds and bodies of all should compose, as it were, one mind and one body." In the mystical tradition we are members of one body; the wish, or fantasy, is taken for the reality. In Spinoza, the demystification of the mystical body takes the notions of communication, community, communion, communism from the imagination and transforms them into rational goals: becoming one body becomes the goal of social action. As a result of his notion of composition, Spinoza's notion of the body politic or social as one body is totally different from all so-called organic or biological theories of the state based on magical (fetishistic) or naturalistic images of the body. The composition of Spinozistic bodies is not hierarchically organized by (functional) subordination of parts to a principal part, the "representative" part, the "head" of the body. Consequently, his political theory of collective participation in one body has nothing to do with medieval (or Hobbesian) notions of unification through the sovereign representative; or with *corpus Christi*, in which Christ is the head of the church (cf. *Love's Body*, chapter 7). When "composing one body," we (or anything else) are not *members* of one body. "Members" of one body are organically, functionally differentiated (head, heart, hands, etc.). Spinozistic composition is not based on functional complementarity or division of labor (or sexes), but on a principle analogous to Leibniz's identity of indiscernibles: "If two individuals of entirely the same nature are joined to one another, they compose a single individual twice as powerful."

This original approach to mass psychology developed in Spinoza's *Ethics* does not, as even Freud's does, envisage dependence on a leader, or head, as the origin or essence of mass formation. I believe this insight, not envisaged in the *Tractatus Theologico-Politicus*, came to Spinoza as he worked out the implications of the *Ethics*; as a result he decided to "apply my mind to politics" and wrote the *Tractatus Politicus*, in spite of the promise in the *Ethics* of a further treatise on epistemology (see above, Part I). In envisaging unification without representation, Spinoza resembles Rousseau: but Spinoza's fundamental rejection of the mythology of the will immediately separates him from Rousseau and all his (revolutionary) posterity. Spinoza's notion of the human community as one body is quite distinct from that corporate and collective identity created by General Will, in an act of will which elevates soul (or "head") above body, general above particular, morality above desire. Spinoza in the *Ethics* outlines the physical foundations for a theory of democracy which he was himself unable to perfect (see above, Part I).

Spinoza demystifies the mystical body by redefining the body physical in a way that is not only ahead of his time but ahead also of our time: it is in principle both Freudian and post-Freudian. "What the body can do no one hitherto has determined. No one has as yet understood the construction [*fabricam*] of the body so accurately as to be able to explain all its functions, not to mention that many things are observed in brutes which far surpass human ingenuity, and that sleepwalkers in their sleep do very many things that they would not dare to do awake: all this showing that the body itself, simply from the laws of its own nature, can do many things which its own mind [*ipsius mens*] is amazed at." The anticipations of the Freudian point of view are truly astonishing. But at the same time Spinoza's body is in principle post-Freudian. Spinoza's body is a *body without organs*. Gilles Deleuze, whose reading of Spinoza is an essential part of the line of thought here being developed, uses the term *body without organs* to dramatize the theoretical novelties proposed in that last ambitious fling at a Marx-Freud synthesis, *Anti-Oedipus, Capitalism and Schizophrenia*: "The body without organs is the immanent substance, in the most Spinozist sense of the word." There is a crisis not only in the Marxist but also in the Freudian tradition of radicalism—I have already referred to Lacan—and from both points of view a turn toward Spinoza can fuel a fresh start. It is evident that Freudian analysis of the body represents only a partial break with naturalistic (Aristotelian) anthropomorphism. Insofar as psychoanalytic theory presents a drama of psychophysical development of organs—oral, anal, genital stages—a teleological sequence of "primacies" climaxing in genital organization, it remains within the limits of the naturalistically conceived body, functionally and hierarchically organized. The deeper aspect of psychoanalysis—precisely the aspect abhorrent to humanistic conservatives like Scruton—is its impersonal analysis of libido as fluid, indefinitely convertible physical energy. Some affinity between the Freudian libido and the Spinozistic *conatus* has long been recognized: but there can be no peace between the Spinozistic body without organs and any notion of "genital primacy" or the "genital character" as the "natural" outcome of psychosexual development, the happy outcome of the Oedipal drama. In Spinoza's one body there is no privileging of the human form or the human species as microcosm. Thus Spinoza achieves in principle what not Freud but Ferenczi envisaged as the outcome of psychoanalysis, not yet achieved: a synthesis of psychic and physical science in an "animism no longer anthropomorphic." (Compare *Life Against Death*, pp. 314–316). In Spinoza all bodies from the simplest to the most complex exist not only as "extended" but also as "thinking." All things are animate, in different degrees. Spinoza recovers the pre-Socratic grasp on (nondualistic) Being, *Physis* (a better term than his *Natura* with its Lucretian and then medieval legacy of personification). He breaks out of the anthropomorphic predicament; breaks the deep spell of human fascination with our own naturalistic image (the "human form divine"), the residue in every human being of the narcissistic "mirror-stage" which is the *fons et origo* of the universal superstition, the soul as shadow or reflection or double.[17]

Spinoza's physics may be called, comparing it to Whitehead's, a philosophy of organism, but it is a ruthlessly post-Aristotelian, antiteleological philosophy of organism. Organisms (bodies) are not defined in terms of naturalistically conceived form, function, or purpose, but in abstract terms of physics, as ratios of motion and rest, interacting, affecting, and being affected; impersonally and objectively conceived as a field of force or forces. The human body is not an (Aristotelian) natural growth but a machinelike construction or energy system, a "high energy construct" (Charles Olson's modification of Ezra Pound's notion of the poem). It is composed not of organs but of very many parts which are individuals, each one of which is itself highly composite. These individuals are not bits of inert matter or extensive parts in what Whitehead calls "simple location in space." They are intensive units of energy, defined in Spinoza's terms by a certain ratio or proportion of motion and rest; each one, individual or body, being a mode which in a certain and determinate manner expresses the essence of God. As in Blake, the opposition of Body and Soul is overwhelmed in the concept of energy.[18]

The units of energy ("parts") which constitute the body (any body) connect it with other bodies. "Bodies are not distinguished in respect to substance; what constitutes the form of the individual consists in the union of bodies." "When a number of bodies, whether of the same or different size, are so constrained by other bodies that they lie upon one another, or if they so move, whether with the same or with different degrees of speed, that they communicate their motions to each other in a certain fixed manner, we shall say that these bodies are united with one another and that they all compose one body or individual which is distinguished from others by the union of bodies." We are complicated energy systems in complicated interaction with other energy systems ("desiring machines," in the provocative terminology of *Anti-Oedipus*). Spinozistic physics, like Whitehead's, is dialectical—i.e., directed against the "Fallacy of Simple Location," the notion that if *here*, then not *there*; if inside, then not outside. Spinoza says what constitutes the form of the individual consists in the union of bodies. Whitehead says reality is unification: reality is not stuff but events which are prehensive unifications, a gathering of here and there, subject and object, into a unity (*Love's Body*, chapter 13). Spinozistic physics places us in a magnetic field of action at a distance, with lines or streams of energy going in all directions, connecting different parts of one body with each other and with other bodies—a conceptual framework leaving room for all those unconscious linkages between bodies of which psychoanalysis has made us conscious—identifications, projections, introjections. Spinoza's Letter 17 shows him interested, as Freud was, in phenomena of telepathic (sympathetic) communication: a father through love participates in the essence of his son so that under certain circumstances he can perceive an image of his son's condition as vivid as if he were present. Spinoza's analysis of the pathology of jealousy recognizes the autonomous, intersubjective connection of parts in the manner explored in the Kleinian school of psychoanalysis and systematized as "schizo-analysis" in *Anti-Oedipus*. "The man who imagines that the woman he loves prostitutes herself to another is not merely troubled because his appetite is restrained, but he turns away from her because he is compelled to connect the image of a beloved object with the privy parts and with what is excremental in another man."[19]

The perfection of the Spinozistic body is not derived from Aristotelian notions of natural development but from the fundamental principles of Spinozistic physics. "That which so disposes the human body that it can be affected in many ways, is profitable to man; the more it renders the body capable of being affected in many ways and to affect other bodies, the more profitable it is." "In this life, therefore, it is our chief endeavor to change the body of infancy, so far as its nature permits and assists, into another body which is fitted for many things."[20] This "body fitted for many things" formally corresponds to the Freudian notion of the original polymorphous perversity of the infantile libido, as opposed to the constrictions imposed on it by the

Oedipal drama and its successive oral, anal, and genital developmental stages (*Life Against Death*, chapter 3 and pp. 46–48). But it is the Freudian notion of the body that is immature in relation to Spinoza's. "Polymorphous perversity" needs to be liberated from its Freudian connection with naturalistically conceived "erogenous zones." By the same token, the theory of sublimation needs to be recast in terms of an inherent polymorphism more polymorphous than anything dreamed of in Freudian orthodoxy.

Spinoza transposes the infantile potentiality for freedom into the adult goal: we are to seize power over our body and perfect it by unlimited expansion of its power: power and perfection and virtue are the same thing. "He who has a body fitted for many things has a mind whose greatest part is eternal." How are we to "change the body of infancy into another body capable of a great many things," thus acquiring "a mind whose greatest part is eternal"? The freedom which is envisaged in the last book of the *Ethics* cannot be purely individual any more than it can be purely mental. Our minds are delivered from error by common notions: our bodies become capable of many things by composition with other bodies; our freedom consists in the intellectual love of God which is identical with God's love of human beings.[21] The highflying language of love corresponds to a real physical process of composition or fusion, going on in the depths; a process of which we are, in the common order of nature, unconscious.

In the modern world our ability to liberate ourselves as energy systems has been frustrated by dualistic social arrangements and dualistic philosophy, which posit, and enforce, an unreal boundary between body and soul, self and other, subject and object, internal world of fantasy and external world of reality. Individualism requires dualism, which frustrates real individuality. Real individuality is the full presence of the whole in every part: in Giordano Bruno's formula, "wholly in the whole and wholly in every part of the whole";[22] in Spinoza's formula, "in a certain and determinate manner expressing the essence of God."

The unreal boundary line separating self and others is at bottom a property line. Personality is the original personal property

(*Love's Body*, chapter 5). As the great philosopher of private property said, "Every man has a 'property' in his own person," and is therefore entitled to annex whatever things he has, by labor, mixed his own person with. And the social institution of property fills out the theoretical gaps in the notion of personal identity: psychological unity at any given time or through time is explained by the notion that we are "owners" of our different states of being. Spinoza opposes the world of ownership to the state of nature: "In the state of nature no one is by common consent the owner of anything, nor is there anything in nature which can be said to belong to this man and not to that man, but all things belong to all." The social contract which institutes the regime of private property and repressive morality corresponds to present conditions of human irrationality; "since men must sin, it is better that they should sin this way." The social contract is the opposite of the true model of perfection, friendship: friends have all things in common, as in the state of nature. The "common consent" which establishes the social contract has nothing to do with the ideal unification based on the discovery of our identical human nature and common good. That ideal unification, which is the only real unification, does not surrender or diminish the powers of conjoining individuals but on the contrary is their expansion.[23]

The aim of the Spinozistic *conatus* is not to *have* but to *be*; it can be likened to Freudian libido only if we distinguish possessive from narcissistic love (in technical Freudian terms "object choice" and "identification"; cf. *Life Against Death*, chapter 4). Like the mystical Narcissus, or the narcissistic libido, the Spinozistic *conatus* seeks to unite with its own likeness; being is multiplied by identification. Beings of the same nature do not compete with each other; they reinforce each other. Hence, "nothing can be evil through what it has in common with our nature"; "in so far as a thing agrees with our nature, it is necessarily good." Conflict arises from differences, and private property creates differences. Peter may be a cause of sorrow to Paul because he alone possesses something which Paul also loves. Peter and Paul are not in conflict insofar as they agree in nature —

that is to say, insofar as they both love the same object—but insofar as they differ from one another. Insofar as they both love the same object, each one's love is thereby strengthened and their joy increased.[24]

Love is joy accompanied by the idea of an external object by means of which the body effects a transition to a greater power or perfection. The transition is effected by composition: if two individuals entirely of the same nature are joined together, they make one individual who is twice as powerful. Hence, "joy posits the existence of the thing which rejoices, and the greater the joy, the more is existence posited." Hence also, "God loves himself with an infinite intellectual love." Not a possessive but a narcissistic love: infinite power enjoying itself as such. Spinoza's doctrine of Amor is not a mystical appendix but the whole (subject) matter. As in Dante, love moves the world, and world unification is the perfection of the body politic. Dante, citing Averroës, argues that the distinctive human capacity for intellectuality cannot be realized in a single human being or in any particular community but only in the multitude of humans taken all together. The human species, made in the likeness of God, resembles God most when it is most unified.[25] So too in Spinoza, but not in the same way. This is as close as we can come to the demystification of the mystical body.

NOTES

1. No. 470 (September 1985); now available in English in *Rethinking Marxism*, 2, no. 3 (Fall 1989), 104–139.

2. *Tractatus Politicus* (hereafter TP), Preface. *Ethics* (hereafter E), II, 40, note 1.

3. TP I, 4. Hobbes, *Leviathan*, chapter 16. TP III, 7. TP VIII, 3. TP VII, 27; IV, 6; IV, 4. TP V, 6.

4. E II, 44, cor 2.

5. E IV, 40. R. Scruton, *Sexual Desire* (New York, 1986), 118.

6. E III, preface.

7. E II, 13, note.

8. E II, 13, letter 7, note.

9. E II, post 4. E IV, 18, note. E IV, app 12.

10. S. Hampshire, *Spinoza* (Harmondsworth, England, 1951), 161, 165, 170.

11. E III, "General Definition of the Emotions." E II, 14. E III, 11. E IV, 38. E V, 39. E V, 29, dem.

12. E II, 29, cor and note. E II, 35, note (cf. E I, app; E III, 2, note). E III, post 2; E II, 13, post 5; E II, 17, 18. E II, 17, note. E II, 12. E III, post 1; E II, 19 and dem.

13. E IV, 4. E IV, 37, note 1. E III, 3, note. E IV, 33. E IV, 34. E III, 59, note.

14. E II, 18, note. E II, 29, cor and note; E II, 40, note 2. E II, 37–40. Heraclitus, fragment 2. Heraclitus, fragment 50.

15. E IV, 35. E IV, 40. E IV, 30–31. E IV, 29. E IV, 32, dem. E IV, 18, note. Letter 32. E III, 7. E II, def 7. E III, 7, dem.

16. E III, 27, dem. E III, 32, note. E III, 17, note. E II, 29, note. E II, 7. E IV, 18, note.

17. E III, 2, note. G. Deleuze and F. Guattari, *Anti-Oedipus: Capitalism and Schizophrenia* (New York, 1972), 327. E II, 13, note. J. G. Frazer, *Golden Bough* (abridged ed.; New York, 1947), chapter 18.

18. E IV, 39, note. E II, 15; E II, 13, letter 7, post 1. E II, 13, note, and letter 3 and 5; E IV, 39, note. E II, def 1.

19. E II, 13, letter 4. E II, 13, letter 3, ax 2, def. E III, 35, note.

20. E IV, 38. E V, 39, note.

21. E IV, def 8. E V, 39. E V, 36 and cor.

22. Cf. M. Wartofsky in M. Grene, ed., *Spinoza, A Collection of Critical Essays* (New York, 1973), 333, note 2.

23. E IV, 37, note 2. E IV, 37, note 2; E IV, 54, note. Letter 44; E IV, 18, note.

24. E IV, 30–31. E IV, 34, dem and note.

25. E III, 21, dem. E V, 35. Dante, *Paradiso* XXXIII, l. 145. Dante, *De Monarchia*, I, ll. 4, 8.

9

Metamorphoses III
The Divine Narcissus

This occasion, in memoriam, inconsolable loss and the futile consolations of poetry: the theme of pastoral elegy. As in Milton's *Lycidas* —

> For Lycidas is dead, dead ere his prime,
> Young Lycidas

Milton's *Lycidas*, or Ovid's *Metamorphoses*.

This is unfinished business. I started to write a Homage to Ovid, his *Metamorphoses*. It was to be the metamorphoses of his *Metamorphoses* through the ages down to our own times; a perpetual poem, or an eternal recurrence of archetypes; as if literature were all one book, just a footnote to Ovid; a book to end all books, like *Finnegans Wake* or Ovid's *Metamorphoses*.

I had done a Daphne, the nymph pursued by Apollo and saved by being transformed into a laurel; and an Actaeon, the hunter who saw Diana bathing, and was transformed into a stag and dismembered by his own hounds.

But Narcissus, another young hunter or shepherd destroyed by what he saw, the reflection of himself in the water—there I

A lecture for Cowell College, University of California at Santa Cruz, April 1989. In memory of Carl Deppe (September 12, 1965–March 6, 1985), student killed by a drunk driver. Published in *Sulfur*, no. 25 (Fall 1989). Reprinted by permission of *Sulfur*.

drowned, like Narcissus; lost in the endless replication of his image in world literature; overwhelmed by the abundance; as in Ovid Narcissus says *inopem me copia fecit*, "Plenty made me poor." Or paralyzed by the proximity: *iste ego sum*—Could it be me? Narcissus is undone discovering his identity with his own reflection; we are undone discovering our identity with Narcissus, our identity made out of identifications. I is an Other; some primordial and universal schizophrenia, as if our first experience of the self were self-alienation.

From mirror unto mirror, an eternal recurrence of meaningless alternatives. Looking into the mirror and seeing nothing. Or *Lost in the Funhouse*: Ovid's *Metamorphoses* turning into black comedy. John Barth says, "He wishes he had never entered the funhouse. But he has. Then he wishes he were dead. But he's not. Therefore he will construct funhouses for others and be their secret operator—though he would rather be among the lovers for whom funhouses are designed."

And on the other hand there was the exhilarating discovery of *El Divino Narciso* by Sor Juana Ines de la Cruz; exhilarating in the way Ezra Pound describes the effect of a literary image or epiphany: "An 'Image' is that which presents an intellectual and emotional complex in an instant of time. It is the presentation of such a 'complex' instantaneously which gives that sense of sudden liberation; that sense of freedom from time limits and space limits; that sense of sudden growth, which we experience in the presence of the greatest works of art."

Sor Juana was exhilarating, but still frustrating. It was as if she had said it all, or all I wanted to say; rendering my encyclopedic scholarship superfluous and vain. There was also a certain inhibiting awe in the presence of Sor Juana, a miraculous phenomenon altogether. A star of the first magnitude in European literature, whose entire life was spent in Mexico, in the seventeenth century, 1648–1695. Her encyclopedic intelligence, her audacity. The first feminist writer in the Western hemisphere; the vertiginous catastrophe of her meteoric end.

This unfinished business—what is there to say about Sor Juana Ines de la Cruz, *El Divino Narciso*?

❧

El Divino Narciso, an *auto sacramental*: sacred drama, or mystery play, attached to the Catholic liturgy; for Corpus Christi Day, the festival of the Body and Blood.

The Divine Narcissus in America. In a stately masque, two by two, the prelude (*loa*) recapitulates the conquest of Mexico. Two personages, el Occidente, native American warrior or brave, and la America, Indian woman in exotic native costume, are celebrating the festival of their "vegetation deity," the great god of the harvest, to the native Indian music of the Tocotin. It is their pagan Corpus Christi Day, an offering of human blood mixed with harvest seed, for the nourishment of the body and the purification of the soul. These two are confronted by their opposite numbers, Christian Zeal (Captain General, Conquistador) and Christian Religion (female). After the conquest by force, Christian Religion in dialogue with the Indians discovers a similarity between pagan ritual and Christian mystery, following the example of St. Paul, who said to the men of Athens (Acts 17:23): "The God whom I proclaim is the one you already worship without knowing it." The Christian sacrament of the Eucharist celebrates the redemptive power of human blood, no less than the Mexican ritual, but without shedding fresh blood. Christ, offering himself to be eaten in the Eucharist, is the true vegetation deity. The demonstration of this mystery must take the form of a visible representation of a metaphorical idea, an allegory, a sacramental drama, to be called *The Divine Narcissus*, recalling an earlier paganism, which, like Aztec religion, also contained demonic parodies of the mystery of the Christian Eucharist. Written in Mexico, the mystery play is to be performed in Madrid, in the presence of their Catholic majesties the King and Queen.

The confrontation between Christianity and Paganism in the New World repeats the original confrontation between Christianity and classical culture in the Old World. The *auto sacramental* begins with an allegorical representation of the origin of Christianity. Judaism ("la Sinagoga") confronts Paganism ("la Gentilidad"): Judaism praises the beauty of God in the language of Psalms ("Praise the Lord all creatures here below"), and Paganism, having its own bible in Ovid's *Metamorphoses*, praises the pastoral beauty of Narcissus ("Praise Narcissus, all ye flowers and fountains"). Human Nature, the mother of both, seeks to combine their voices, to make Christianity by combining Judaism and Paganism, and make Narcissus into Christ.

Herself plunging into the story and opening another level of play within the play, Human Nature discovers herself to be that very image of himself with which Narcissus seeks to be united. As the Bible tells us, Human Nature was made in the image of God; but Human Nature has been so disfigured by the muddy waters of sin that the Divine Narcissus cannot recognize her as his own image. It is the moment of the Incarnation; Human Nature seeks a pure fountain in which her image will be cleansed and she can be reunited with the Divine Nature, the Divine Narcissus.

Into this cosmic drama reenacting the moment of the Incarnation, Satan must insert himself, to sow confusion. Continuing his bitter jealousy of the Divine Narcissus who rejected him (the story of *Paradise Lost*), he is now bent on frustrating the love between the Divine Narcissus and his own image, Human Nature. Satan plunges into the drama, identifying his own tragedy with that of Echo in Ovid's story, the nymph who desperately tries to seduce Narcissus, but who, like Satan, can never do more than ape or echo the actions of God. In a reenactment of Christ's temptation in the wilderness (*Paradise Regained*), Narcissus has been fasting forty days and nights on a high mountain in Mexico; Echo offers him all the riches of the New World, and is steadfastly rejected.

Meanwhile, in a pastoral symphony combining pagan and biblical motifs, Human Nature in her longing for Narcissus becomes the distraught seeker of the Song of Songs: "I charge you, Nymphs that inhabit this flowery field, if ye find my beloved, tell him that I am sick with love." Narcissus is the Beloved who says, "I am the flower of the field, the lily of the valley. My beloved is mine and I am his. He feedeth among the lilies." He is also the Good Shepherd of the New Testament, calling everywhere for his one lost sheep.

They meet at the fountain: a garden enclosed is my sister, my spouse, a spring shut up, a fountain sealed. A little fountain became a river, and there was light, and the sun and much water: this river is Esther, whom the king married; the River of Paradise, the Well of Life; the figure of the Virgin Mary, in whom the divine image and the human coalesce, the Virgin Mary of the Immaculate Conception. In the pure fountain Narcissus sees the reflection of Human Nature, and seeing in it his own image, he falls in love with his own image. Open the crystal seal of this clear cold spring, that my love may enter in!

In love with his own perfection, perfect love makes the immortal mortal. "Love that has power to wound, in me has shown its power: in love with my own image, from heaven I came to die." He suffers unto death. He humbled himself, consumed himself; tenderly melted in the sweet fire; died in the end in love's voluntary crucifixion. It is finished. Truly this was the Son of God.

Human Nature leads the pastoral world in lamentation, but there is the comfort of the Resurrection: he remains with us, transfigured; into a white flower. Transparent disguise; jealous spouse of the soul, he looketh forth at the windows, showing himself through the lattice. The pageantry of Corpus Christi displays the Fountain, and beside it the Chalice with the Host above it. See in the crystal margin of the clear fountain the fair white flower of which the Beloved said, "This is my body and my blood, martyred for your sakes. In memory of my death, repeat it."

❧

What is there to say about *El Divino Narciso*? First the *loa*: the New World as a religious experience. Everywhere in the New World "A New Age Now Begins"; but in North America's City on the Hill the natives formed no part of it. We complacently think of Cortés and the conquistadors in Mexico as more ruthless than our frontier. But Sor Juana's *loa* dramatizes the different view from south of the border. Christian Zeal and Christian Religion are separate personages. In the Catholic tradition church and state, spiritual and temporal powers, remain distinct and even opposed. In the *loa*, after the conquest, Christian Zeal says, "Now insolent America must die." Christian Religion checks Christian Zeal, saying, "Wait, do not put her to death; I need America alive." "I need America alive," said Christian Religion in Mexico. The Catholic church used the key of baptism to open the doors of society to the Indians. "This possibility of belonging to a living order, even if it was at the bottom of the social pyramid, was cruelly denied to the Indians by the Protestants of New England."[1] That is Octavio Paz speaking: shall we contradict him?

The Pilgrims in North America—they too said, "A New Age Now Begins." For them it was a reenactment of the Old Testament. Pilgrims interpret themselves as another Mosaic community, in exodus from Egypt to the Promised Land, a holy nation like the Jews, with the same theological permission or rather commandment to exterminate the native inhabitants. Deuteronomy 7:1–2, 6:

> When the Lord thy God shall bring thee into the land whither thou goest to possess it, and hath cast out many nations before thee, the Hittites, and the Girgashites, and the Amorites, and the Canaanites, and the Perizzites, and the Hivites, and the Jebusites, seven nations greater and mightier than thou:
>
> And when the Lord thy God shall deliver them before thee; thou shalt smite them, and utterly destroy them: thou shalt make no covenant with them, nor shew mercy unto them:
>
> For thou art an holy people unto the Lord thy God: the Lord thy God hath chosen thee to be a special people unto himself, above all people that are upon the face of the earth.

In the spiritual Conquest of Mexico—the historical drama corresponding to Sor Juana's *loa*—the original representatives of Christian Religion, saying to Christian Zeal, "Wait, do not put her to death: I need America alive," were the Franciscans: *The Millennial Kingdom of the Franciscans in the New World.*[2] The advent of the first twelve Franciscan "apostles" in Mexico City in 1524, an event of vast prophetic significance. It was the Second Coming not of Moses but of Christ. Francis and the Fran-

ciscans were imitating Christ. The book of the Bible being reen-
acted was not Deuteronomy but Revelation.

The pursuit of the millennium. I didn't know that Columbus
was a Franciscan and wrote a book titled *The Book of Prophecies*. Both Columbus and the leader of the twelve apostles in
Mexico, Brother Martin de Valencia, acknowledged the inspiration of Joachim of Fiore, the revolutionary theologian who re-
directed Christian thought toward the eternal pursuit of the millennium.

Joachim, in the twelfth century, opened Christianity to the
thought of the historical future. Human history is religious history, divided into three stages: the age of the Father, the Son, and
the Holy Spirit. The age of the Father, the Old Testament, from
Adam to Christ, is the age of patriarchal piety, located in patriarchal families. The age of the Son, the New Testament, from
Christ down to the present, is the age of ecclesiastical or priestly
piety, located in churches and prescribing the active life of good
works. In the future age of the Spirit, ecclesiastical piety will be
superseded by mendicant, monastic piety, now made universal by
outpouring of the Spirit. All men—I follow Joachim in omitting
the mention of women as a separate category—all men will practice apostolic poverty and lead lives of contemplation. It will be
a higher form of Christianity, a new gospel, which will spiritu-
alize the meaning of the New Testament even as the New Testament spiritualized the meaning of the Old Testament. Thus, it
will be the Second Coming of Christ, and the Eternal Gospel
prophesied in Revelation: "And what is this Gospel? That of
which Jesus speaks in *Revelations:* I saw an angel flying in the
midst of heaven, and he had the eternal Gospel. And what is in
this Gospel? All that goes beyond the Gospel of Christ. For the
letter kills and the spirit gives life."[3]

The Franciscans were certain that St. Francis was the fulfillment of Joachim's prophecy of a messianic leader to inaugurate
the new age. The Franciscan missionaries were certain that the
discovery of the New World was the unfolding of the drama of
the end of the world as prophesied in Revelation; their task was
to realize eschatology in actual history, to bring about the end of

history. "The Gospel must first be published among all the nations" (Mark 13:10). In the Apocalyptic as opposed to the Exodus perspective, the natives of North America are the lost tribes of Israel; or, if that cannot be proved, at least welcome guests at that final apocalyptic banquet at which all nations will be gathered into one body: and there shall be one fold, one shepherd (John 17:21). Franciscan missionaries saw the Holy City, the New Jerusalem, coming down from God out of Heaven and settling in Mexico; an evangelical utopia based not only on the perception of America as the rediscovered Garden of Eden, but also on the uncorrupted character of the noble Indian savages. The radical innocence exemplified in the angelic Indians opened up the possibility of a more perfect realization of Christianity in the New World, in an Indian church administered by Franciscan millenarians. The New World could attain angelic perfection while Europe, apocalyptically speaking, would go to Hell.

The disastrous history of the New World. *The Indian Ecclesiastical History* by the Franciscan Jeronimó de Mendieta, written in the 1590s, but publication suppressed till 1870, long after the end of Spanish rule in Mexico, records the defeat of the dream of an evangelical millennium, an Indian church, defeated by the old idol of Mammon, the accursed love of gold which Christ came into the world to overthrow.

But hope creates from its own wreck the things it contemplates. The new spiritual men of the seventeenth century were the Jesuits; they too, like the Franciscans, seeing themselves as the fulfillment of the prophecies of Joachim of Fiore. The utopian dream took a new form: the dream of an ecumenical Christian order embracing all religions. Franciscan fundamentalism was succeeded by Jesuit syncretism. "Syncretism": the attempted union or reconciliation of conflicting parties or principles in philosophy or religion; "almost always in a derogatory sense"; as if it were a utopian project, unrealistic, if not unprincipled. The word comes to us from Plutarch's treatise on *philadelphia*, that is to say, brotherly love. When differences arise among brothers, he says, we must imitate the practice of the Cretans, who though they often quarreled and fought with one another, made up their differences and united when outside enemies attacked; this was what they called their "syncretism."

In the service of the ecumenical aspirations of the Counter-Reformation, the Jesuits developed a sophisticated doctrine of the preestablished harmony among all religions, justifying the Jesuit missionary practice of accommodation—i.e., syncretistic adaptation of Christian revelation to local language, belief, and custom. It was not a new theology but a renewal of an ancient tradition. The early Fathers of the Church had arrived at the notion that the reception of the Gospel among the heathen had been prepared by prefigurations, anticipations of Christianity in paganism. Seventeenth-century Jesuit intellectuals modernized this idea by combining it with the Hermetic strain in Renaissance humanism: the notion of a primordial revelation of occult wisdom identified with the name of Hermes Trismegistus and with Egyptian hieroglyphs.

There was Father Athanasius Kircher—more frequently cited by Sor Juana than any other contemporary—professor of mathematics at the Roman College, the hub of the Jesuit order in Rome, author of *Oedipus Aegyptiacus*, which expounds Egyptian hieroglyphics as instituted by Hermes Trismegistus and constituting symbolic pictures of divine and universal truths.[4] And there was in Mexico Athanasius Kircher's Mexican correspondent and Sor Juana's friend, Don Carlos de Siguenza y Gongora, who laid the intellectual foundations for Mexican creole national consciousness, finding a place for the native Indian Aztec civilization in the Christian scheme of universal history; syncretism. Just listen to the titles of some of his books: *The Phoenix of the West, the Apostle St. Thomas, Found Under the Name of Quetzalcoatl Among the Ashes of Ancient Traditions Preserved on Toltec Stones and Teomoxtles and in Teochichimec and Mexican Songs*; *Primavera Indiana—the Indian Springtime, Sacro-Historical Poem, Idea of the Most Holy Mary of Guadalupe*. The dark, little Indian, Virgin of Guadalupe, who took the place of the Aztec Mother Goddess Tonantsin at Tepeyac, the most potent manifestation of syncretism in the New World. The Indian Springtime: a new age now begins, with the foundation of the

Virgin of Guadalupe; identified with the woman of Revelation 12:1. "And there appeared a great wonder in heaven: a woman clothed with the sun, and the moon under her feet, and upon her head a crown of twelve stars."[5]

This baroque synthesis—the culture which produced Sor Juana—preserved the core of Joachite millenarianism in a new form. In this new form it prepared the way, in the next age, for the heavenly city of the eighteenth-century philosophers; the Enlightenment apotheosis of progress; the Enlightenment dream of universal history from a cosmopolitan point of view; the Enlightenment science of comparative religion. The work of syncretism, in the service of world unification—to gather the limbs of Osiris—still goes on. Sor Juana's *auto sacramental* dramatizes the three principal players: pagan or heathen religion; Hebrew or Christian religion; and classical mythology, the reinterpretation of pagan religion by the free spirit of the poetic imagination, as authorized by the example of Ovid.

Christ as the Divine Narcissus; syncretism. "Western Civilization"—that old bag—a synthesis of Hebraism and Hellenism, or Christianity and classical culture; the medieval synthesis. My original project was a "Western Civilization" project: the metamorphoses of Ovid's *Metamorphoses* inside "Western Civilization." Daphne and Actaeon had already led me to the medieval *Ovide Moralisé*. Ovid moralized is Ovid Christianized: Actaeon dismembered by his hounds is Christ crucified; or (even more unlikely!) Daphne transformed into a laurel wreath round Apollo's head is the Virgin Mary round Christ incarnate in her womb.

Daphne, Actaeon, Narcissus: these quaint medieval Christological interpretations, these baroque conceits—they go too far. There is a leap of faith. *Credo quia absurdum*, the theologians say; but also poetry is impossibility made credible: the circle squared, the opposites unified, in the end; in an eschatological (anagogic) or utopian or beatific vision. It is not just "Christianity and classical culture," abstract scholastic categories; it is as if this antithesis recapitulated deep contradictions in our "western way of life": the contradiction between sacred and profane love; between the body and the soul; between the physical and the spiritual; between love and death.

The vehicle which carries Sor Juana in *The Divine Narcissus* to the threshold of heaven, the vehicle which mediates the reconciliation of opposites, is not Revelation but Song of Songs. The Song of Songs, the Song of Solomon:

> The unexpressive nuptial song
> In the blest Kingdoms meek of joy and love.

The miracle is the marriage of the idyllic Ovidian pastoral with the paradisical landscape of the Song of Songs; a transubstantiation of the pastoral. In the footsteps of her namesake, whose name she chose for herself when she joined his order, the order of Reformed Carmelites, Sor Juana Ines de la Cruz in the footsteps of San Juan de la Cruz.

First the Franciscans, then the Jesuits, then the Carmelites. Carmelite mysticism, a different spiritual elite: "Our desire is that they should be like mirrors, like shining lamps, glaring torches, brilliant stars, illuminating and guiding the wanderers in this dark world . . . raised above themselves by raptures both ineffable and indescribable."[6] Raised above themselves by raptures both ineffable and indescribable: conquistadors at heaven's gate; in Dionysian delirium, or Sufi ecstasy.

San Juan de la Cruz, St. John of the Cross. *The Spiritual Canticle*: songs between the Soul and the Bridegroom; a pastoral dialogue in which the Lover and the Beloved converse and make love among the woods, mountains, and rivers; as in Ovid's *Metamorphoses*.

> Shepherds, you who wander
> There by sheepfolds to the summit,
> If you chance to see
> The one I most desire
> Tell him I am sick, I suffer and I die.

The identity of sacred and profane love. The lyric poetry of San Juan is based on a fusion of three ingredients: the exalted rapture of the Song of Songs; the refined, sublimated eroticism of

Renaissance neoclassical poetry; and the vulgar love poetry of the street music, the pop songs of the day, the rhythms of which are preserved in his lyrics. The subject of the pop songs was nearly always love, but religious writers interpreted them *a lo divino*, that is, as expressing love for Christ or the Virgin. In prison (imprisoned by the unreformed Carmelites), where the first great burst of poetry came to him, one evening, when he was in very low spirits, he heard a voice singing a *villancico* (popular ballad) in the street outside, and it sent him at once into ecstasy. The words were

> Muérome de amores
> Carillo. Que haré?
>   —Que te mueras, alahé.
> "I am dying of love, darling. What
> shall I do?—Die, hey, hey!"

Overcoming the antitheses of sacred and profane love. It could have been Madonna. One of San Juan's great lyrics has the refrain *Que muero por que no muero*: I die because I do not die.

Interpreting *a lo divino*, we get *El Divino Narciso*. There was an anonymous, ordinary love poem in the pastoral mode:

> A shepherd boy, all alone, was suffering
> Far away from all pleasure and joy,
> Every thought on his shepherdess lay
> His heart deeply wounded by love.
>
> The shepherd boy said, "Ah woe to the one
> Who has taken my love away;
> She does not wish to enjoy me or stay."
> His heart deeply wounded by love.

San Juan made a few changes and added a stanza:

> In the end climbing high on a tree
> He opened his lovely arms full and wide;
> Held by them he stayed there and died
> His heart deeply wounded by love.

The song is included in San Juan's collected poems under the title "Canciones a lo Divino de Cristo y el Alma"; "Verses *a lo divino* on Christ and the Soul."[7]

Protestant heretics need the great Protestants and heretics who stayed inside the church, Joachim of Fiore, Francis of Assisi, San Juan de la Cruz. Intoxicated by the saint's ecstasy; not knowing what we are getting into; "all knowledge transcending"— *entréme donde no supe*—we may not realize how heterodox it all is.

> "Let us enjoy ourselves, my love,
> And let us go to see ourselves in thy beauty,
> To the mountain and to the hillside
> Where flows the pure water;
> Let us enter more deeply into the thicket."

This could be an erotic moment in Ovid's *Metamorphoses*, Jupiter incarnate as mortal man making improper advances to a nymph. Or it could be from a duet between the Divine Narcissus and Human Nature. But it is from San Juan's *Spiritual Canticle*, and his own prose commentary goes as follows:

And let us go to see ourselves in thy beauty.

. . . that is, that I may be so transformed in Thy beauty that, being alike in beauty, we may both see ourselves in Thy beauty, since I shall have Thy own beauty; so that, when one of us looks at the other, each may see in the other his beauty, the beauty of both being Thy beauty alone, and I being absorbed in Thy beauty; and thus I shall see Thee in Thy beauty and Thou wilt see me in Thy beauty; and I shall see myself in Thee in Thy beauty; and Thou wilt see Thyself in me in Thy beauty; so that thus I may be like to Thee in Thy beauty and Thou mayest be like to me in Thy beauty, and my beauty may be Thy beauty, and Thy beauty my beauty; and thus I shall be Thou in Thy beauty and Thou wilt be I in Thy beauty, because Thy beauty itself will be my beauty, and thus we shall each see the other in Thy beauty.

The rhapsody goes on and on like a Sufi chant inducing ecstasy; and the Spanish word *hermosura* is twice as long and twice as seductive.

"Giving birth in beauty," Plato said. We become what we behold. We are saved by what we see. Redemption is vision, not a vicarious redemption of a literal victim on a literal cross. In *The Divine Narcissus* the crucifixion is the contemplation of the

beauty. Only as an aesthetic phenomenon are existence and the
world eternally justified. That is Nietzsche speaking. But I take
my theology from William Blake. Blake: Protestant, mystic, but
also revolutionary; not just the Song of Songs, but also Revelation and the spirit of Joachim of Fiore. Blake's stunning heterodoxy.

> Prayer is the Study of Art.
> Praise is the Practise of Art.
> Fasting &c., all relate to Art.
> The outward Ceremony is Antichrist.
> The Eternal Body of Man is The Imagination, that is,
> God himself $\Big\}$ יש[ו]ע, Jesus: we are his Members.
> The Divine Body
> It manifests itself in his Works of Art (In Eternity All is
>   Vision).

Eternity is the eternal pursuit of the millennium. Eternity is in
love with the productions of time.

In San Juan there is the Dark Night:

> amado con amada
> amada en el Amado transformada!

Lover and Beloved, complete union with God; identification with
the Absolute, that crime for which some of the great Sufi masters
were put to death. Yet San Juan explicitly says, "God absorbs the
soul above all being in the being of God, deifying its substance
and making it divine." Deifying, *endiosando*: enthusiasm in the
full etymological sense of the word, "en-god-ment." Enthusiasm:
the word is Greek and comes to us from the Greek god Dionysus.
San Juan's heterodoxy should be called Dionysian rather than
pantheist.

A heterodox redemption requires a heterodox creation. The
mirror of Narcissus is not the mirror of vanity, or the Fall, but
the mirror of creation. What is implicit in San Juan de la Cruz is
explicit in the mystical tradition of Islam, in Sufism; in the Sufism
of Ibn Arabi. The Breath of Creation is the "Sigh of Compas-
sion," Allah al-Rahman, yearning to be known: "I was a hidden
Treasure and I yearned to be known. Then I created creatures in

order to be known by them." God becomes a mirror in which the spiritual man contemplates his own reality, and man in turn becomes the mirror in which God contemplates his names and qualities.[8]

The story of creation, Genesis 1:2: "And the Spirit of God moved upon the face of the waters." Reinterpreted spiritually, *a lo divino*, that will be God as Narcissus, imagining his own image in the face of the waters. A Gnostic text, preserved in Coptic Christianity, a meditation on the first words of the Gospel according to St. John, "In the beginning was the Word," says "He 'thought' His own likeness when He saw it in the pure Light-water that surrounded Him. And His Thought became efficacious and made herself manifest. Out of the splendor of the Light she stood herself before Him: the Light that is the image of the Light, the likeness of the Invisible. . . . She is the first Thought, His likeness."[9]

There actually is a sequence of poems by San Juan de la Cruz, titled "Ballad on the Gospel 'In the Beginning Was the Word': About the Most Holy Trinity," in which he actually dares, like Blake, to give in popular ballad form (romance) his own version of creation. It is pure Gnosticism, or Sufism; I follow the commentary of Gerald Brenan, no Gnostic or Sufi or even mystic; he wrote the best book on the Spanish Civil War. The three Persons of the Trinity, though distinct in substance, are made one by love; this love, which in the manner of an electric generator they manufacture among themselves, spills over and manifests itself in the creation of the world. In ballad-style dialogue the Father, out of his immense love for the Son, offers to give him a Bride, and on his acceptance the creation takes place. The whole of creation from angels to man makes up the body of the Bride of Christ, but there is a distinction: whereas in the upper compartment of the palace the angels possess the Bridegroom in full enjoyment, in the lower compartment the marriage remains unconsummated. There is no mention of Eve's sin, or of the Fall. Human Nature was created inferior to the angels—we are not told why—but endowed with faith and hope. The rest of the poem develops the long history of this hope until with the Incarnation the Son enters the womb of his Bride and the original purpose of creation, the marriage of Divine with Human Nature, is finally fulfilled.[10]

NOTES

1. O. Paz, *The Labyrinth of Solitude* (New York, 1961).

2. J. L. Phelan, *The Millennial Kingdom of the Franciscans in the New World*, 2nd ed. (Berkeley, 1970).

3. J. Lafaye, *Quetzalcoatl and Guadalupe: The Formation of Mexican National Consciousness, 1513–1813* (Chicago, 1976), 32. Cf. M. Reeves, *Joachim of Fiore and the Prophetic Future* (London, 1976).

4. O. Paz, *Sor Juana* (Cambridge, Mass., 1988), 165–166.

5. Lafaye, *Quetzalcoatl and Guadalupe*, 64–64.

6. G. Brenan, *St. John of the Cross* (Cambridge, 1973), 12.

7. Ibid, 32, 126.

8. H. Corbin, *Creative Imagination in the Sufism of Ibn Arabi* (Princeton, 1969), 114–115. Cf. L. Lopez Baralt, *San Juan de la Cruz y el Islam* (Mexico, 1985), 395–401.

9. H. Jonas, *The Gnostic Religion* (Boston, 1963), 106.

10. Brenan, *St. John of the Cross*, 128–129.

10

Revisioning Historical Identities

This is work in progress; for fellow students, fellow workers; I need a friendly audience, in order to be as vulnerable as I want to be; in this intertextual autobiography; a life made out of books. "Revisioning Historical Identities," the title of your conference, is the story of my life.

I was introduced as the author of *Life Against Death* and *Love's Body*. *Life Against Death* (1959) records the first revision of my historical identity, from Marx to Marx and Freud. I am here today because I was, I am, a premature post-Marxist. My first book, *Hermes the Thief* (1947) is a good Marxist interpretation of classical mythology. My first historical identity, my Marxist ideology, was wrecked in the frozen landscape of the Cold War, the defeat of the simplistic hopes for a better world that inspired the Henry Wallace campaign for the Presidency in 1948. Things were happening in history that Marxism could not explain. Psychoanalysis was to supply Marxism with the psychology it seemed desperately to lack.

Revisioning as I have experienced it is not a luxury but life itself, a matter of survival; trying to stay alive in history; improvising a raft after shipwreck, out of whatever materials are available. Out of whatever materials are available: bits of books, the fragments we shore up against our ruin. Historical identity is made out of identifications: ancestral figures we identify with, the authors who are our authorities. Carving our own *persona* ("mask") in their image. "Identification: psychological process

Keynote address to the second annual interdisciplinary conference of University of California graduate students in the humanities, May 1989; revised. Printed in *Tikkun*, November–December 1990, pp. 36–40, 107–110.

whereby the subject assimilates an aspect, property or attribute of the other and is transformed, wholly or partially, after the model the other provides. It is by means of a series of identifications that the personality is constituted and specified."[1] Trying to stay alive: it is always an emergency operation; "emergency after emergency of swift transformations."[2] One doesn't know what one is getting into: *entréme donde no supe.*

At the end of *Life Against Death* I repeat Freud's prayer, at the end of *Civilization and Its Discontents*, for a rebirth of Eros, to counter the threat of nuclear suicide. I didn't know that the commitment to Eros would take me to poetry. At that uncertain juncture in my life,[3] fate led me to California. It was Robert Duncan who introduced me to modern poetry, the New American Poetry stemming from Ezra Pound and William Carlos Williams. Pound and Williams, and their successors Olson and Duncan, took their place inside my mind as authors having authority over me. And so there was a movement set up from modern politics to modern poetry. The last sentence in *Love's Body* is "There is only poetry." I am sentenced by my own sentence: how do you live with that? A movement or a tension, a dissension, a schism in the soul; between politics and poetry, between two kinds of revolutionism or vanguardism, between political vanguard and poetical avant-garde. The murky politics in the poetry of Ezra Pound highlights the contradictions. And the deep poetic connection between Ezra Pound and poets whose politics were the opposite of his, Olson and Duncan.

One has no choice; one must keep blundering ahead. As Malcolm X said, the chickens come home to roost. In 1968, a world turned upside down, it seemed that the poetic imagination might come to power.[4] More sober thoughts took over with the victory of Mrs. Thatcher, the failure of the Left, the experience of defeat; and a deeper identification with Ezra Pound, the later Pound, the Pound of the defeat, the defeat of all his politics. In 1985 at the Pound centennial over in San Jose I read with feeling Canto 116. Canto 116: Pound's large sense of failure draped around Dante's sestina *al poco giorno e al gran cerchio d'ombra*, "a little light / in great darkness." Pound's shipwreck, like Odysseus': "My errors and wrecks lie about me." His identification with Mussolini: the *Pisan Cantos* open with Mussolini hung by the heels from a butcher's hook, killed by the Italian Partisan Resistance; Canto 116 compares Pound's own *Cantos* to the futile jumble of legislation left by Mussolini, "a tangle of works unfinished." And some deeper notes of self-criticism: "a nice quiet paradise / over the shambles"; "if love be not in the house there is nothing."

Ezra Pound. The mysterious ways in which poetry and history are related. The *Cantos* were to be "a poem including history." Already in Canto 1 Pound identified himself with Odysseus and predicted his own shipwreck. The new American poetry: Open or Naked Poetry. Put yourself in the open; open to all the winds that blow, as winds veer in periplum. To be a poet is to be vulnerable. Odysseus on his raft. Only in 1985 did I discover in our library a copy of the periodical put out by Pound in 1927–1928, *The Exile*. Only then did I get down to work; reconsidering the revolutions—fascist and communist, political and poetical, Marxist and modernist—in the history of the twentieth century; seeing more deeply the hidden interconnections.

In *The Exile*, Pound, the autocratic leader, lays down the law: "Quite simply," he says, "I want a new civilisation." I remember one of the early landmarks in my political development, Sidney and Beatrice Webb's *Soviet Communism: A New Civilization?* The first edition (1935) had a question mark: later editions struck the question mark. And now what should the punctuation be? Pound, the extremist, goes all the way in identifying aesthetic modernism with political revolutionism: "I want a new civilization. We have the basis for a new poetry, and for a new music. The government of our country is hopelessly low-brow, there are certain crass stupidities that it is up to the literate members of the public to eradicate."[5] The elitist pretension, the fascist potential is clear. Pound's imprudent candor makes me think twice before dismissing the thought because it is fascist. The conflict between low-brow mass culture and the high-brow avant-garde will not go away. Even Whitman, in *Democratic Vistas*, sees himself as facing "the appalling dangers of universal suffrage in the United States."

Even more disturbing food for thought, to this early admirer of Soviet Communism, is Pound's effort, in the pages of *The Exile*, 1927–1928, to fuse what he calls the Soviet idea with the fascist idea, in the overall idea of modernism. "This century has seen two ideas move into practice," he says. Issue no. 2 of *The Exile* has a page with the banner headline MODERN THOUGHT, featuring first Mussolini saying, "We are tired of government in which there is no responsible person having a hind-name, a front-name and an address"; and then Lenin saying, "The banking business is declared a state monopoly."[6] The Soviet idea needs no explanation; the fascist idea is the attack on bureaucracy. Hannah Arendt defined bureaucracy as the rule of nobody; the fascist idea so defined we will have around as long as there is bureaucracy. The pages of *The Exile* show Pound straining to include communist intelligence in the struggle for renewal: debating the ABC of economics with *New Masses* editor and Communist Party literary boss Mike Gold; proposing Lenin as the model of modernist style: "Lenin is more interesting than any surviving stylist. He probably never wrote a single brilliant sentence; he quite possibly never wrote anything an academic would consider a 'good sentence' but he invented or very nearly invented a new medium, something between speech and action (language as cathode ray) which is worth any writer's study."[7]

In the pages of *The Exile*, I found Louis Zukofsky, the communist, collaborating with Ezra Pound, the future fascist; Louis Zukofsky, Semite, collaborating with Ezra Pound, the future anti-Semite. Their correspondence, 1927–1963; we need a complete edition. Louis Zukofsky, patron saint of the contemporary leftist sect of "language poets"; Zukofsky, whose work, especially the tour de force modernist translation of Catullus, I had previously looked at with amazement but not with identification. Only in 1985 did Zukofsky become alive for me: Zukofsky functioning in himself as the link between the two phases of my life, the Marxist and the modernist.

Louis Zukofsky contributed to *The Exile* no. 4 (1928) an elegy on the death of Lenin, "Constellation: In Memory of V. I. Ulianov" —

O white
O orbit-trembling
Star—

It is a beautiful recall of Whitman's elegy on Lincoln; a way of saying, "Communism is twentieth-century Americanism"—the slogan of the Communist Party in the 1930s, the time when Pound would claim that fascism was twentieth-century Americanism, as he did in that outrageous title, *Jefferson and/or Mussolini* (1935).

But there was a more personal message for me in the quotations from Bunyan's *Pilgrim's Progress* with which Zukofsky studded his work at this time. "Constellation" is introduced with a quotation, "Wherefore, being come out of the River, they saluted them saying, We are ministering Spirits, sent forth to minister for those that be heirs of salvation." Zukofsky contributes an explanatory "Preface":

Because Bunyan, who had a conception of Deliverance by the right way, straight and narrow, was, if similitudes are employed, a Revolutionary pessimist with a metaphysics such as George Sorel wrote of in his Reflections on Violence. . . . In these 18 poems, then, the pessimistic philosophy of proletarian violence, the only contemporary Deliverance to minds thinking in terms of destiny and necessity.[8]

Glossing Bunyan's *Pilgrim's Progress* with Sorel's *On Violence*; Sorel, like Pound, an admirer of both Lenin and Mussolini. Those who keep up with the actual twists of desperate New Left thought will know that Sorel is being currently rediscovered and rehabilitated.[9] But even more significant for me is Zukofsky's turn to Bunyan. My life-long friend and fellow traveler with a nonconformist conscience, Christopher Hill, Marxist historian of the English Revolution—like Zukofsky thinking in terms of destiny and necessity—after his book on *Milton and the English Revolution* has written a book on Bunyan and the English Revolution. Bunyan's *Pilgrim's Progress* and Milton's *Paradise Lost* were written after the defeat of the revolution in which their whole beings had been involved. *The Experience of Defeat* is the title of a collection of essays by Christopher Hill, inscribed in friendship's name for Norman O. Brown. Christopher Hill is fond of quoting the Puritan revolutionaries themselves ruefully acknowledging "The Lord hath spit in our faces."

The experience of defeat. Those great works of literature written in "the bright light of shipwreck." The motto is taken from George Oppen's poem—George Oppen another defeated revolutionary, who had to take refuge in exile from McCarthyism— Oppen's poem "Of Being Numerous"; poem which he says asks the question "whether or not we can deal with humanity as something which actually does exist."[10]

The bright light of shipwreck, sometimes uncannily predicted in the prophetic soul. Christopher Hill titles the first part of *Milton and the English Revolution* "Shipwreck Everywhere," and cites the title page of Milton's *Lycidas*, published four years before the revolution broke out; where the motto is taken from (of all things!) Petronius' *Satyricon: si recte calculum ponas, ubique naufragium est*: "If you add it up aright, everywhere is shipwreck." Everywhere is shipwreck, and then we start moving. We start moving because we have to. It is a matter of life against death.

The sea in which we are shipwrecked is history. The highstrung equilibrium, in the 1920s, between the Soviet and the fascist ideas could not survive into the 1930s. 1934: the Spanish Civil War; my first (Marxist) historical identity. 1933–1935, Pound's *Jefferson and/or Mussolini*. The parting of the ways between Pound and Zukofsky; miraculously the correspondence, between anti-Semite and Semite, went on. 1934: Zukofsky's "Mantis," and "Mantis Interpreted," dated November 4, 1934. (The anniversary of the Russian Revolution is supposed to be on November 7.)

"Mantis" and "Mantis Interpreted"; two poems which are one poem, though so far apart in form.[11] "Mantis Interpreted," the genesis and growth of the poem, "The actual twisting of many and diverse thoughts" in the poet's mind, in the concrete historical situation. "Mantis," the finished product, so finished, so formal: a sestina, an exact reproduction of that exacting trou-

badour formal invention: a tour de force, a miracle. The sestina
so heavenly, so unearthly; "Mantis Interpreted," so fragmentary,
so ungainly, so down to earth.

The genesis of the poem, the concrete situation as articulated
in "Mantis Interpreted":

> "The mantis opened its body
> It had been lost in the subway
> It steadied against the drafts
> It looked up—
> Begging eyes—
> It flew at my chest"
>
> > —The ungainliness
> > of the creature needs stating.

The ungainliness of the creature needed stating. The impulse to
articulate the poet's identification with the mantis becomes the
vehicle for articulating his identification with the poor:

> One feels in fact inevitably
> About the coincidence of the mantis lost in the subway,
> About the growing oppression of the poor—
> Which is the situation most pertinent to us—,

The Hunger Marches of the 1930s. Resulting in the second line
of the sestina:

> And your terrified eyes, pins, bright, black and poor
> Beg—

Under the pressure of what "Mantis Interpreted" calls "The actual twisting / Of many and diverse thoughts" (condensed in the
sestina to "thoughts' torsion") the theme expands: "the mantis /
the poor's strength / the new world." The mantis is the praying
mantis; the Greek word means prophet. The sestina calls the
mantis prophetess, and ends with a prophetic summons:

> Fly, mantis, on the poor, arise like leaves
> The armies of the poor, strength: stone on stone
> And build the new world in your eyes, Save it!

Those who are old enough to remember the 1930s—the Hunger Marches, the trade union struggles, the Spanish Civil War—

can recognize in Zukofsky's sestina the Communist hymn, the Internationale, set to new measures—

> Arise, ye prisoners of starvation;
> Arise ye wretched of the earth;
> For justice thunders condemnation;
> A better world's in birth.

Zukofsky is rewriting the Communist Internationale, and also updating Shelley's "Ode to the West Wind," the most revolutionary poem in the anthology-canon of English poetry. O wild West Wind—

> Drive my dead thoughts over the universe
> Like withered leaves to quicken a new birth!

The Communist Internationale, and Shelley's "Wild West Wind," and Dante's sestina, *al poco giorno e al gran cerchio d'ombra.* "Mantis Interpreted" gives Zukofsky's translation, stronger than Pound's—"To the short day and the great sweep of shadow." Zukofsky revisioning historical identities; reamalgamerging them, making them new. The Communist Internationale set to new measures, new music. The new music is the old music of the sestina: the formal tour de force, the unearthly formality of the sestina. The unique combination of "Mantis Interpreted" with "Mantis"—a poem on a poem—forces us to think about the sestina in a new way. Zukofsky says,

> Is the poem then, a sestina
> Or not a sestina?
>
> The word sestina has been
> Taken out of the original title. It is no use (killing oneself?)
>
> > —Our world will not stand it,
> > the implications of a too regular form.

He strikes the word from the title but persists in his quixotic project, linking Dante and the proletarian revolution. The political vanguard (Mike Gold) did not see the connection.

Dante's sestina. A sestina ("a sixer") is 6 × 6 + 3: 6 stanzas of 6 lines plus 3 concluding, wrapping it up, the envoi. Six times six lines, with what they in Dante's day called crucified retrogression: no rhymes, but six key words at the end of the line ("monorhymes"), which change places with each other at the end of the line in a tortured regressive pattern.

> The sestina, then, the repeated end words
> Of the lines' winding around themselves,
> Since continuous in the Head, whatever has been read,
>> whatever is heard,
>>> whatever is seen
> Perhaps goes back cropping up again with
> Inevitable recurrence again in the blood

The sestina as a form of thinking:

>> "I think" of the mantis
>> "I think" of other things—

A form of thinking not like the Cartesian *cogito*. Tortured thinking, Dantesque thinking:

>> "(thoughts' torsion)"
>> la battaglia delli diversi pensieri . . .
>> the battle of diverse thoughts—
>> The actual twisting
>> Of many and diverse thoughts

La battaglia delli diversi pensieri, the battle of diverse thoughts, a quotation from Dante's *Vita Nuova* (chapter 19). Zukofsky links the form of the sestina to the deep philosophy of Amor in Dante's *Vita Nuova*, that deep level where love itself is a battle: *questa battaglia d'Amore* (chapter 16).

The sestina form, as a kind of thinking. The poet Karl Shapiro says, "The sestina would seem to require the poet's deepest love and conviction, as these take on a rather obsessive quality. . . . If such an obsessive vision does not in fact exist or come into existence as the poem's written, the six key words will seem unmotivated and the whole poem will turn out to be an academic exercise."[12] And in a beautiful tribute to the Dante sestina, Leslie Fiedler says, "It is only too easy to make the sestina an embodiment of ingenuity rather than necessity. . . . The successful sestina must make it seem that each monorhyme is seven times fled and seven times submitted to; that the poet is ridden by a passion which forces him back on the six obsessive words, turn and twist as he may. . . . The sestina seems, in this sense, a dialogue of freedom and necessity, like, say, Bach's *Art of the Fugue*, but it is one loaded heavily on the side of necessity—a predestinarian dialogue."[13] Or like Bunyan's *Pilgrim's Progress*. Or like Sorel: "the pessimistic philosophy of proletarian violence, the only contemporary Deliverance to minds thinking in terms of destiny and necessity."

The sestina: obsession, depression; the Great Depression.

> the most pertinent subject of our day—
> The poor—

Louis Zukofsky's sestina sent me back to Dante, first of all to read Dante's sestina with new eyes. The last line of Zukofsky's sestina: build the new world in your eyes. Dante's sestina—

> si è barbato ne la dura petra
> che parla e sente come fosse donna—

"so rooted in the hard *stone* / which speaks and senses as if it were a *woman*" is not about his lady giving him a hard time. We must break through the literalism and poverty of our thought about love.[14] Love, believe it or not, is what moves the sun and all the stars; as well as any political or social movements that may be moving. And the Dante who wrote the sestina is the tortured exile, the defeated revolutionary; like Ezra Pound, like Louis Zukofsky; like Osip Mandelstam and many others also. *Al poco giorno e al gran cerchio d'ombra.* He is blocked. "Mantis Interpreted" quotes *la calcina pietra*, "cement locks stone," and *pietra sott'erba*, "stone under grass." William Carlos Williams, another contributor to *The Exile* in 1927–1928, opens "Paterson II" (1948—the frozen landscape of the Cold War) with

> Blocked.
>   (Make a song out of that: concretely)
> By whom?

By whom? The answer is Dante.

Louis Zukofsky went back to Dante in order to recharge his batteries with the tremendous power of Dante's overriding idealism, that idealism which brought him to Paradise even after his political shipwreck, the defeat of all his life seemed meant for. That idealism carries Zukofsky in the last line of his sestina to the new world—"and build the new world in your eyes." New world, new life: a better world's in birth.

Incipit Vita Nova. Zukofsky sent me back to Dante's *Vita Nuova.* "Mantis Interpreted" begins by linking the revolutionary sestina with *Incipit Vita Nova,* the rubric with which Dante opens that Book of Memory in which he tells the absurd story of his Love, his Beatrice. Absurd as it may seem; Love's Body is absurd. There is a connection between Beatrice and the Revolution; communist politics must be grounded in Amor. It will be like squaring the circle: making room in modern materialism for *The Figure of Beatrice* (Charles Williams). The full meaning of concretely embodied experience is not limited to the literal but is polysemously symbolic. Beatrice is Blake's City, yet a Woman; the New Jerusalem, beautiful as a bride adorned to meet her husband.

Love, that topic that Marxists can't handle: the topic this post-Marxist addressed in *Love's Body:* the topic Zukofsky addressed in "*A*"-9. Zukofsky's "*A*," his "poem including history."[15] "*A*"-1 begins:

> The Passion According to Matthew,
> Composed seventeen twenty-nine,
> Rendered at Carnegie Hall,
> Nineteen twenty-eight,
> Thursday evening, the fifth of April.
> The autos parked, honking.

"*A*"-9 is the secret history of the crisis (inner and outer, political and personal) in the lives of the generation preceding mine (Louis Zukofsky, 1904–1978). It is a secret history, a *trobar clu,* a closed trope, a tour de force of hermetic modernism, open if at all only to those who know that "*A*"-9 is metrically and musically a reprise of Cavalcanti's (Dante's friend Cavalcanti) canzone "Donna Mi Pregha," a lady is asking me a question. The question is: What is Love? It is the same canzone of Cavalcanti which obsessed Pound, who did two translations of it and placed one of them at the very center of the first half of the *Cantos*, "Canto 36." "*A*"-9 is a diptych, composed of two exactly equal and symmetrical parts: two answers to the question printed as if they were one "*A*"-9, concealing the fact that they were composed ten years apart, the first part in 1938–1939, the second part in 1948–1950. Concealing the great turning point, the hinge of fate ("minds thinking in terms of destiny and necessity"), the revision of historical identity in the life of Zukofsky.

The first part of "*A*"-9 recapitulates the contradictions—between prose and poetry, between avant-garde and masses, between two soi-distant avant-gardes, the political and the poetical—that I have experienced in my life. It is nothing less than an attempt to set the economics of Karl Marx, *Das Kapital*, to the music of Cavalcanti.[16] It is that tour de force promised by Zukofsky to Rakosi in a letter of 1931: "The only thing left for me to do is to make a canzone out of economics, which I'll do some day, wait and see."[17] He wasn't able to do it till 1939. In the 1930s the Soviet and the fascist ideas came to the parting of the ways. "*A*"-9 is a reply to Pound's *ABC of Economics* (1933), in which the Social Credit theories of C. H. Douglas are expounded. We can use Poundian aesthetics in order to see the superiority of Zukofsky's economics; both poetically and politically superior. We are trying "to construct a method of thought from the imagist intensity of vision" (Oppen); scrutinizing capitalism through the lens of poetry. And the result in "*A*"-9 is Marxism made over into something rich and strange. In a letter to Pound (June 7, 1935) Zukofsky writes, "There is more material fact and more imaginative poetic handling of fact in that first chapter of Marx than has been guessed at in your economic heaven." In that first chapter of *Das Kapital* Marx says, "If commodities could speak, they would say. . . ." In "*A*"-9 this becomes "So that were the things words they could say. . . ." And they speak of the labor theory of value ("The measure all use is time congealed labor"); use value versus exchange value ("Use hardly enters into their exchanges"); surplus value; the fetishism of commodities (things taking on a queer life of their own); the alienation of labor ("The labor speeded while our worth decreases"); the crisis of capitalism ("Times have subverted the plenty they point to"). Summarized in the concluding envoi:

> We are things, say, like a quantum of action
> Defined product of energy and time, now
> In these words which rhyme now how song's exaction
> Forces abstraction to turn from equated
> Values to labor we have approximated.

Why clothe the poetry of *Das Kapital* in a recondite imitation of Cavalcanti? Why alienate the masses with esoteric *trobar clu*?

> —Our world will not stand it,
> the implications of a too regular form.

Pound distinguished three elements of poetry—*phanopoeia*, the casting of images upon the imagination; *logopoeia*, the dance of the intellect among words; *melopoeia*, the music.[18] The dance of the intellect among the words, turning *Das Kapital* into a dance. But the deepest is the *melopoeia*, the music. The music of Cavalcanti in "*A*"-9, the music asking, What is Love? The music mutely, mutely, tells us that the Marxist theory of Labor must be grounded in a theory of Amor. And that for a musical, or adequately political, theory of Amor we have to go back, believe it or not, to Cavalcanti and Dante.

Love, the unmentionable subject of Part I of "*A*"-9, is the only subject of Part II. The two parts together thus constitute an effort to supplement the doctrine of Labor with a doctrine of Amor, or to move from Labor to Amor. As in *Life Against Death* and *Love's Body*. But in "*A*"-9 Part II the new force called in to remedy the defect in Karl Marx is not Freud but Spinoza and Wittgenstein. Turning from book to book, revisioning historical identities, we have the record of Zukofsky's wandering in the wood in the second half of his life in *Bottom: On Shakespeare*, begun in 1947. "*A*"-9 Part II was begun in 1948 (1948–1950:

the beginning of my post-Marxist wandering; after the defeat of the Henry Wallace Third Party campaign for the Presidency, 1948).

In Zukofsky poetry is in the driver's seat: the question is, What is Love? And for an answer we turn principally to Shakespeare.

All of Shakespeare's writing embodies a definition . . . the definition of love as the tragic hero. He is Amor, identified with the passion of the lover falling short of perfection. . . . The more detailed precision or obscurities of this definition of love in early Renaissance writing are beside the point. Its origins and changes are many and complex: Greek mysteries, Ovid (as compared to whose work Shakespeare's conjures with a difference), Oriental and Arabian sources, Provençal extensions and intensities, Continental and English philosophy of the 13th century, configurations of Cavalcanti, Dante and other Italians.

About thirty-five years after the publication of the First Folio, Spinoza may have been looking into similar matter: ". . . love is of such a nature that we never strive to be released from it."[19]

All of Shakespeare's plays are glossed as disclosing what is enclosed, as in a *trobar clu*, in Shakespeare's "The Phoenix and the Turtle," which Zukofsky calls "probably the greatest English metaphysical poem."[20] "The Phoenix and the Turtle" as quoted toward the end of *Love's Body*.[21]

> So they lov'd, as love in twain
> Had the essence but in one;
> Two distincts, division none:
> Number there in love was slain.
>
> Reason, in itself confounded,
> Saw division grow together;
> To themselves yet either neither,
> Simple were so well compounded;
>
> That it cried, "How true a twain
> Seemeth this concordant one!
> Love hath reason, reason none,
> If what parts can so remain."

Zukofsky is reaching far into the future: anticipating not only *Life Against Death* (1959), but also *Love's Body* (1966). The point to be arrived at is the coincidence of opposites—"Love hath reason, reason none."

Out of Shakespeare, to the music of Cavalcanti, with the aid of Spinoza and Wittgenstein, Zukofsky makes a new *trobar clu*, a new hymn to the Mysterium Amoris; celebrated in the conclusion:

> No one really knows us who does not love us,
> Time does not move us, we are and love, searing
> Remembrance—veering from guises which cloak us,
> So defined as eternal, men invoke us.

And yet . . .

Perhaps Zukofsky's error, if it is an error—the author of *Love's Body* is in no position to say—the physics, that is to say the politics, of Amor is still the undiscovered New Atlantis for which we set out—

Perhaps Zukofsky's error was to take Wittgenstein instead of Freud as the representative of modern thought who "appears to have traveled with the flame of *The Phoenix and the Turtle*."[22] With Wittgenstein and without Freud, Zukofsky ends up with Love's mind—"Nor hath Love's mind of any judgement taste." Love's mind rather than Love's Body: "Love looks not with the eyes but with the mind."[23] Without Freud there can be no psychopathology of modern life, no sociopathology of the twentieth century, the insanity in politics and in economics; the filthiness of filthy lucre, in order to surpass Pound's effort in "Canto 14" to depict the obscenity of money in purely Dantesque terms.

Even Spinoza is no substitute for Freud. Spinoza is indeed a communist, and philosopher of Love's Body: "Whatever things conduce to the communalization of human society (*ad hominum communem societatem conducunt*), or cause men to live in concord (*concorditer*) are useful." "Men can desire, I say, nothing more excellent for the preservation of their being than that all should so agree in all things that the minds and bodies of all should compose, as it were, one mind and one body."[24] But that is not what Zukofsky is seeing in Spinoza. Spinoza's doctrine of perfection—"REALITY and PERFECTION I understand to be one and the same thing"—haunts "*A*"-9—"desired perfection," "reason, the perfect real," "any compassed perfection"—and aggravates a contradiction in the poetics which Zukofsky shared with Pound. Zukofsky interpreted Spinoza's notion of perfection as reinforcing a traditional notion, sanctioned by the authority of Dante, of movement as movement toward perfection, and therefore as *defect*. Zukofsky cites Dante: "Everything that moves, moves for the sake of something which it has not, and which is the goal of its motion; . . . Everything that moves, then, has some defect, and does not grasp its whole being at once."[25] Amor, in Zukofsky's explication of Shakespeare, is identified with the "tragic hero, the passion of the lover falling short of perfection." Activity then, whether in art or in life, is the manifestation of "desire longing for perfection" ("*A*"-1, p. 2); equated with Spinoza's "love towards a thing immutable and eternal." Perfection itself (par excellence the music of Bach) is static: Zukofsky says, "Properly no verse should be called a poem if it does not convey the totality of perfect rest."[26] Perfection: others call it Beauty, Art, Poetry. The poem including history then has two voices: "desire for what is objectively perfect," and "the direction of historic and contemporary particulars."[27]

The poem including history has to be action poetry. It is part of "an impulse to action" ("*A*"-9, first line); it is poetry responding to Karl Marx's challenge, "the philosophers have interpreted the world in various ways but the thing is to change it." There is a historical agenda. Vita Nova; new life, new thinking. A poetic kind of thinking: renewal is the revivifying power of metaphorical troping.[28] The poem participates in the movement of history. The movement is everything, the kinetics, the energy. It all becomes a matter of energy, unblocking energy (that frozen landscape of the Cold War, the hardened stone of Dante's sestina). Charles Olson, another coming after Louis Zukofsky, who attempted to appropriate the legacy of Ezra Pound and divert the energy into "progressive movement," in his famous manifesto "Projective Verse" lays out "the *kinetics* of the thing. A poem is energy transferred from where the poet got it to . . . by way of the poem itself to, all the way over to, the reader. The poem itself must, at all points, be a high energy-construct and, at all points, an energy-discharge."[29] The advice is, keep moving.

If there is movement in history, there is violence and struggle (Sorel's "philosophy of proletarian violence"). Not necessarily class struggle; there is also *la battaglia delli diversi pensieri*; and even *la battaglia d'Amore*. Pound called his work an "explosion in an art museum," and dedicated, even in the 1930s, his *Guide to Kulchur* "To Louis Zukofsky and Basil Bunting, strugglers in the desert." But in the same *Guide to Kulchur* he speaks (with reference to his own *Cantos*) of "the defects inherent in a record of struggle."[30]

We need a new philosophy of movement, and it is not to be found in Spinoza. We need a philosophy of process, not of substance. A philosophy of energy, and therefore also of Amor: it is Amor which moves the sun and all the stars. It will not be a philosophy of perfection, but of struggle; and violence; and death. All part of the process; creative destruction. As Freud taught us, a philosophy of Amor must be also a philosophy of Death; including all that Hegel objected as omitted from the philosophy of Spinoza: the pain, the patience, and the labor of the negative. Omitted from Spinoza, for whom there is no death. "A free man thinks of nothing less than of death." "A thing has nothing in itself through which it can be destroyed, or which can negate its existence." Negation is the work of the death instinct, without which we cannot live, according to Freud. According to Spinoza negation is impotence, i.e., defect.[31]

Nature, *Natura naturans*, is not an orderly Spinozistic or Dantesque cosmos; Nature is Heraclitean fire. And the fire and the rose are one. And so, in spite of Dante, Heaven and Hell are the same place. Augustine said that the torments of the damned are part of the felicity of the redeemed; but he thought of these as two separate peoples, two cities. Modern, or is it postmodern, thought begins with Blake's *Marriage of Heaven and Hell*. Not the longing for perfection, but "Selige Sehnsucht" —

> Das Lebendge will ich preisen,
> Das nach Flammentod sich sehnet.[32]

celebrating life; life that longs for death by fire.

A poetics, then, not of perfection (Art, Beauty, etc.), but of incarnation. As in Mandelstam, another defeated revolutionary; who identified with Dante as defeated revolutionary: "A heroic era has begun in the life of the word. The word is flesh and bread. It shares the fate of bread and flesh: suffering."[33] Not perfect but open, that is to say broken, form. Against Beauty as such. Like the Suffering Servant in Isaiah 53:2: "No form nor comeliness; no beauty that we should desire him." Rejecting Spinoza's equation of reality with perfection, and perfection with power; to be is to be vulnerable.[34]

The death instinct, like a rejected lover, takes its revenge on all immortal longing for perfection. "*A*"-9 Part II goes dead:

> goaded
> Voice holding the node at heart, song, unfaded
> Understanding whereby action is aided.

Go dead voice. In each of the stanzas Zukofsky places a flower, as in a cemetery. *Et in Arcadia ego.* Immediately after the dead voice comes the envoi:

> Love speaks: "in wracked cities there is less action,
> Sweet alyssum sometimes is not of time; now
> Weep, love's heir, rhyme now how song's exaction
> Is your distraction—related is equated,
> How else is love's distance approximated."

After "*A*"-9 Part II, the political commitment completely drops out of the life of Zukofsky. His voluminous journal, 1947–1960, contains not a single mention of Marx or Lenin; or of Stalin for that matter. "*A*"-10, placed after "*A*"-9 but composed in 1940 ("wracked cities"), is a record of political disillusionment. In "*A*"-11 Zukofsky finds his Vita Nova. "*A*"-11 is inscribed for wife Celia and son Paul. The love that Zukofsky discovered is what Blake called "soft family-love" (and puts next door to "cruel Patriarchal pride").[35] In his retreat from the public to the personal, from the political to the domestic, Zukofsky was traveling the path traced by many members of his generation.[36] But not by me. The body in *Love's Body* includes the body politic. Though not a sestina, *Love's Body* is obsessive: *Nondom amabam, et amare amabam; quaerebam quid amarem, amans amare.* I need Augustine's Latin: "Not yet loving, but loving to love; seeking an object for my love, in love with love." A *trobar clu* perhaps; a hermetic game of hide-and-seek with esoteric erudition; very far from the masses which constitute the body of love, Whitman's en masse.

There is no blame. There is no defect inherent in a record of struggle. The assignment remains, to not cease from exploration. There is no blame. We all survive as best we can; always after shipwreck; improvising our own raft; revisioning our historical identity; to tell another story. As the Japanese Zen Buddhist lady eye-doctor said, "Going to Paradise is good, and to fall into Hell is also a matter of congratulation."[37] All shall be well. After being shipwrecked you become a "Sea Marke." Charles Olson includes in his *Maximus Poems* the poem called "The Sea Marke" by the navigator-explorer John Smith, and set by him as the epigraph for his last book "ADVERTISEMENTS for the Unexperienced Planters of New-England" (1630). The Sea Marke, some actual buoy afloat to mark the spot of a previous shipwreck:

THE SEA MARKE

It reads (Smith died,
that year):

"Aloofe, aloofe; and come no neare,
    the dangers doe appeare;
Which if my ruine had not beene
    you had not seene:
I onely lie upon this shelfe
    to be a marke to all
    which on the same might fall,
That none may perish but my selfe.[38]

NOTES

1. J. Laplanche and J.-B. Pontalis, *The Language of Psychoanalysis* (London, 1973), 205.

2. R. Buckminster Fuller, *Education Automation* (Carbondale, Ill., 1962), 87.

3. See Chapter 1 in this book.

4. See Chapter 3 in this book.

5. *The Exile*, no. 3 (1927–1928): 108.

6. *Exile*, no. 2:117.

7. *Exile*, no. 4:115–116.

8. *Exile*, no. 4:87.

9. Cf. E. Laclau and C. Mouffe, *Hegemony and Socialist Strategy: Towards a Radical Democratic Politics* (London, 1985).

10. G. Oppen, interview in *Contemporary Literature* 10 (1964): 162.

11. L. Zukofsky, *All: The Collected Short Poems, 1923–1958* (New York, 1965), 73–80.

12. K. Shapiro and R. Baum, *A Prosody Handbook* (New York, 1965), 120.

13. L. Fiedler, *No! in Thunder* (Boston, 1960), 24.

14. Cf. C. Williams, *The Figure of Beatrice* (New York, 1961).

15. L. Zukofsky, *"A"* (Berkeley, 1978).

16. Cf. D. Byrd, "The Shape of Zukofsky's Canon," *Paideuma* 7 (1978): 455–477.

17. B. Ahearn, *Zukofsky's "A": An Introduction* (Berkeley, 1983), 100.

18. E. Pound, *Literary Essays* (New York, 1968), 25.

19. L. Zukofsky, *Bottom: On Shakespeare* (Berkeley, 1987), 15.

20. Ibid., 25.

21. N. O. Brown, *Love's Body* (New York, 1966), 252.

22. Zukofsky, *Bottom*, 45.

23. Cf. Ibid., 16–19; quoting *A Midsummer Night's Dream*, act 1, scene 1, and glossing with Spinoza.

24. *Ethics* IV, 40. *Ethics* IV, 18, note; see Chapter 8 in this book.

25. L. Zukofsky, *Prepositions: The Collected Critical Essays* (Berkeley, 1981), 63.

26. Ibid., 13.

27. Zukofsky, *"A"*-6, 24.

28. Cf. R. Rorty, *Contingency, Irony, and Solidarity* (Cambridge, 1989), 66.

29. C. Olson, *Selected Writings*, ed. R. Creeley (New York, 1966), 16.

30. E. Pound, *Guide to Kulchur* (New York, 1968), 135.

31. *Ethics* IV, 67. *Ethics* III, 6. *Ethics* III, 3; *Ethics* IV, 33, Dem.

32. Cf. *Love's Body*, chapter 10.

33. O. Mandelstam, *Selected Essays*, trans. S. Monas (Austin Tex., 1977), 52. Cf. Mandelstam, "Conversation about Dante," in *Selected Essays*, 3–44.

34. Cf. *Love's Body*, chapter 11.

35. W. Blake, *Jerusalem*, pl. 27.

36. Cf. B. Hatlen, "Art and/as Labor: Some Dialectical Patterns in 'A'-1 Through 'A'-10, *Contemporary Literature* 25 (1984): 205–234.

37. R. H. Blyth, *Haiku*, vol. 1 of *Eastern Culture* (Tokyo, 1964), 9.

38. C. Olson, *The Maximus Poems* (New York, 1960), 69.

11

Dionysus in 1990

Contemplating the collapse of "actually existing socialism" in 1990, and dissenting from the opinion that we are witnessing the triumph of liberal capitalism and the end of history, in what post-Marxist terms can we begin to rethink the premises of a future science of political economy? Does the apparent triumph of capitalism mean the worldwide triumph of consumerism coupled with capitalism's ability to deliver the goods, or does it require a fundamental reconsideration of what do human beings really want?

In my first exuberant surge of premature post-Marxist energy (*Life Against Death*, 1959), I wagered my intellectual life on the idea of finding in Freud what was missing in Marx. I found in Freud's analysis of the pathological dimension in human desires the basis for a post-Marxist critique of capitalism. *Life Against Death*, chapter 15, "Filthy Lucre": the amazing Freudian discovery of the connection between money and anality. My Marxist background had given me a healthy prejudice against money-making. Imagine my excitement when I discovered Sandor Ferenczi's article called "The Ontogenesis of the Interest in Money"; with its immortal conclusion, "After what has been said money is seen to be nothing other than deodorized, dehydrated shit that has been made to shine."[1] "Nothing other than": it is the exaggeration which grabbed me. Years later I discovered the epigram of Theodor Adorno, "In psychoanalysis the only true thing is the exaggerations." That I now recognize as the cornerstone of a Dionysian epistemology.

A lecture for the History of Consciousness Program at the University of California, Santa Cruz, given on October 3, 1990.

The turn to Freud was irreversible; but where it led to was surprising. *Love's Body* (1966) begins with "Freud . . . ," and ends with "there is only poetry." It was as if the change of direction taken from Freud, resolutely pursued, in the end dictated a massive breakdown of categories of traditional "rationality" still accepted as authoritative by both Marx and Freud; that massive breakdown of traditional categories of rationality which Nietzsche baptized with the name of Dionysus. Already the last chapter in *Life Against Death*, not really knowing what it was saying, proposes "Dionysian consciousness" as a "way out."

What does it mean to take one's stand under the Dionysian, rather than the Freudian (or the Marxist) flag? It means to discard the pseudo-scientific posture of clinical detachment or political rationality, and recognize madness as the universal human condition, not the distinctive stigma of a separate class distinguished as insane. It means that madness is not an individual but a social phenomenon in which we all participate collectively: we are all in one and the same boat or body. It means also that madness is inherent in life and in order to live with it we must learn to love it. That is the point of honoring it with the name of a god. "Our greatest blessings," says Socrates in the *Phaedrus*, "come to us by way of madness—provided," he adds, "that the madness comes from a god" (see above, Chapter 1).

"Dionysus, the god of madness, is also death" (Heraclitus). Ever since I read Freud's *Beyond the Pleasure Principle* I have pursued the idea that Life against Death, Eros and Thanatos, were the ultimate terms in which to think about human behavior, or "the psychoanalytical meaning of history." At the same time it was clear to me even in *Life Against Death* that at that deep level which can only be expressed in myth or metaphor, Freud's "instinct theory" needed to be remythologized in terms of Dionysus, that is to say in terms of instinctual dialectics rather than instinctual dualism. Or, to use another metaphor, in terms of Heraclitus rather than Empedocles. In his last, characteristically obstinate reaffirmation of his "dualistic theory, according to which an instinct of death, destruction or aggression claims equal partnership with Eros"—"Analysis, Terminable and Interminable," 1937—Freud expresses his delight to find himself returning to pre-Socratic forms of thought, and identifies his pre-Socratic precursor as Empedocles, who conceived of the world-process as a constant battle, with alternating supremacy, between two principles forever in conflict with each other, named *philia*, love, and *neikos*, strife.

We are once amore—once amor, once à mort, thank heaven!—in a world made fresh for fundamental metaphors; where it makes all the difference, the difference between Life and Death, whether one goes with Empedocles or with Heraclitus; a difference dawning on me with new light in this year of 1990. Only in this year of 1990, exhilarated by the Dionysian manifestations of new life in Eastern Europe—replaying or redeploying, this time to more general acclaim, the Dionysian manifestations in Western Europe in 1968—soon, very soon, says the chorus in Euripides' *Bacchae*, the whole world will join the dance. Also only in 1990 for the first time hearing clearly the testimony of that fellow traveler on the Dionysian path, Georges Bataille. Already in 1947 Bataille had been mad enough to offer a Dionysian interpretation of an earlier turning point in the history of the twentieth century: "Truman would appear to be blindly fulfilling the prerequisites for the final—and secret—apotheosis. It will be said that only a madman could perceive such things in the Marshall and Truman plans. I am that madman."[2]

Georges Bataille in appropriately unruly ways bears precious testimony to the need for a Dionysian transvaluation of the Freudian revolution. The style and the stance is as significant as the substance. His 1939 manifesto—when his lifelong obsession with violent death had been transfigured by the advent of World War II—"The Practice of Joy Before Death"—with its prefatory motto taken from Nietzsche: "All this I am, and I want to be: at the same time dove, serpent, and pig"—and the concluding "Heraclitean Meditation," beginning I MYSELF AM WAR—covers with exemplary candor and directness ground laboriously crawled in

Love's Body.[3] I am reminded of Freud's concluding gesture at the end of *Beyond the Pleasure Principle*: "What we cannot reach flying we must reach limping."

Bataille helped me to reformulate the difference between Freudian dualism and the Dionysian or Heraclitean principle of the unity of opposites. Both Bataille and Freud find themselves once more on the terrain of pre-Socratic mythologization, finding it necessary to tell a story about the origin of life in order to account for human sexuality in general, and in particular to give the necessary weight and earnestness to the various, mysterious, and frightening phenomena gathered together under the name of masochism.

Freud summarizes his doctrine in the (pre-Socratic style) aphorism "The goal of all life is death," and mythologizes an origin of life resulting from a disturbance in an originally inanimate condition of matter, a condition to which all forms of animate (organic or living) matter seek to return. Thus in Freud the emphasis is on psychic entropy, elevated to a cosmic principle, "the urge of animate matter to return to an inanimate state." The entropic emphasis was aggravated by Freud's negative, homeostatic interpretation of the pleasure-principle — "Pleasure is in some way connected with lessening, lowering or extinguishing the amount of stimulation present in the mental apparatus." The opposition to all forms of violent or excessive pleasure, implicitly condemned as counterproductive or pathological, is plain. The good bourgeois principle of self-preservation, and the good rational (Apollonian) principle of moderation are in command. The ironical effect, as Freud came later to realize, is to place the pleasure-principle, which Lucretius had celebrated as *dux vitae*, the guide to life, entirely at the service of the death instinct: it becomes, Freud says, a Nirvana-principle, aiming at the reduction of the "throbbing energy of life" to the lowest possible level.[4] The whole picture depends on a nineteenth-century fixation on a distinction between animate and inanimate "matter"; as a product of the times, it is not really intelligible without assuming some fin-de-siècle weariness with life, aggravated by the trauma of World War I.

> Sleepe after toyle, port after stormy seas,
> Ease after warre, death after life does greatly please.

That Copernican revolution which Freud thought he was in-augurating, by showing that the human ego is not even master in its own house, is not complete until the human ego is forced to admit another master, the Dionysian principle of excess; Nietzsche called it drunkenness. It takes a madman like Bataille, and a libertine like Bataille, to challenge the homeostatic pleasure-principle in terms of another definition of pleasure and another definition of life. In Bataille's Heraclitean vision we are suffering not from some repressed longing for death but from excess of life—the Dionysian principle of excess, Blake's principle of exuberance. There is a contradiction built into the pleasure-principle: there is no such thing as satis-faction; there is no such thing as "enough." There is a built-in need for toomuchness, for flamboyance (flaming), for exaggeration (*Love's Body*, Chapter 15). That is why, in the last resort, there is only poetry. We cannot live without imagination; adorning and exaggerating life; lavishing of itself in change. This property of the imagination is not a human aberration, but a manifestation of the fundamental nature of life. So far from there being, as Freud assumed, a fundamental tendency to stability, Bataille says,

The living organism, in a situation determined by the play of energy on the surface of the globe, ordinarily receives more energy than is necessary for maintaining life; the excess energy (wealth) can be used for the growth of a system (e.g., an organism); if the system can no longer grow, or if the excess cannot be completely absorbed in its growth, it must necessarily be lost without profit; it must be spent, willingly or not, gloriously or catastrophically.[5]

Already Freud, for example in "The Economic Problem of Masochism," had envisaged the distribution and discharge (expenditure) of sexual energy on the model of the classical (closed) system of economics. Bataille's vision assimilated biological energy to the explosive character of solar and cosmic energy on the one hand, and on the other to the explosive character of human energy as manifested in economic development—that explosion which leads from paleolithic food-gathering to the Industrial Revolution of the last century, and to whatever lies ahead in the next. The movement of energy on the earth—from geophysics to political economy, by way of sociology, history, and biology—all manifests that universal effervescence of superfluous prodigality which is best honored as a god or as God. Science becomes religious in deference to the awesome facts.

> The scholar of one candle sees
> An Arctic effulgence flaring on the frame
> Of everything he is. And he feels afraid.

As in *Love's Body* (Chapter 10, "Fire"), and whatever the laws of thermodynamics may say, Bataille finds in Heraclitean Fire the best metaphor for the universal unity of eternal creation and eternal destruction—Blake's tiger burning. I still can do no better than quote the scripture that is authoritative for me: Gerard Manley Hopkins saying "That Nature is a Heraclitean Fire and of the comfort of the Resurrection." Gerard Manley Hopkins, Jesuit priest and poet, leaping over the distance separating Christianity and pre-Socratic paganism. And Goethe; in the *West-östlicher Divan*—the "Western-Eastern Divan,"—leaping over the distance separating "western" from "eastern" civilization. Goethe, one of the greatest spirits of "Western Civilization," writing in the spirit of, in imitation of, one of the greatest spirits of Islam, the fourteenth-century Sufi master, Hafiz of Shiraz, the Dionysian poet of intoxication and unappeasable passion.

> Das Lebendge will ich preisen,
> Das nach Flammentod sich sehnet.

Celebrating life, life that longs for death by fire. Goethe is not less the scientist for being a Sufi. Love is all fire; and so Heaven and Hell are the same place. Satan is the primordial Sufi, the model of the perfect monotheist and lover, who, cursed by God, accepts this curse as a robe of honor, preferring eternal separation willed by the beloved to the union for which he longs.[6] Why is this mystic or Dionysian consciousness so rare? What Bataille called the "apotheosis of the perishable"; what Goethe called the law of *Stirb und werde*, die to live.[7]

Bataille's special contribution is to show the connection between the mystic vision, "the apotheosis of the perishable," and the economic system. In so doing, he gave us a first sketch of that post-Marxist science of political economy which is the crying need of this hour of 1990, in his book *La Part Maudite*, first published in 1949; first published in translation, *The Accursed Share* (Zone Books), in 1988. The idea-nucleus was outlined in a short article in the anti-Stalinist Marxist review edited by Boris Souvarine, *La Critique Sociale*, January 1933; in translation, "The Notion of Expenditure," in Georges Bataille, *Visions of Excess*, 1985.

The key move in Bataille's transvaluation of economic value is to deflect the traditional Marxist notion of a "surplus" by connecting it with the Dionysian notion of life as the manifestation of a universal principle of excess. The whole notion of "surplus" then begins to waver: if there is no distinction between necessary and wasteful expenditure, if there is a necessity to waste, where is the "surplus"? The focus shifts from modes of production to modes of unproductive expenditure; from production to consumption; unnecessary, unconditional, exuberant, i.e., wasteful consumption. This perspective liberates us from the necessity of having to take "growth" as the self-evident destiny of all economic activity, and from the necessity of taking "demand," or desire manifested in the marketplace, as the ultimate and unquestionable indicator of human needs. Pandora's box, what do human beings really want, is open. It always has been open; now our eyes are opened. We can no longer continue with the conventional Marxist distinction between economic base, governed by technological rationality and economic necessity ("relations of production"), and ideological superstructures identified with a ruling class. A Marxist view of history shows a (loose) distinction between a class or classes that produce a surplus, and a class or classes that play games with it, games of war, religion, art, etc.; Bataille shows how the social structure is for the sake of these games, and not for the sake of productivity. Freud sees everywhere compromise formations in the eternal contest between Eros and Thanatos; Bataille suggests that Eros and Thanatos are one.

Just as Freud can bring out of darkness into light a whole sector of human irrationality by means of a single case history, Bataille focuses on the institution of potlatch, the gift-giving institution which energized and organized the prodigious economic life of the Indians of the Northwest Coast.

pot·latch *also* **pot·lach** [Chinook Jargon, fr. Nootka *patshatl* giving, gift] 1 : a ceremonial feast or festival of the Indians of the northwest coast given for the display of wealth to validate or advance individual tribal position or social status and marked by the host's lavish destruction of personal property and an ostentatious distribution of gifts that entails elaborate reciprocation.

First reported by Boas at the end of the nineteenth century, in the 1920s Marcel Mauss made potlatch a key instance of archaic gift-giving, taken by him as the key to an archaic mode of establishing human reciprocity and solidarity, antecedent and corresponding to the modern institution of the contract. Developing Mauss's idea of the socializing effect of gift-giving, Levi-Strauss in the 1940s explained the incest taboo and kinship systems in general as based on the primordial gift of women. In the 1970s Mauss's view of the role of gift-giving in archaic economies was updated and given currency in Anglo-American academic anthropology by Marshall Sahlins in *Stone Age Economics*. All these interpretations see in archaic gift-giving an organizing principle of human solidarity more primitive than, and antithetical to, the modern institutions of contract or (egoistic, acquisitive) barter in the market place. As Marshall Sahlins showed, the underlying psychological assumption is the Hobbesian assumption of innate human aggressive tendencies, leading to the war of everyman against everyman, unless contradicted by an institution which elaborately denies the innate aggressive tendencies and lays the basis for rational reciprocity. "It is the triumph of human rationality over the folly of war." The gift lays the foundation of human culture, by the repression of human nature.[8]

The human tendency that Bataille sees at work in the potlatch is not aggression but death: the need to lose, the need to spend, to give away, to surrender; the need to *sacrifice*; the need for ruin. Power is the ability to lose. Wealth was accumulated in order to be sacrificed, in a solemn competition for prestige, in which rival chiefs staked their whole being, for the purpose of challenging, humiliating, and obligating the other. The rivalry even entailed the return of a greater gift, i.e., a return with interest; in order to get even the giver must not only redeem himself by repayment, but must also in his turn impose "the power of the gift" on his rival.[9] The analogy with clashes between rival male animals in the rutting season is unmistakable; in the notion of "expenditure," sexuality and economics cannot be separated. One of the potlatch tribes called their festival "killing wealth." Slaves were killed. Chiefs burned their own houses. Emblazoned copper bars, worth a fortune, were broken in pieces or thrown into the sea. Bataille notes the relevance of psychoanalytic interpretations insisting on the primordial connection between excrement and jewelry, between the worthless and priceless, between anal eroticism and anal sadism. In Melanesia the donor designates as his excrement magnificent gifts, which he deposits at the feet of the rival chief.[10]

The game that is played with the surplus is gambling, with a built-in risk of self-destruction, a built-in need for competition, and a built-in demand for new goods to replenish the store and be in turn destroyed (as in "planned obsolescence"). A need for hemorrhage is built into the system. "This process of Creative Destruction is the essential fact about capitalism" (Schumpeter).[11] The whole thing amounts to a masochistic game of playing with fire, or Russian roulette playing with death or bankruptcy; The Bonfire of the Vanities. The best, full-blooded account of potlatch as an integral element in the culture of the Kwakiutl Indians is in Ruth Benedict's *Patterns of Culture*. Ruth Benedict notes that "the manipulation of wealth on the Northwest Coast is clearly enough in many ways a parody of our own economic arrangements."[12] Her whole interpretation is based on the idea that here we can see what Nietzsche meant by Dionysian. (L. Hyde, *The Gift: Imagination and the Erotic Life of Property* [New York, 1979], is an interesting discussion of the analogies between gift-giving and poetry; but he sees too little of the dark side of Dionysus, in spite of having written on John Berryman; and too little of the self-destructive side of potlatch. Following Mauss and Sahlins, he is too romantic in his antithesis between gift-giving and poetry on the one hand and capitalistic profit-taking on the other; as if it were an antithesis between life and death. He needs, as I needed, some influence from Bataille.)

≥♠

In 1990, with the need to rethink the foundations of economics so clearly urgent, Bataille tells us that the problem is not the production of wealth, nor even its distribution, but consumption; unproductive expenditure. What are we to do with the surplus, the toomuchness we produce? What do human beings really want?

In *The Accursed Share* Bataille gets away from the traditional Marxist sequence of modes of production. The human sacrifices of Aztecs, Islamic jihad, Tibetan monasteries of Buddhist contemplation, as well as potlatch, are all seen as alternative ways of obeying the imperative social need to squander wealth. They all illustrate the connection between the problem of disposing of the economic surplus and the institutions of religion; "Religion is the satisfaction that a society gives to the use of its excess resources, or rather to their destruction."[13] That intimate connection is enigmatically displayed in the word "sacrifice"—as if the proper thing to do with the economic surplus (painfully accumulated by economic sacrifices) is to give it away; and as if gods exist to receive it—i.e., that religion is essentially the theater of masochism.

It is enough to make one fear for the future of humanity, after the death of God. The scholar of one candle feels afraid. Protestantism-capitalism carried the masochistic logic inherent in religion to a new and higher level, piercing the soul far more deeply than any Roman Catholic penitential exercises, while at the same time making the religious solution to the problem of masochism no longer viable. Liberal capitalism—the world run as a purely secular business proposition—depends on a religious revolution which it can neither repudiate nor live with. Luther and Calvin legitimated a desacralization of human life on a scale which took the ground from under conspicuous consumption conceived as for the glory of God. At the same time it inculcated an ascetic abstention of enjoyment, the worthlessness of the things of this world, which still hopelessly confuses both public policy and private pleasures. The glorification of God by the nullification of man carries the masochistic potential of religion to a new level: our nullification, our humiliation as worthless creatures in the sight of God, is our sanctification. After the death of God the theology of human nullity becomes the pathology of nihilism.

Capitalism has proven itself more dynamic—i.e., Dionysian—than socialism. Its essential nature is to be out of control: exuberant energy, exploiting every opportunity, to extract a surplus. That is what free enterprise means. We can (masochistically) lament forces beyond our control, but the self-destructive, ruinous process goes on. Death and Dionysus get their due, deny them as we may. "If we do not have the force to destroy the surplus energy ourselves, it cannot be used, and, like an unbroken animal that cannot be trained, it is this energy that destroys us: it is we who pay the price of the inevitable explosion."[14] The schizophrenic symbiosis of spendthrift symbolic projects with a mainline dynamic of thrifty accumulation aggravates the situation. Appeals for conservation or limits to growth are only futile additions to the discordant noise, the Dionysian tumult of modern times; as long as we refuse to recognize the divinity of the mad god, as long as we go on kidding ourselves that man is a rational (Apollonian) animal. The forces not of production but of wasteful destruction have been unleashed and will not get back into the cage.

It is an open question what difference a more realistic view of human nature, call it psychoanalytical awareness or Dionysian consciousness, would make. The excess, says Bataille, must be spent, willingly or not, gloriously or catastrophically; it is not so easy as bourgeois or clerical optimists have imagined to distinguish gloriously from catastrophically; or to avoid both by opting for "comfort." This world was, is, and always will be, everliving fire. It will never be a safe place; it will never be a pastoral scene of peace and pleasure, *luxe calme et volupté*, Baudelaire's utopian image invoked by Marcuse in *Eros and Civilization*.[15] Traces of this misleading light disfigure the last chapter of *Life Against Death*. The dichotomy between pleasure and pain is socially constructed to make the economy work.

But one does not have to have utopian dreams of a peaceful or even a "better" future in order to recognize the historical exigencies, the demands of Eros, of Life, at this particular moment. The human race is facing the problem of consumption in a new way, a way that forces us to ask in a new way the question, what do human beings really want. There is a hidden harmony between the advent of Freud and the crisis of capitalism. "In the propitious darkness a new truth turns stormy" (Bataille).[16]

The new truth that cannot be avoided is the advent of the spendthrift masses, the advent of that new era designated in *Finnegans Wake* by the letters HCE: Here Comes Everybody. It is a truth promoted by socialist ideology (the "mass line") and capitalist reality. Ascetic intellectuals (I am one of them), schooled in cultural criticism by such models of resistance as Herbert Marcuse, have assailed mass consumerism as "repressive desublimation," controlled by a ruling class in order to "buy off" potentially revolutionary discontent. In this way Marcuse was able to combine (utopian) political radicalism with cultural elitism: the sacred heart of radicalism was located in great works of Art. But in the era of Here Comes Everybody, ascetic intellectuals have to rejoin the human race. Pushpin may be as good as poetry. A new age now begins. We will, as Euripides says in the *Bacchae*, have to submit to the verdict of the common man.[17] The dependence of the world economy on mass consumption, and the intrusion of mass demands for consumer goods, to the frustration of the best-laid plans of the Central Committee, are the most hopeful signs in the most recent events (1988–1990). "His producers are they not his consumers?" (*Finnegans Wake*). "Here Comes Everybody" means that the human race is getting ready to discard the (childish, Oedipal) game whereby the mass of Slaves left the mystery (the burden, the guilt) of surplus consumption to their Masters. It would be something new in world history, something like an apocalyptic novelty, if our social and economic arrangements came to reflect a collective consensus that we are all members of one body, with a collective problem of surplus production and surplus consumption. There is no other way out of the flagrant maldistribution, and the futile quest for justice.

All economies are systems of mutual interdependence. The Dionysian energy of the free enterprise market economy, like the potlatch economy of the Kwakiutl, is a violent assertion of interdependence in the negative form of mutual competition and aggression; under these circumstances addictive self-abuse becomes the only outlet for the need for self-abandon, and whole economies become organized round the traffic in drugs. That strengthening of the forces of Eros for which Freud prayed might create new institutions of individual generosity and public joy such as the world has not seen since Mont-Saint-Michel and Chartres. (Beethoven said *Freude*, not *Freiheit*, but they are the same thing. Freedom remains an empty abstraction until it is returned to its root meaning, *jouissance*. "Fredome mays [= 'makes'] man to haiff liking." Anglo-Saxon *freo* means both "free" and "joyful." It all comes from Freyja, the Teutonic Venus, the goddess of sexuality, and Friday. Bacchus is Liber; liberty is lust, *libido*.[18]) Gift-giving, a primary manifestation of Dionysian exuberance, might be able to revel in its own intrinsic self-sacrificial nature, instead of being inhibited and distorted, in bondage to primary social institutions of self-assertion. And public joy might manifest itself in carnivalesque extravaganzas uninhibited by the resentment of the exploited, the excluded, the deprived.

ə♪

Expelling God from the scientific exploration of the universe and the scientific management of the economy, human beings finally come face to face with the uncomfortable Dionysian realities of their own human nature. René Girard's book *Violence and the Sacred*, better known than Bataille's, looks into the Pandora's box opened by Bataille, in order to frighten us back into orthodox religion; Pope John Paul II really liked it.

After the death of God—that external God to whom we (masochistically) surrendered the glory, saying *Non nobis, Domine*, not unto us, O Lord—a gruesome Christian ritual. After victory in battle the triumphant army piously disclaims credit for the slaughter, saying they didn't do it; God did it. After the death of God, Love Calls Us to the Things of This World. "The unconditional splendor of material things" (Bataille). Bataille remains faithful to Marxist materialism; he speculates on the connection between his Blakean paradise and that utopian promise to replace the "government of men" with the "government of things."[19]

Love calls us to the things of this world, and capitalism, like God, produces them in unprecedented variety, and glamour. It brought the Berlin Wall down. In this strange new world the masses move as strangers, exploring. Things in a strange way remain shadows, or estranged. The science of enjoyment which, as Ruskin said, has nothing to do with either the science of production, or the science of accumulation, still lies in the future.

Bataille says that everything that exists exists to be consumed—a hard truth for Apollonian conservationism, saying "nothing in excess." It is because we do not know how to consume that so much energy is spent on accumulating excrement, or money, which cannot be consumed. Wherefore do ye spend money for that which is not bread? (Isaiah 55:2). To really enjoy is to consume; consumption is the way separate beings communicate; and real consumption is inseparable from Dionysian violence; the consuming fire.

If I thus consume immoderately, I reveal to my fellow beings that which I am *intimately*: Consumption is the way in which *separate* beings communicate. Everything shows through, everything is open and infinite between those who consume intensely. But nothing counts then; violence is released and it breaks forth without limits, as the heat increases.[20]

As in *Love's Body*, Chapter 9, "Food," Chapter 10, "Fire," Chapter 11, "Fraction." Fraction, the solemn moment of consecration, the breaking of the bread over the cup in the Communion. "The image of the tiger reveals the truth of eating" (Bataille); "to eat and to be eaten; this is union, since desire is beyond measure" (John Ruysbroeck, the fourteenth-century Flemish mystic; but the original is in Euripides. Dionysus likes it raw).[21] These are all metaphors to grasp the full reality of an embodied life of polymorphous bodily intercommunication, to contradict the spectral world of entertainment, and narcissistic dreams of pleasure without pain. (These metaphors apply even to such "incorporeal" things as books. It is an approximation to the truth to see, with Milton, the Eucharist in every book consumption, the precious lifeblood of master spirit, treasured up for a life beyond life. It is a further step forward to see the cannibalism in the Eucharist. The Dionysian is strong enough to take responsibility: the meaning is her own. The book sets the reader on fire. The meaning is the fresh creation, the eruption of poetry; meaning is always surplus meaning, an excess extracted; the toomuchness, the fartoomanyness of *Finnegans Wake*.)

To be is to be vulnerable. Bataille is of no importance if he does not pierce us with fragments of this Dionysian truth.

The wound of incompleteness opens me up. Through what could be called incompleteness or animal nakedness or the wound, the different separate beings *communicate*, acquiring life by losing it in *communication* with each other.

The fate of finite beings leaves them at the edge of themselves. And this edge is torn.[22]

Bataille's originality is to have seen in erotic mysticism, the Marriage of Heaven and Hell, the key to a new science of economics. It is an attempt to go beyond Blake (I leave the text in all its original toomuchness):

The Giants who formed this world into its sensual existence, and now seem to live in it in chains, are in truth the causes of its life & the sources of all activity; but the chains are the cunning of weak and tame minds which have power to resist energy; according to the proverb, the weak in courage is strong in cunning.

Thus one portion of being is the Prolific, the other the Devouring: to the Devourer it seems as if the producer was in his chains; but it is not so, he only takes portions of existence and fancies that the whole.

But the Prolific would cease to be Prolific unless the Devourer, as a sea, received the excess of his delights.

Some will say: "Is not God alone the Prolific?" I answer: "God only Acts & Is, in existing beings or Men."

These two classes of men are always upon earth, & they should be enemies: whoever tries to reconcile them seeks to destroy existence.

Religion is an endeavour to reconcile the two.

Note: Jesus Christ did not wish to unite, but to seperate them, as in the Parable of sheep and goats! & he says: "I came not to send Peace, but a Sword."

Messiah or Satan or Tempter was formerly thought to be one of the Antediluvians who are our Energies.[23]

The uncomfortable truth at the end of the road—the road taken by the masochistic love of truth—is the truth of masochism. The science of enjoyment is also a science of death; this Ruskin did not know. To speak in pre-Socratic style: it is a universal principle of biological life that growth leads to excess: and excess leads to laceration and loss.

> Give me excess of it; that, surfeiting,
> The appetite may sicken, and so die.

Or in another style, the children's story *The Velveteen Rabbit*, cited by Susan Farr in the collection of lesbian S/M writing *Coming to Power*:

"Real isn't how you are made," said the Skin Horse. "It's a thing that happens to you."

"Does it hurt?" asked the Rabbit.

"Sometimes," said the Skin Horse, for he was always truthful.
"When you are Real, you don't mind being hurt."

"Does it happen all at once, like being wound up," he asked, "or bit by bit?"

"It doesn't happen all at once," said the Skin Horse. "You become. It takes a long time. That's why it doesn't often happen to people who break easily, or have sharp edges, or who have to be carefully kept. Generally, by the time you are Real, most of your hair has been loved off, and your eyes drop out and you get loose in the joints and very shabby. But these things don't matter at all, because once you are Real, you can't be ugly, except to people who don't understand."[24]

Freud, often treated as a masculinist antagonist by feminists, always insisted on a special connection between masochism and femininity. Erotic mysticism has always known that the wound is the woman, and we are all not made whole until we are first wounded. "The wound of incompleteness opens me up." When the need to participate in mothering is institutionalized inside the family, there is the custom of couvade.

cou·vade fr. *couver, cover* to sit on (as a female bird on eggs): a custom among primitive peoples in many parts of the world in accordance with which when a child is born the father takes to his bed as if he himself had suffered the pains of childbirth, cares for the child, and submits himself to fasting, purification, or various taboos.

Baudrillard's critique of Marxist "productionism" and the fetishistic conceptualization of labor as the essence of human nature[25] needs to be transformed by a deconstruction, that is to say Freudian resexualization, of the idea of labor; see above, Chapter 3, "My Georgics: A Palinode in Praise of Work." A palinode, revoking the celebration of "play"—*homo ludens*—in *Life Against Death*. Transform the nature of work, returning it to life, to labor, the labor of childbirth; making men into women, in our work. Painstaking work; couvade; spending. John Donne, "To His Mistris Going to Bed":

> Come, Madam, come, all rest my powers defy,
> Until I labour, I in labour lie.

In the mysticism of the Moravian Brethren, who called themselves Unitas Fratrum, Christ's wounds are his womb, in which
we are reborn.[26] In London, in 1943, H.D.—H.D. leaped from
her Moravian background into the poetic company of Ezra
Pound, and into the psychoanalytical company of Freud (her
Tribute to Freud)—in London, in 1943, H.D. heard Christian
Renatus saying:

> Wound of Christ,
> Wound of God,
> Wound of Beauty,
> Wound of Blessing,
> Wound of Poverty,
> Wound of Peace

and it went on and on.[27] Gift-giving, what Charles Williams in
The Figure of Beatrice calls largesse—courtesy, generosity, humility, charity—is the woman's gift; that is what qualifies her in
patriarchal structures to become the primordial object given, a
poisoned gift (Pandora). Plato knows that the aim is "giving birth
in beauty." Dante is taught that "if he is not afraid of an agony
of sighs," he will come to the Beatricean moment and say, "Love,
true lord, behold thy handmaid, do what thou wilt." *Ecce ancilla
Domini, fiat mihi secundum verbum tuum*; the words of the Virgin Mary. His own soul is to be the feminine, the mother of Love.
Here, in the first canzone of the *Convivio*, Charles Williams says,
there is already proposed that mortal maternity of God which is
fully exposed in the conclusion of the *Paradiso*.[28] Teilhard de
Chardin, in *The Eternal Feminine*, shows how far orthodox
Christianity, in the twentieth century, can go in this direction.[29]

The developments in feminism—including excesses, lacera-
tions, splits—have brought us all, including feminists, face to face
with Death. Jessica Benjamin, in *The Bonds of Love*, putting
Bataille and *The Story of O* together, says, "We are as islands,
connected yet separated by a sea of death. Eroticism is the per-
ilous crossing of that sea."[30] After Freud, human culture, in all
of its interconnected aspects, private and public, is to be seen as
an unending search for an accommodation, a modus vivendi,

between Eros and Thanatos. Bataille's personal erotic excesses are potlatches. "In its cruelty, eroticism brings indigence, demands ruinous outlays."[31] The injunction of Spinoza stands: not to mock, lament, or execrate, but to understand.

ਣੈ

Political economy needs a theory of sacrifice; and sacrifice necessarily involves the sacred. The unconditional splendor of material things is accessible only to a newborn sense of religious awe; with Blake, saying everything lives; and everything that lives is holy. If the masses consolidate their presence on the stage of history, a new religion will emerge to take the place of the old religions administered by specialists in public consumption. It cannot be the obsolete Nature worship that conservationism is vainly trying to resuscitate. Consumption cannot not be sacrificial, and sacrifice cannot not be sacrilegious. Freud understood the "antithetical sense of primal words": the word *sacer* means both "sacred" and "accursed."[32] A sacred act must involve violence and rupture, breaking the boundary.

With any tangible reality, for each being, you have to find the place of sacrifice, the wound. A being can only be touched where it yields. For a woman, this is under her dress; and for a god it's on the throat of the animal being sacrificed.[33]

Human culture is human sacrifice. It is the truth of Actaeon; the wounded deer leaps highest. That heroical frenzy which was the life of Giordano Bruno; or Jimi Hendrix.

There is no telling how it will all turn out in the end. At the present moment, in this phase of exploration, the picture is confused by the novelty of the situation, the predominance of vicarious entertainment in the life of the masses, what Blake would call spectral enjoyment—everything on TV; the life-styles of the rich and famous offering vicarious participation in spectacles of waste; spectator sports offering vicarious agonistics; democracy restricted to mass voting for media stars. Not only bread but also circuses. It is not clear whether this half-hearted arrangement is an interregnum or the final solution. The Grand Inquisitor is betting that circuses will satisfy. The Dionysian bets the Grand Inquisitor is wrong.

We do not know to what degree individual excesses can be drowned in collective consciousness. Dionysian is a consciousness which does not need a ruling class or a divine scapegoat. Such strength can only be collective. Bataille says Christianity is left behind at the stage of exuberance; Blake did not think so. And Nietzsche said that the whole question was Dionysus versus Christ. Bataille himself could never free himself from the need for Christian pedagogy toward the sado-masochistic truth, the Suffering Servant. "I open my eyes on a world in which I have no meaning unless I'm wounded, torn apart and *sacrificed*, and in which divinity, in the same way, is just a tearing apart or being torn apart, is executing or being executed, is sacrifice."[34] Christianity, except for the mystics who (violently) anticipate in their own bodies the final apotheosis, must always be a religion of vicarious redemption. It may well be that human beings can tolerate the Dionysian truth only if it is held at a distance, projected onto human or divine scapegoats, admitted under the sign of negation. Reality may be too much for us. We may, like Job, have uttered what we cannot understand.

The vision of exuberance requires identification with the exuberant life of the whole. Materialists must come to understand what Spinoza called the intellectual love of God. We do not know how far the human race can go in this direction. But there is no doubt in my mind that Spinoza was right in seeing the connection between that mystic vision and the concrete development of polymorphous intercommunication between all bodies; and the maximalization, to the greatest possible degree, of the communist principle: "Men, I say, can wish for nothing more excellent for the preservation of their being than that all should so agree in all things that the minds and bodies of all would compose, as it were, one mind and one body" (*Ethics* IV, 18, note). Spinoza was wrong in thinking that self-preservation could bring us to the mystical body. As it says in the Gospel, "Anyone who finds his own life will lose it; anyone who loses his life for my sake will find it."[35] The notion of energy as self-destructive self-expenditure was beyond the scientific imagination of the seventeenth century. We participate each other, connected as well as separated by a sea of death; living each other's death, and dying each other's life.

NOTES

1. S. Ferenczi, *Sex in Psychoanalysis* (New York, 1950), 327.

2. G. Bataille, *The Accursed Share* (New York, 1988), 190 and note 22.

3. G. Bataille, *Visions of Excess: Selected Writings 1927–1939*, ed. A. Stoekl (Minneapolis, 1985), 235, 239.

4. S. Freud, *General Introduction to Psychoanalysis* (New York, 1963), 365; Freud, "The Economic Problem of Masochism," in *Collected Papers* (London, 1953), 2:255–268. Cf. *Life Against Death*, 88–89.

5. Bataille, *Accursed Share*, 21.

6. A. Schimmel, *Mystical Dimensions of Islam* (Chapel Hill, 1975), 195.

7. Bataille *Visions of Excess*, 237.

8. M. Sahlins, *Stone Age Economics* (Chicago, 1972), 175.

9. Bataille, *Accursed Share*, 70.

10. Bataille, *Visions of Excess*, 119, 122.

11. J. Schumpeter, *Capitalism, Socialism, and Democracy*, 4th ed. (London, 1952), 83.

12. R. Benedict, *Patterns of Culture* (New York, 1946), 174.

13. Bataille, *Accursed Share*, 120.

14. Ibid., 24.

15. H. Marcuse, *Eros and Civilization* (Boston, 1955), 164.

16. Bataille, *Accursed Share*, 133.

17. Cf. N. O. Brown, *Closing Time* (New York, 1973), 119.

18. R. B. Onians, *The Origins of European Thought* (New York, 1973), 472–476.

19. Bataille, *Accursed Share*, 135–141.

20. Ibid., 58–59.

21. Cf. M. Idel, *Kabbalah, New Perspectives* (New Haven, 1988), 70.

22. G. Bataille, *Guilty* (San Francisco, 1988), 27, 154.

23. W. Blake, *The Marriage of Heaven and Hell*, pl. 16.

24. S. Farr, "The Art of Discipline," in ed. Samois, *Coming to Power* (Boston, 1981), 188.

25. J. Baudrillard, *The Mirror of Production* (St. Louis, 1975), 33–41.

26. N. Hall and W. R. Dawson, *Broodmales* (Dallas, 1989), 26.

27. H.D. *The Gift* (New York, 1982), 141.

28. C. Williams, *The Figure of Beatrice* (New York, 1983), 57–58, 61.

29. Cf. H. de Lubac, *The Eternal Feminine: A Study on the Poem by Teilhard de Chardin* (New York, 1971).

30. J. Benjamin, *The Bonds of Love* (New York, 1988), 63.

31. Bataille, *Guilty*, 22.

32. Freud, *General Introduction to Psychoanalysis*, 187.

33. Bataille, *Guilty*, 26.

34. Bataille, *Guilty*, 45.

35. Cf. *Love's Body*, 161.

Designer: Barbara Jellow
Text: 10/13 Sabon
Display: Sabon
Compositor: Auto-Graphics, Inc.
Printer: Edwards Brothers, Inc.
Binder: Edwards Brothers, Inc.